Contents

Chapter 1

Introduction

1.1 Caviar

This article is about sturgeon roe. For other uses, see Caviar (disambiguation).

"Black caviar" redirects here. For the Australian racehorse, see Black Caviar.

Caviar is a delicacy consisting of salt-cured fish-eggs of

Salmon roe (left) and sturgeon caviar (right) served with mother of pearl caviar spoons to avoid tainting the taste of the caviar.

The rarest and costliest caviar comes from the critically endangered beluga sturgeon that swim in the Caspian Sea

the Acipenseridae family. The roe can be "fresh" (non-pasteurized) or pasteurized, with pasteurization reducing its

culinary and economic value.*[1]

Traditionally, the term *caviar* refers only to roe from wild sturgeon in the Caspian and Black Sea*[2] (Beluga, Ossetra and Sevruga caviars). Depending on the country, *caviar* may also be used to describe the roe of other fish such as salmon, steelhead, trout, lumpfish, whitefish,*[3] and other species of sturgeon.*[4]*[5]

Caviar is considered a delicacy and is eaten as a garnish or a spread.

1.1.1 Terminology

Beluga caviar

Russian and Iranian caviar tins: Beluga to the left, Ossetra in middle, Sevruga to the right

Ossetra caviar, salmon creme fraiche, potato shallot croquette, basil oil, egg whites and yolks
  According to the United Nations' Food and Agricul-

Trout roe with bread

ture Organization, roe from any fish not belonging to the Acipenseriformes species (including Acipenseridae, or sturgeon *sensu stricto*, and Polyodontidae or paddlefish) are not caviar, but "substitutes of caviar." *[6] This position is also adopted by the Convention on International Trade in Endangered Species of Wild Fauna and Flora,*[7] the World Wide Fund for Nature,*[8] the United States Customs Service,*[9] and France.*[10]

The term is also used to describe dishes that are perceived to resemble caviar, such as "eggplant caviar" (made from eggplant or aubergine) and "Texas caviar" (made from black-eyed peas).

1.1.2 Varieties

The four main types of caviar are Beluga, Sterlet, Ossetra, and Sevruga. The rarest and costliest is from beluga stur-

geon that swim in the Caspian Sea, which is bordered by Iran, Kazakhstan, Russia, Turkmenistan, and Azerbaijan. Wild caviar production was suspended in Russia between 2008 and 2011 to allow wild stocks to replenish. Azerbaijan and Iran also allow the fishing of sturgeon off their coasts. Beluga caviar is prized for its soft, extremely large (pea-size) eggs. It can range in color from pale silver-gray to black. It is followed by the small golden sterlet caviar which is rare and was once reserved for Russian, Iranian and Austrian royalty. Next in quality is the medium-sized, gray to brownish osetra (ossetra), and the last in the quality ranking is smaller, gray sevruga caviar.

Cheaper alternatives have been developed from the roe of whitefish and the North Atlantic salmon. The American caviar industry got started when Henry Schacht, a German immigrant, opened a business catching sturgeon on the Delaware River. He treated his caviar with German salt and exported a great deal of it to Europe. At around the same time, sturgeon was fished from the Columbia River on the west coast, also supplying caviar. American caviar was so plentiful that it was given away at bars for the same reason modern bars give away peanuts - to make patrons thirsty.*[11] In the wake of overfishing, the harvest and sale of black caviar was banned in Russia in 2007. There was an unsuccessful effort to resume export (in 2010, limited to 150 kg).*[12]

1.1.3 Royal sturgeons

The British Royal family has held a long affinity with the sturgeon since 1324, when Edward II decreed it a Royal Fish, whereby all sturgeons found within the foreshore of the Kingdom are decreed property of the monarch. Today, in the British Isles there is only one producer of sturgeon caviar, Exmoor Caviar. Prior to starting caviar production in the United Kingdom, the company received a letter from Buckingham Palace confirming that the Queen would not extend the royal prerogative and that the sturgeons held by Exmoor Caviar would therefore remain the property of the company.*[13]

1.1.4 Suppliers

In the early 20th century, Canada and the United States were the major caviar suppliers to Europe; they harvested roe from the lake sturgeon in the North American midwest, and from the Shortnose sturgeon and the Atlantic sturgeon spawning in the rivers of the Eastern coast of the United States. Today the Shortnose sturgeon is rated *Vulnerable* in the IUCN Red List of endangered species and rated *Endangered* per the Endangered Species Act. With the depletion of Caspian and Black Sea caviar, production of farmed or "sustainable" caviar[14] has greatly increased. As well as Canada and the United States, Uruguay has become a major producer and exporter.[15] In particular, northern California is reported to account for 70% to 80% of U.S. production.[16] In addition, a "no-kill" caviar harvesting technique has been developed in Germany[17] and implemented in California.[18]

In 2009, Iran was the world's largest producer and exporter of caviar, with annual exports of more than 300 tons, followed by Russia.[19][20] Iranian expertise helped China produce ten tons of farmed caviar in 2013.[21]

According to Eric Ripert, chef and proprietor of Le Bernadin, a leading seafood restaurant in New York, and Jean Francois Bruel, chef of Daniel, a Michelin-rated restaurant in Manhattan, the best caviar on the market is produced by Kibbutz Dan in Israel.[22] The kibbutz produces 4 tons of caviar a year. The farm is fed by the Dan River, a tributary of the Jordan River.[23]

Uruguay produces Black River caviar from *Acipenser gueldenstaedtii* (Russian surgeon). The production process is organic and 100% sustainable. The sturgeon is raised in 8,000 hectares of river delta, allowing the fish to live as conditions in the wild.

Italy is the world's largest producer and exporter of farmed caviar, delivering 25 tons in 2013.

The ban on sturgeon fishing in the Caspian Sea has led to the development of aquaculture as an economically viable means of commercial caviar production.[24] Caviar Court, in Dammam, Saudi Arabia, was established in 2001 and began harvesting caviar in 2007. It produced about five tons per year in 2011 and is building a larger facility in Abu Dhabi hoping to produce 35 tons by 2015.[25] In Spain, a fish farm called Caviar de Riofrio produces organic caviar.[26] In Canada, a sturgeon farm called Target Marine Hatcheries is now the first producer of organic caviar in North America called "Northern Divine" .[27]

1.1.5 Ecology

Over-fishing, smuggling and pollution caused by sewage entry into the Caspian Sea have considerably reduced the sea's sturgeon population.[28]

In September 2005, the United States Fish and Wildlife Service banned the import of Caspian Sea Beluga caviar to protect the endangered Beluga sturgeon; a month later, the ban was extended to include Beluga caviar from the entire Black Sea basin. In January 2006, the Convention on the International Trade in Endangered Species of Wild Flora and Fauna (CITES) supported an international embargo on caviar export.[29] In January 2007, this ban was partly lifted, allowing the sale of 96 tons of caviar, 15% below

the official 2005 level.[30] In July 2010, Russia and some other CIS countries restarted the export of caviar.[31] The 2010 quotas allow for the export of three tons of beluga, 17 tons of sevruga and 27 tons of osetra.[31] In September 2010, Kazakhstan launched a state monopoly brand, Zhaik Balyk, from the Kazakh word for the Ural River. Under the CITES agreement, Kazakhstan was granted the right to produce 13 out of the 80 tons allowed up until February 28, 2011.[32]

1.1.6 Extraction

Commercial caviar production historically involved stunning the fish and extracting the ovaries. Another method is extracting the caviar surgically (C section) which allows the females to continue producing roe but this method is very painful and stressful for the fish and is illegal in some countries. Other farmers use a process called "stripping", which extracts the caviar from the fish without surgical intervention. A small incision is made along the urogenital muscle when the fish is deemed to be ready to be processed. An ultrasound is used to determine the correct timing.[33] This is the most humane approach towards fish that is presently available but not all farmers use it due to the lack of knowledge in this field.[34]

1.1.7 Caviar preparation

Preparation follows a sequence that has not significantly changed over the last century. First, the ovaries are removed from a sedated female sturgeon and passed through a sieve to remove the membrane. Freed roes are rinsed to wash away impurities. Roes are now ready to become caviar by adding a precise amount of salt for taste and preservation. The fresh product is tasted and graded according to quality. Finally, the golden eggs are packed into lacquer-lined tins that will be further processed or sold directly to customers.[35]

1.1.8 Caviar substitutes

In Scandinavia, a cheaper version of caviar is made from mashed and smoked cod roe (*smörgåskaviar* meaning "sandwich caviar") sold in tubes as a sandwich spread, however this Swedish "Felix Sandwich Caviar" cannot be called "caviar" in Finland. Instead it is called "Felix Roe Paste" . When sold outside Scandinavia, the product is referred to as *creamed smoked roe* or in French as *Caviar de Lysekil*.

A sturgeon caviar imitation is a black or red coloured lumpsucker caviar sold throughout Europe in small glass jars. A more expensive alternative sold in Sweden and

Caviar substitutes

Finland is caviar from the vendace. In Finland caviars from burbot and common whitefish are also sold, but not as "caviar", since the word "caviar" is exclusively reserved for sturgeon roe.

There are also kosher and vegan caviar substitutes made of seaweeds such as *Laminaria hyperborea*. They closely resemble beluga caviar in appearance and are either used as a food prop for television and film, or enjoyed by vegetarians and other people throughout the world.[36][37][38]

Another common technique is to use spherification of liquids to recreate the texture, albeit not the flavour, of caviar.

1.1.9 History of caviar production in Italy

The Caspian Sea had not always been the only source of caviar. Beluga sturgeon were common in the Po river in Italy in the 16th century, and were used to produce caviar.

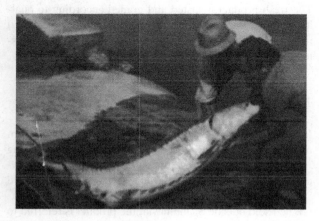

Sturgeon fishing in the Po river in 1950, Italy

Cristoforo da Messisbugo in his book *Libro novo nel qual si insegna a far d'ogni sorte di vivanda*, Venice, 1564, at page 110, gave the first recorded recipe in Italy about extraction of the eggs from the roe and caviar preparation "to be consumed fresh or to preserve".[39] The writer and voyager Jérôme Lalande in his book "*Voyage en Italie*", Paris, 1771, vol. 8 page 269, noted that many sturgeon were caught in the Po delta area in the territory of Ferrara.[40] In 1753 a diplomatic war broke out between the Papal States, governing the Ferrara territory, and the Venetian Republic about sturgeon fishing rights in the Po river, the border between the two states.[41] From about 1920 and until 1942 there was a shop in Ferrara, named "Nuta" from the nickname of the owner Benvenuta Ascoli, that processed all the sturgeons caught in the Po river for caviar extraction, using an elaboration of the original Messisbugo recipe, and shipped it to Italy and Europe. Production was sporadically continued by a new owner until 1972, when sturgeon stopped swimming up the Po river.

1.1.10 Storage and nutritional information

Caviar is extremely perishable and must be kept refrigerated until consumption. Pasteurized caviar has a slightly different texture. It is less perishable and may not require refrigeration before opening. Pressed caviar is composed of damaged or fragile eggs and can be a combination of several different roes. It is specially treated, salted, and pressed.

Although a spoonful of caviar supplies the adult daily requirement of vitamin B_{12}, it is also high in cholesterol and salt. 1 tablespoon (16 g) of caviar contains:[42]

- Energy: 42 kcal
- Fat: 2.86 g
- Carbohydrates: 0.64 g
- Fibers: 0 g
- Protein: 3.94 g
- Sodium: 240 mg
- Cholesterol: 94 mg
- Zinc: 12.18 mg

1.1.11 In popular culture

The film *God Loves Caviar* is based on the true story of Ioannis Varvakis, a Greek caviar merchant and benefactor from Psara who was a former pirate.

In a play on his surname, science fiction author Theodore Sturgeon titled an anthology of his best short stories *Caviar*.

1.1.12 See also

- List of hors d'oeuvre
- Snail caviar

1.1.13 References

[1] According to Jean-Pierre Esmilaire, *Directeur Général* of Caviar House & Prunier: "two-thirds of caviar's taste is lost through pasteurisation." (in "Three-star caviar", Caterersearch - The complete information source for hospitality, 1 February 2001). Also Judith C. Sutton states that "pasteurized caviar doesn't taste as good or have the consistency of fresh caviar, and caviar lovers avoid it." (in Judith C. Sutton, *Champagne & Caviar & Other Delicacies*, New York, Black Dog & Leventhal, 1998, p. 53.)

[2] Ian Davidson, Tom Jaine, *The Oxford companion to food*, Oxford University Press, 2006, ISBN 0-19-280681-5, ISBN 978-0-19-280681-9, p. 150.

[3] "Smith Bros. Whitefish Caviar". *web44.net*.

[4] "Caviar, American Caviar, Sturgeon Caviar, Black Caviar, Salmon Caviar". Affordablecaviar.com. Retrieved 2012-08-18.

[5] "Romanoff® Caviar". Marzetti.com. Retrieved 2012-08-18.

[6] "Roe coming from a fish other than Acipenseriformes is not caviar, and is often classified as «caviar substitute»." in Catarci, Camillo (2004), "Sturgeons (Acipenseriformes)", in *World markets and industry of selected commercially-exploited aquatic species with an international conservation profile*, FAO Fisheries Circulars - C990, FAO Corporate Document Repository, Fisheries and Aquaculture Department.

[7] "Caviar: processed roe of Acipenseriformes species." in CITES (2002), "Annex 1 - CITES guidelines for a universal labelling system for the trade in and identification of caviar", in *Resolution Conf. 12.7 - Conservation of and trade in sturgeons and paddlefish*, Twelfth meeting of the Conference of the Parties, Santiago (Chile), 3-15 November 2002.

[8] "Caviar is made from the unfertilized eggs of female sturgeon and paddlefish, among the oldest and largest species of fish living on earth." in World Wide Fund for Nature, Wildlife Trade - Caviar Trade FAQs.

[9] "The United States of America Custom Service (US Customs & Border Protection, 2004) defines caviar thus: Caviar is the eggs or roe of sturgeon preserved with salt. It is prepared by removing the egg masses from freshly caught fish and passing them carefully through a fine-mesh screen to separate the eggs and remove extraneous bits of tissue and fat. At the same time, 4–6 percent salt is added to preserve the eggs and bring out the flavour. Most caviar is produced in Azerbaijan, Russia and Iran from fish taken from the Caspian Sea, the Black Sea, and the Sea of Azov." in Johannesson, J. (2006), "1. Fish roe products and relevant resources for the industry: Definitions of caviar", *Lumpfish caviar – from vessel to consumer*, FAO Fisheries Technical Paper No. 485, Rome, FAO, p.1.

[10] Arrêté du 23 février 2007 (NOR: DEVN0750874A; Version consolidée au 06 mai 2007), Article 1: "a) Caviar : oeufs non fécondés, traités, des espèces d'acipenseriformes dont la liste figure en annexe du présent arrêté;".

[11] Linda Stradley. "Culinary Dictionary - C, Food Dictionary, Whats Cooking America". *whatscookingamerica.net*.

[12] "After a nine year ban Russia has begun exporting sturgeon caviar to the European Union", Newzy.net, 21 February 2011

[13] Wilkes, Davis (19 November 2013). "The caviar produced in DEVON! Fish farm becomes first in Britain to sell expensive delicacy". *The Daily Mail*. Retrieved 14 January 2014.

[14] http://www.ifis.org/resources/features/sustainable-caviar-production-save-our-sturgeon!/

[15] "Uruguayan Aquaculture Farming Techniques Perfecting Caviar - WSJ. Magazine - WSJ". *wsj.com*.

[16] "California caviar is big fish on this side of the pond". *Los Angeles Times*.

[17] http://www.awi.de/index.php?id=5946&type=123&filename=awi.pdf

[18] "California Caviar Co.'s Sausalito tasting room one of a kind". *SFGate*.

[19] "Crunch time for Caspian caviar". *BBC News*. 2001-06-19. Retrieved 2010-04-28.

[20] "Iransaga - Iran The Country, The Land". Art-arena.com. Retrieved 2010-09-21.

[21] "China employs Iranian expertise to farm caviar". *yjc.ir*.

[22] "New York's finest caviar: All the way from a socialist kibbutz in northern Israel". *Haaretz.com*. 27 April 2012.

[23] ABC News. "Caviar, Israel's Latest Weapon Against Iran". *ABC News*.

[24] California Farm Bureau Federation - Farmers tame prehistoric fish to make food fit for a king

[25] The Fish that Lay the Golden Eggs, by Anglea Shah, New York Times, 5 July 2011

[26] "More than one fish egg in the sea". *boston.com*.

[27] "Canadian Organic Aquaculture Standards". *gtcert.com*.

[28] "No Operation". Presstv.com. Retrieved 2010-09-21.

[29] "BBC NEWS - Business - International caviar trade banned". *bbc.co.uk*.

[30] "BBC NEWS - Science/Nature - UN lifts embargo on caviar trade". *bbc.co.uk*.

[31] Orange, Richard (July 25, 2010). "Caviar producers to restart wild caviar exports". London: The Daily Telegraph, UK. Retrieved July 2010.

[32] Orange, Richard (October 4, 2010). "Kazakhstan launches state caviar monopoly". London: The Daily Telegraph, UK. Retrieved October 4, 2010.

[33] mottra.co.uk – The link to the Latvian farm which pioneered commercial "stripping" in 2007

[34] Walsh, John (24 September 2009). "The new black: Can a revolutionary sustainable caviar make the grade?". Independent.co.uk. Retrieved August 18, 2012.

[35] Welch, James (22 March 2014). "Caviar Production". http://caviarbase.com. Retrieved March 23, 2014.

[36] Vegan Caviar. "Vegan Caviar, Seaweed Caviar, Vegetarian Caviar :: Buy Vegan Gourmet Food". *vegancaviar.com*.

[37] http://www.caviarkelp.com/the-process/

[38] http://oukosher.org/index.php/common/article/kelp_caviar_receives_ou_kosher_certification/

[39] Cristoforo da Messisbugo (1564). "Libro novo nel qual si insegna a far d'ogni sorte di vivanda". Venezia.

[40] Joseph-Jérôme De Lalande (1771). "Voyage en Italie". Paris.

[41] Archivio di Stato di Roma, Commissariato Generale della Reverenda Camera Apostolica, busta 546, Controversia coi veneziani sulla pesca nel Po di Corbola

[42] National Agricultural Library. "National Nutrient Database for Standard Reference, Release 25, Nutrient data for caviar". USDA. Retrieved 15 November 2012.

1.1.14   Further reading

- Peter G. Rebeiz, *Caviar - a magic history*, ISBN 978-88-6373-103-3, Sagep Editori, Genova, Italy, 2010.

1.1.15   External links

- Cooking For Engineers: Caviar

- Sturgeon population in Hudson River - Once-Endangered Sturgeon Rebounding in Hudson River, Study Says

- Caspian caviar in peril

- Russian caviar: an old fish learns some new tricks

- Black Gold: Russian caviar

Chapter 2

Further Reading

2.1 Aquaculture

Aquaculture

Aquaculture installations in southern Chile

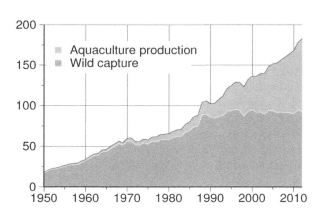

Global harvest of aquatic organisms in million tonnes, 1950–2010, as reported by the FAO [1]

Aquaculture, also known as **aquafarming**, is the farming of aquatic organisms such as fish, crustaceans, molluscs and aquatic plants.[2][3] Aquaculture involves cultivating freshwater and saltwater populations under controlled conditions, and can be contrasted with commercial fishing, which is the harvesting of wild fish.[4] Broadly speaking, the relation of aquaculture to finfish and shellfish fisheries is analogous to the relation of agriculture to hunting and gathering.[5] Mariculture refers to aquaculture practiced in marine environments and in underwater habitats.

According to the FAO, aquaculture "is understood to mean the farming of aquatic organisms including fish, molluscs, crustaceans and aquatic plants. Farming implies some form of intervention in the rearing process to enhance production, such as regular stocking, feeding, protection from predators, etc. Farming also implies individual or corporate ownership of the stock being cultivated." [6] The reported output from global aquaculture operations would supply one half of the fish and shellfish that is directly consumed by humans;[7] however, there are issues about the reliability of the reported figures.[8] Further, in current aquaculture practice, products from several pounds of wild fish are used to produce one pound of a piscivorous fish like salmon.[9]

Particular kinds of aquaculture include fish farming, shrimp farming, oyster farming, mariculture, algaculture (such as seaweed farming), and the cultivation of ornamental fish. Particular methods include aquaponics and integrated multi-trophic aquaculture, both of which integrate fish farming and plant farming.

2.1.1 History

The indigenous Gunditjmara people in Victoria, Australia, may have raised eels as early as 6000 BC. There is evidence that they developed about 100 square kilometres (39 sq mi) of volcanic floodplains in the vicinity of Lake Con-

Workers harvest catfish from the Delta Pride Catfish farms in Mississippi

dah into a complex of channels and dams, and used woven traps to capture eels, and preserve them to eat all year round.[*][10][*][11]

Aquaculture was operating in China circa 2500 BC.[*][12] When the waters subsided after river floods, some fishes, mainly carp, were trapped in lakes. Early aquaculturists fed their brood using nymphs and silkworm feces, and ate them. A fortunate genetic mutation of carp led to the emergence of goldfish during the Tang Dynasty.

Japanese cultivated seaweed by providing bamboo poles and, later, nets and oyster shells to serve as anchoring surfaces for spores.

Romans bred fish in ponds and farmed oysters in coastal lagoons before 100 CE.[*][13]

In central Europe, early Christian monasteries adopted Roman aquacultural practices.[*][14] Aquaculture spread in Europe during the Middle Ages since away from the seacoasts and the big rivers fish had to be salted so they did not rot.[*][15] Improvements in transportation during the 19th century made fresh fish easily available and inexpensive,

even in inland areas, making aquaculture less popular. The 15th Century fishponds of the Trebon Basin in the Czech Republic are maintained as a UNESCO World Heritage Site.[*][16]

Hawaiians constructed oceanic fish ponds (see Hawaiian aquaculture). A remarkable example is a fish pond dating from at least 1,000 years ago, at Alekoko. Legend says that it was constructed by the mythical Menehune dwarf people.[*][17]

In first half of 18th century German Stephan Ludwig Jacobi experimented with external fertilization of brown trouts and salmons. He wrote an article *"Von der künstlichen Erzeugung der Forellen und Lachse"*. By the latter decades of the 18th Century, oyster farming had begun in estuaries along the Atlantic Coast of North America.[*][18]

In 1859, Stephen Ainsworth of West Bloomfield, New York, began experiments with brook trout. By 1864, Seth Green had established a commercial fish hatching operation at Caledonia Springs, near Rochester, New York. By 1866, with the involvement of Dr. W. W. Fletcher of Concord, Massachusetts, artificial fish hatcheries were under way in both Canada and the United States.[*][19] When the Dildo Island fish hatchery opened in Newfoundland in 1889, it was the largest and most advanced in the world. By the 1920s, the American Fish Culture Company of Carolina, Rhode Island founded in the 1870s was one of the leading producers of trout. During the 1940s, they had perfected the method of manipulating the day and night cycle of fish so that they could be artificially spawned year around.[*][20]

Californians harvested wild kelp and attempted to manage supply circa 1900, later labeling it a wartime resource.[*][21]

2.1.2   21st-century practice

Harvest stagnation in wild fisheries and overexploitation of popular marine species, combined with a growing demand for high quality protein, encouraged aquaculturists to domesticate other marine species.[*][22][*][23] At the outset of modern aquaculture, many were optimistic that a "Blue Revolution" could take place in aquaculture, just as the Green Revolution of the 20th century had revolutionized agriculture.[*][24] Although land animals had long been domesticated, most seafood were still caught from the wild. Concerned about the impact of growing demand for seafood on the world's oceans, prominent ocean explorer Jacques Cousteau wrote in 1973: "With earth's burgeoning human populations to feed, we must turn to the sea with new understanding and new technology." [*][25]

About 430 (97%) of the species cultured as of 2007 were domesticated during the 20th and 21st centuries, of which an estimated 106 came in the decade to 2007. Given the long-term importance of agriculture, it is interesting to note that to date only 0.08% of known land plant species and 0.0002% of known land animal species have been domesticated, compared with 0.17% of known marine plant species and 0.13% of known marine animal species. Domestication typically involves about a decade of scientific research.[26] Domesticating aquatic species involves fewer risks to humans than do land animals, which took a large toll in human lives. Most major human diseases originated in domesticated animals,[27] including diseases such as smallpox and diphtheria, that like most infectious diseases, move to humans from animals. No human pathogens of comparable virulence have yet emerged from marine species.

Biological control methods to manage parasites are already being used such as cleaner fish (e.g. lumpsuckers and wrasse) to control sea lice populations in salmon farming.[28] Models are being used to help with spatial planning and siting of fish farms in order to minimize impact.[29]

The decline in wild fish stocks has increased the demand for farmed fish.[30] However, it is necessary to find alternative sources of protein and oil for fish feed so the aquaculture industry can grow sustainably; otherwise it represents a great risk for the over-exploitation of forage fish.[31]

Another recent issue following the banning in 2008 of organotins by the IMO (International Maritime Organization) is the need to find environmentally friendly, but still effective, compounds with antifouling effects.

Many new natural compounds are discovered every year, but it is almost impossible to produce them on a large enough scale for commercial purposes.

It's highly probable that future developments in this field will rely on microorganisms, but greater funding and further research is needed to overcome the lack of knowledge in this field.[32]

2.1.3 Species groups

Global aquaculture production in million tonnes, 1950–2010, as reported by the FAO [1]

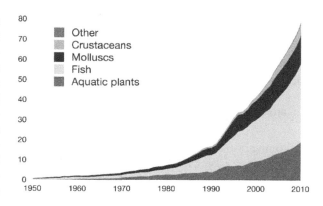

Main species groups

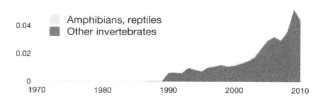

Minor species groups

Aquatic plants

Cultivating emergent aquatic plants in floating containers

See also: Algaculture and Seaweed farming

Microalgae, also referred to as phytoplankton, microphytes, or planktonic algae constitute the majority of cultivated algae.

Macroalgae, commonly known as seaweed, also have many commercial and industrial uses, but due to their size and specific requirements, they are not easily cultivated on a large scale and are most often taken in the wild.

Fish

Main article: Fish farming

The farming of fish is the most common form of aquaculture. It involves raising fish commercially in tanks, ponds, or ocean enclosures, usually for food. A facility that releases juvenile fish into the wild for recreational fishing or to supplement a species' natural numbers is generally referred to as a fish hatchery. Worldwide, the most important fish species used in fish farming are, in order, carp, salmon, tilapia and catfish.[1]

In the Mediterranean, young bluefin tuna are netted at sea and towed slowly towards the shore. They are then interned in offshore pens where they are further grown for the market.[33] In 2009, researchers in Australia managed for the first time to coax tuna (Southern bluefin) to breed in land-locked tanks.

A similar process is used in the salmon farming section of this industry; juveniles are taken from hatcheries and a variety of methods are used to aid them in their maturation. For example, as stated above, one of the most important fish species in the industry, the salmon, can be grown using a cage system. This is done by having netted cages, preferably in open water that has a strong flow, and feeding the salmon a special food mixture that will aid in their growth. This process allows for year-round growth of the fish, and thus a higher harvest during the correct seasons.[34][35]

Crustaceans

See also: Shrimp farm and Freshwater prawn farm

Commercial shrimp farming began in the 1970s, and production grew steeply thereafter. Global production reached more than 1.6 million tonnes in 2003, worth about 9 billion U.S. dollars. About 75% of farmed shrimp is produced in Asia, in particular in China and Thailand. The other 25% is produced mainly in Latin America, where Brazil is the largest producer. Thailand is the largest exporter.

Shrimp farming has changed from its traditional, small-scale form in Southeast Asia into a global industry. Technological advances have led to ever higher densities per unit area, and broodstock is shipped worldwide. Virtually all farmed shrimp are penaeids (i.e., shrimp of the family *Penaeidae*), and just two species of shrimp, the Pacific white shrimp and the giant tiger prawn, account for about 80% of all farmed shrimp. These industrial

monocultures are very susceptible to disease, which has decimated shrimp populations across entire regions. Increasing ecological problems, repeated disease outbreaks, and pressure and criticism from both NGOs and consumer countries led to changes in the industry in the late 1990s and generally stronger regulations. In 1999, governments, industry representatives, and environmental organizations initiated a program aimed at developing and promoting more sustainable farming practices through the Seafood Watch program.[36]

Freshwater prawn farming shares many characteristics with, including many problems with, marine shrimp farming. Unique problems are introduced by the developmental life cycle of the main species, the giant river prawn.[37]

The global annual production of freshwater prawns (excluding crayfish and crabs) in 2003 was about 280,000 tonnes of which China produced 180,000 tonnes followed by India and Thailand with 35,000 tonnes each. Additionally, China produced about 370,000 tonnes of Chinese river crab.[38]

Molluscs

Abalone farm

See also: Oyster farming and Geoduck aquaculture

Aquacultured shellfish include various oyster, mussel and clam species. These bivalves are filter and/or deposit feeders, which rely on ambient primary production rather than inputs of fish or other feed. As such shellfish aquaculture is generally perceived as benign or even beneficial.[39] Depending on the species and local conditions, bivalve molluscs are either grown on the beach, on longlines, or suspended from rafts and harvested by hand or by dredging. Abalone farming began in the late 1950s and early 1960s in Japan and China.[40] Since the mid-1990s, this industry has become increasingly successful.[41] Over-fishing and poaching have reduced wild populations to the extent that farmed abalone now supplies most abalone meat. Sustainably farmed molluscs can be certified by Seafood Watch and other organizations, including the World Wildlife Fund (WWF). WWF initiated the "Aquaculture Dialogues" in 2004 to develop measurable and performance-based standards for responsibly farmed seafood. In 2009, WWF co-founded the Aquaculture Stewardship Council with the Dutch Sustainable Trade Initiative (IDH) to manage the global standards and certification programs.*[42]

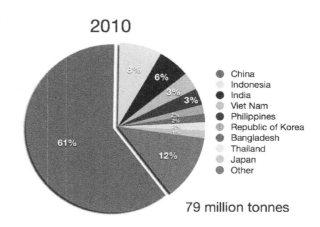

Main aquaculture countries in 2010

Other groups

Other groups include aquatic reptiles, amphibians, and miscellaneous invertebrates, such as echinoderms and jellyfish. They are separately graphed at the top right of this section, since they do not contribute enough volume to show clearly on the main graph.

Commercially harvested echinoderms include sea cucumbers and sea urchins. In China, sea cucumbers are farmed in artificial ponds as large as 1,000 acres (400 ha).*[43]

2.1.4 Around the world

Global aquaculture production in million tonnes, 1950–2010, as reported by the FAO *[1]

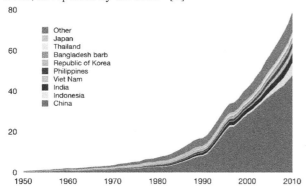

Main aquaculture countries, 1950–2010

See also: Aquaculture by country

In 2012, the total world production of fisheries was 158 million tonnes of which aquaculture contributed 66.6 million tonnes, about 42 percent.*[44] The growth rate of worldwide aquaculture has been sustained and rapid, averaging about 8 percent per annum for over thirty years, while the take from wild fisheries has been essentially flat for the last decade. The aquaculture market reached $86 billion*[45] in 2009. *[46]

Aquaculture is an especially important economic activity in China. Between 1980 and 1997, the Chinese Bureau of Fisheries reports, aquaculture harvests grew at an annual rate of 16.7 percent, jumping from 1.9 million tonnes to nearly 23 million tonnes. In 2005, China accounted for 70% of world production.*[47]*[48] Aquaculture is also currently one of the fastest growing areas of food production in the U.S.*[2]

Approximately 90% of all U.S. shrimp consumption is farmed and imported.*[49] In recent years salmon aquaculture has become a major export in southern Chile, especially in Puerto Montt, Chile's fastest-growing city.

A United Nations report titled *The State of the World Fisheries and Aquaculture* released in May 2014 maintained fisheries and aquaculture support the livelihoods of some 60 million people in Asia and Africa.*[50]

National laws, regulations, and management

Laws governing aquaculture practices vary greatly by country*[51] and are often not closely regulated or easily traceable. In the United States, land-based and nearshore aquaculture is regulated at the federal and state levels;*[52] however, there are no national laws governing offshore aquaculture in U.S. exclusive economic zone waters. In June 2011, the Department of Commerce and National Oceanic and Atmospheric Administration released national aquaculture policies*[53] to address this issue and "to meet the growing demand for healthy seafood, to create jobs in coastal communities, and restore vital ecosystems." In 2011, Congresswoman Lois Capps introduced the *National Sustainable Offshore Aquaculture Act of 2011*[54] "to establish a regulatory system and research program for sustainable offshore aquaculture in the United States exclusive economic zone;" however, the bill was not enacted into law.

2.1.5 Over reporting

China overwhelmingly dominates the world in reported aquaculture output,*[55] reporting a total output which is double that of the rest of the world put together. However, there are issues with the accuracy of China's returns.

In 2001, the fisheries scientists Reg Watson and Daniel Pauly expressed concerns in a letter to *Nature*, that China was over reporting its catch from wild fisheries in the 1990s.*[8]*[56] They said that made it appear that the global catch since 1988 was increasing annually by 300,000 tonnes, whereas it was really shrinking annually by 350,000 tonnes. Watson and Pauly suggested this may be related to China policies where state entities that monitor the economy are also tasked with increasing output. Also, until recently, the promotion of Chinese officials was based on production increases from their own areas.*[57]*[58]

China disputes this claim. The official Xinhua News Agency quoted Yang Jian, director general of the Agriculture Ministry's Bureau of Fisheries, as saying that China's figures were "basically correct".*[59] However, the FAO accepts there are issues with the reliability of China's statistical returns, and currently treats data from China, including the aquaculture data, apart from the rest of the world.*[60]*[61]

2.1.6 Aquacultural Methods

Mariculture

Carp are the dominant fish in aquaculture

Mariculture off High Island, Hong Kong

The adaptable tilapia is another commonly farmed fish

Main article: Mariculture

Mariculture refers to the cultivation of marine organisms in seawater, usually in sheltered coastal waters. The farming of marine fish is an example of mariculture, and so also is the farming of marine crustaceans (such as shrimps), molluscs (such as oysters) and seaweed.

Integrated

Main article: Integrated Multi-trophic Aquaculture

Integrated Multi-Trophic Aquaculture (IMTA) is a practice in which the by-products (wastes) from one species are recycled to become inputs (fertilizers, food) for another. Fed aquaculture (for example, fish, shrimp) is combined with inorganic extractive and organic extractive (for example, shellfish) aquaculture to create balanced systems for environmental sustainability (biomitigation), economic stability (product diversification and risk reduction) and social acceptability (better management practices).[62]

"Multi-Trophic" refers to the incorporation of species from different trophic or nutritional levels in the same system.[63] This is one potential distinction from the age-old practice of aquatic polyculture, which could simply be the co-culture of different fish species from the same trophic level. In this case, these organisms may all share the same biological and chemical processes, with few synergistic benefits, which could potentially lead to significant shifts in the ecosystem. Some traditional polyculture systems may, in fact, incorporate a greater diversity of species, occupying several niches, as extensive cultures (low intensity, low management) within the same pond. The "Integrated" in IMTA refers to the more intensive cultivation of the different species in proximity of each other, connected by nutrient and energy transfer through water.

Ideally, the biological and chemical processes in an IMTA system should balance. This is achieved through the appropriate selection and proportions of different species providing different ecosystem functions. The co-cultured species are typically more than just biofilters; they are harvestable crops of commercial value.[63] A working IMTA system can result in greater total production based on mutual benefits to the co-cultured species and improved ecosystem health, even if the production of individual species is lower than in a monoculture over a short term period.[64]

Sometimes the term "Integrated Aquaculture" is used to describe the integration of monocultures through water transfer.[64] For all intents and purposes however, the terms "IMTA" and "integrated aquaculture" differ only in their degree of descriptiveness. Aquaponics, fractionated aquaculture, IAAS (integrated agriculture-aquaculture systems), IPUAS (integrated peri-urban-aquaculture systems), and IFAS (integrated fisheries-aquaculture systems) are other variations of the IMTA concept.

2.1.7 Netting materials

Various materials, including nylon, polyester, polypropylene, polyethylene, plastic-coated welded wire, rubber, patented rope products (Spectra, Thorn-D, Dyneema), galvanized steel and copper are used for netting in aquaculture fish enclosures around the world.[65][66][67][68][69] All of these materials are selected for a variety of reasons, including design feasibility, material strength, cost, and corrosion resistance.

Main article: Copper alloys in aquaculture

Recently, copper alloys have become important netting materials in aquaculture because they are antimicrobial (i.e., they destroy bacteria, viruses, fungi, algae, and other microbes) and they therefore prevent biofouling (i.e., the undesirable accumulation, adhesion, and growth of microorganisms, plants, algae, tubeworms, barnacles, mollusks, and other organisms). By inhibiting microbial growth, copper alloy aquaculture cages avoid costly net changes that are necessary with other materials. The resistance of organism growth on copper alloy nets also provides a cleaner and healthier environment for farmed fish to grow and thrive.

2.1.8 Issues

See also: Issues with salmon aquaculture

Aquaculture can be more environmentally damaging than exploiting wild fisheries on a local area basis but has considerably less impact on the global environment on a per kg of production basis.[70] Local concerns include waste handling, side-effects of antibiotics, competition between farmed and wild animals, and using other fish to feed more marketable carnivorous fish. However, research and commercial feed improvements during the 1990s and 2000s have lessened many of these concerns.[71]

Aquaculture may contribute to propagation of invasive species. As the cases of Nile perch and Janitor fish show, this issue may be damaging to native fauna.

Fish waste is organic and composed of nutrients necessary in all components of aquatic food webs. In-ocean aquaculture often produces much higher than normal fish waste concentrations. The waste collects on the ocean bottom, damaging or eliminating bottom-dwelling life. Waste can also decrease dissolved oxygen levels in the water column, putting further pressure on wild animals.[72]

Fish oils

Further information: Tilapia § Nutrition

Tilapia from aquaculture has been shown to contain more fat and a much higher ratio of omega-6 to omega-3 oils.

Impacts on wild fish

Some carnivorous and omnivorous farmed fish species are fed wild forage fish. Although carnivorous farmed fish represented only 13 percent of aquaculture production by weight in 2000, they represented 34 percent of aquaculture production by value.[*][73]

Farming of carnivorous species like salmon and shrimp leads to a high demand for forage fish to match the nutrition they get in the wild. Fish do not actually produce omega-3 fatty acids, but instead accumulate them from either consuming microalgae that produce these fatty acids, as is the case with forage fish like herring and sardines, or, as is the case with fatty predatory fish, like salmon, by eating prey fish that have accumulated omega-3 fatty acids from microalgae. To satisfy this requirement, more than 50 percent of the world fish oil production is fed to farmed salmon.[*][74]

Farmed salmon consume more wild fish than they generate as a final product, although the efficiency of production is improving. To produce one pound of farmed salmon, products from several pounds of wild fish are fed to them - this can be described as the "fish-in-fish-out" (FIFO) ratio. In 1995, salmon had a FIFO ratio of 7.5 (meaning 7.5 pounds of wild fish feed were required to produce 1 pound of salmon); by 2006 the ratio had fallen to 4.9.[*][75] Additionally, a growing share of fish oil and fishmeal come from residues (byproducts of fish processing), rather than dedicated whole fish. In 2012, 34 percent of fish oil and 28 percent of fishmeal came from residues.[*][76] However, fishmeal and oil from residues instead of whole fish have a different composition with more ash and less protein, which may limit its potential use for aquaculture.

As the salmon farming industry expands, it requires more wild forage fish for feed, at a time when seventy five percent of the worlds monitored fisheries are already near to or have exceeded their maximum sustainable yield.[*][9] The industrial scale extraction of wild forage fish for salmon farming then impacts the survivability of the wild predator fish who rely on them for food. An important step in reducing the impact of aquaculture on wild fish is shifting carnivorous species to plant-based feeds. Salmon feeds, for example, have gone from containing only fishmeal and oil to containing 40 percent plant protein.[*][77] The USDA has also experimented with using grain-based feeds for farmed trout.[*][78] When properly formulated (and often mixed with fishmeal or oil), plant-based feeds can provide proper nutrition and similar growth rates in carnivorous farmed fish.[*][79]

Another impact aquaculture production can have on wild fish is the risk of fish escaping from coastal pens, where they can interbreed with their wild counterparts, diluting wild genetic stocks.[*][80] Escaped fish can become invasive, out-competing native species.[*][81][*][82][*][83]

Coastal ecosystems

Aquaculture is becoming a significant threat to coastal ecosystems. About 20 percent of mangrove forests have been destroyed since 1980, partly due to shrimp farming.[*][84] An extended cost–benefit analysis of the total economic value of shrimp aquaculture built on mangrove ecosystems found that the external costs were much higher than the external benefits.[*][85] Over four decades, 269,000 hectares (660,000 acres) of Indonesian mangroves have been converted to shrimp farms. Most of these farms are abandoned within a decade because of the toxin build-up and nutrient loss.[*][86][*][87]

Salmon farms are typically sited in pristine coastal ecosystems which they then pollute. A farm with 200,000 salmon discharges more fecal waste than a city of 60,000 people. This waste is discharged directly into the surrounding aquatic environment, untreated, often containing antibiotics and pesticides." [*][9] There is also an accumulation of heavy metals on the benthos (seafloor) near the salmon farms, particularly copper and zinc.[*][88]

Genetic modification

A type of salmon called the AquAdvantage salmon has been genetically modified for faster growth, although it has not been approved for commercial use, due to controversy.[*][89] The altered salmon incorporates a growth hormone from a Chinook salmon that allows it to reach full size in 16-28 months, instead of the normal 36 months for Atlantic salmon, and while consuming 25 percent less feed.[*][90] The U.S. Food and Drug Administration reviewed the AquAdvantage salmon in a draft environmental assessment and determined that it "would not have a significant impact (FONSI) on the U.S. environment." [*][91]

2.1.9   Animal welfare

See also: Pain in fish and Pain in invertebrates

As with the farming of terrestrial animals, social attitudes influence the need for humane practices and regulations in farmed marine animals. Under the guidelines advised by the Farm Animal Welfare Council good animal welfare means both fitness and a sense of well being in the animal's physical and mental state. This can be defined by the Five Freedoms:

- Freedom from hunger & thirst

- Freedom from discomfort

- Freedom from pain, disease, or injury

- Freedom to express normal behaviour

- Freedom from fear and distress

However, the controversial issue in aquaculture is whether fish and farmed marine invertebrates are actually sentient, or have the perception and awareness to experience suffering. Although no evidence of this has been found in marine invertebrates,*[92] recent studies conclude that fish do have the necessary receptors (nociceptors) to sense noxious stimuli and so are likely to experience states of pain, fear and stress.*[92]*[93] Consequently, welfare in aquaculture is directed at vertebrates; finfish in particular.*[94]

Common welfare concerns

Welfare in aquaculture can be impacted by a number of issues such as stocking densities, behavioural interactions, disease and parasitism. A major problem in determining the cause of impaired welfare is that these issues are often all interrelated and influence each other at different times.*[95]

Optimal stocking density is often defined by the carrying capacity of the stocked environment and the amount of individual space needed by the fish, which is very species specific. Although behavioural interactions such as shoaling may mean that high stocking densities are beneficial to some species,*[92]*[96] in many cultured species high stocking densities may be of concern. Crowding can constrain normal swimming behaviour, as well as increase aggressive and competitive behaviours such as cannibalism,*[97] feed competition,*[98] territoriality and dominance/subordination hierarchies.*[99] This potentially increases the risk of tissue damage due to abrasion from fish-to-fish contact or fish-to-cage contact.*[92] Fish can suffer reductions in food intake and food conversion efficiency.*[99] In addition, high stocking densities can result in water flow being insufficient, creating inadequate oxygen supply and waste product removal.*[96] Dissolved oxygen is essential for fish respiration and concentrations below critical levels can induce stress and even lead to asphyxiation.*[99] Ammonia, a nitrogen excretion product, is highly toxic to fish at accumulated levels, particularly when oxygen concentrations are low.*[100]

Many of these interactions and effects cause stress in the fish, which can be a major factor in facilitating fish disease.*[94] For many parasites, infestation depends on the host's degree of mobility, the density of the host population and vulnerability of the host's defence system.*[101] Sea

lice are the primary parasitic problem for finfish in aquaculture, high numbers causing widespread skin erosion and haemorrhaging, gill congestion, and increased mucus production.*[102] There are also a number of prominent viral and bacterial pathogens that can have severe effects on internal organs and nervous systems.*[103]

Improving welfare

The key to improving welfare of marine cultured organisms is to reduce stress to a minimum, as prolonged or repeated stress can cause a range of adverse effects. Attempts to minimise stress can occur throughout the culture process. During grow out it is important to keep stocking densities at appropriate levels specific to each species, as well as separating size classes and grading to reduce aggressive behavioural interactions. Keeping nets and cages clean can assist positive water flow to reduce the risk of water degradation.

Not surprisingly disease and parasitism can have a major effect on fish welfare and it is important for farmers not only to manage infected stock but also to apply disease prevention measures. However, prevention methods, such as vaccination, can also induce stress because of the extra handling and injection.*[96] Other methods include adding antibiotics to feed, adding chemicals into water for treatment baths and biological control, such as using cleaner wrasse to remove lice from farmed salmon.*[96]

Many steps are involved in transport, including capture, food deprivation to reduce faecal contamination of transport water, transfer to transport vehicle via nets or pumps, plus transport and transfer to the delivery location. During transport water needs to be maintained to a high quality, with regulated temperature, sufficient oxygen and minimal waste products.*[94]*[96] In some cases anaesthetics may be used in small doses to calm fish before transport.*[96]

Aquaculture is sometimes part of an environmental rehabilitation program or as an aid in conserving endangered species.*[104]

2.1.10 Prospects

Global wild fisheries are in decline, with valuable habitat such as estuaries in critical condition.*[105] The aquaculture or farming of piscivorous fish, like salmon, does not help the problem because they need to eat products from other fish, such as fish meal and fish oil. Studies have shown that salmon farming has major negative impacts on wild salmon, as well as the forage fish that need to be caught to feed them.*[106]*[107] Fish that are higher on the food chain are less efficient sources of food energy.

Apart from fish and shrimp, some aquaculture undertakings, such as seaweed and filter-feeding bivalve mollusks like oysters, clams, mussels and scallops, are relatively benign and even environmentally restorative.*[23] Filter-feeders filter pollutants as well as nutrients from the water, improving water quality.*[108] Seaweeds extract nutrients such as inorganic nitrogen and phosphorus directly from the water,*[62] and filter-feeding mollusks can extract nutrients as they feed on particulates, such as phytoplankton and detritus.*[109]

Some profitable aquaculture cooperatives promote sustainable practices.*[110] New methods lessen the risk of biological and chemical pollution through minimizing fish stress, fallowing netpens, and applying Integrated Pest Management. Vaccines are being used more and more to reduce antibiotic use for disease control.*[111]

Onshore recirculating aquaculture systems, facilities using polyculture techniques, and properly sited facilities (for example, offshore areas with strong currents) are examples of ways to manage negative environmental effects.

Recirculating aquaculture systems (RAS) recycle water by circulating it through filters to remove fish waste and food and then recirculating it back into the tanks. This saves water and the waste gathered can be used in compost or, in some cases, could even be treated and used on land. While RAS was developed with freshwater fish in mind, scientist associated with the Agricultural Research Service have found a way to rear saltwater fish using RAS in low-salinity waters.*[112] Although saltwater fish are raised in off-shore cages or caught with nets in water that typically has a salinity of 35 parts per thousand (ppt), scientists were able to produce healthy pompano, a saltwater fish, in tanks with a salinity of only 5 ppt. Commercializing low-salinity RAS are predicted to have positive environmental and economical effects. Unwanted nutrients from the fish food would not be added to the ocean and the risk of transmitting diseases between wild and farm-raised fish would greatly be reduced. The price of expensive saltwater fish, such as the pompano and combia used in the experiments, would be reduced. However, before any of this can be done researchers must study every aspect of the fish's lifecycle, including the amount of ammonia and nitrate the fish will tolerate in the water, what to feed the fish during each stage of its lifecycle, the stocking rate that will produce the healthiest fish, etc.*[112]

Some 16 countries now use geothermal energy for aquaculture, including China, Israel, and the United States.*[113] In California, for example, 15 fish farms produce tilapia, bass, and catfish with warm water from underground. This warmer water enables fish to grow all year round and mature more quickly. Collectively these California farms produce 4.5 million kilograms of fish each year.*[113]

2.1.11   See also

- Agroecology

- Alligator farm

- Aquaponics

- Copper alloys in aquaculture

- Fish hatchery

- Fisheries science

- Industrial aquaculture

- List of harvested aquatic animals by weight

- Recirculating aquaculture system

2.1.12   Notes

[1] Based on data sourced from the FishStat database

[2] Environmental Impact of Aquaculture

[3] Aquaculture's growth continuing: improved management techniques can reduce environmental effects of the practice.(UPDATE)." Resource: Engineering & Technology for a Sustainable World 16.5 (2009): 20-22. Gale Expanded Academic ASAP. Web. 1 October 2009.

[4] "Answers - The Most Trusted Place for Answering Life's Questions". Answers.com.

[5] Klinger, D. H. et al. 2012. Moving beyond the fished or farmed dichotomy. Marine Policy.

[6] Global Aquaculture Production Fishery Statistical Collections, FAO, Rome. Retrieved 2 October 2011.

[7] Half Of Fish Consumed Globally Is Now Raised On Farms, Study Finds Science Daily, September 8, 2009.

[8] Watson, Reg and Pauly, Daniel (2001). "Systematic distortions in world Fisheries catch trends". Nature 414 (6863): 534. doi:10.1038/35107050.

[9] Seafood Choices Alliance (2005) It's all about salmon

[10] Aborigines may have farmed eels, built huts ABC Science News, 13 March 2003.

[11] Lake Condah Sustainability Project. Retrieved 18 February 2010.

[12] "History of Aquaculture". Food and Agriculture Organization, United Nations. Retrieved August 23, 2009.

[13] McCann, Anna Marguerite (1979). "The Harbor and Fishery Remains at Cosa, Italy, by Anna Marguerite McCann". Journal of Field Archaeology 6 (4): 391–411. doi:10.1179/009346979791489014. JSTOR 529424.

[14] Jhingran, V.G., Introduction to aquaculture. 1987, United Nations Development Programme, Food and Agriculture Organization of the United Nations, Nigerian Institute for Oceanography and Marine Research.

[15] Salt: A World History Mark Kurlansky

[16] "Fishpond Network in the Trebon Basin". UNESCO. Retrieved 1 Oct 2015.

[17] Costa-Pierce, B.A., (1987) Aquaculture in ancient Hawaii. Bioscience 37(5):320-331. web access

[18] "A Brief History of Oystering in Narragansett Bay". URI Alumni Magazine, University of Rhode Island. 22 May 2015. Retrieved 1 October 2015.

[19] Milner, James W. (1874). "The Progress of Fish-culture in the United States". United States Commission of Fish and Fisheries Report of the Commissioner for 1872 and 1873. 535 – 544 <http://penbay.org/cof/cof_1872_1873.html>

[20] Rice, M.A. 2010. A brief history of the American Fish Culture Company 1877-1997. Rhode Island History 68(1):20-35. web version

[21] Peter Neushul, Seaweed for War: California's World War I kelp industry, Technology and Culture 30 (July 1989), 561-583.

[22] "'FAO: 'Fish farming is the way forward.'(Big Picture)(Food and Agriculture Administration's 'State of Fisheries and Aquaculture' report)." The Ecologist 39.4 (2009): 8-9. Gale Expanded Academic ASAP. Web. 1 October 2009. <http://find.galegroup.com/gtx/start.do?prodId=EAIM.>.

[23] "The Case for Fish and Oyster Farming," Carl Marziali, University of Southern California Trojan Family Magazine, May 17, 2009.

[24] "The Economist: 'The promise of a blue revolution', Aug. 7, 2003. <http://www.economist.com/node/1974103>

[25] "Jacques Cousteau, The Ocean World of Jacques Cousteau: The Act of life, World Pub: 1973."

[26] "Science Magazine: Sign In". sciencemag.org.

[27] Guns, Germs, and Steel. New York, New York: W.W. Norton & Company, Inc. 2005. ISBN 978-0-393-06131-4.

[28] Imsland, Albert K.; Reynolds, Patrick; Eliassen, Gerhard; Hangstad, Thor Arne; Foss, Atle; Vikingstad, Erik; Elvegård, Tor Anders (2014-03-20). "The use of lumpfish (Cyclopterus lumpus L.) to control sea lice (Lepeophtheirus salmonis Krøyer) infestations in intensively farmed Atlantic salmon (Salmo salar L.)". Aquaculture. 424–425: 18–23. doi:10.1016/j.aquaculture.2013.12.033.

[29] "DEPOMOD and AutoDEPOMOD —Ecasa Toolbox". www.ecasatoolbox.org.uk. Retrieved 2015-09-24.

[30] Naylor, Rosamond L.; Goldburg, Rebecca J.; Primavera, Jurgenne H.; Kautsky, Nils; Beveridge, Malcolm C. M.; Clay, Jason; Folke, Carl; Lubchenco, Jane; Mooney, Harold (2000-06-29). "Effect of aquaculture on world fish supplies". Nature 405 (6790): 1017–1024. doi:10.1038/35016500. ISSN 0028-0836.

[31] "Turning the tide" (PDF).

[32] "Qian, P. Y., Xu, Y. & Fusetani, N. Natural products as antifouling compounds: recent progress and future perspectives. Biofouling 26, 223-234". ResearchGate. Retrieved 2015-09-24.

[33] Volpe, J. (2005). "Dollars without sense: The bait for big-money tuna ranching around the world". BioScience 55 (4): 301–302. doi:10.1641/0006-3568(2005)055[0301:DWSTBF]2.0.CO;2. ISSN 0006-3568.

[34] Asche, Frank (2008). "Farming the Sea". Marine Resource Economics 23 (4): 527–547. JSTOR 42629678.

[35] Goldburg, Rebecca; Naylor, Rosamond (February 2005). "Future Seascapes, Fishing, and Fish Farming". Frontiers in Ecology and the Environment 3 (1): 21–28. doi:10.2307/3868441. JSTOR 3868441.

[36] "About Seafood Watch". Monterey Bay Aquarium.

[37] New, M. B.: Farming Freshwater Prawns; FAO Fisheries Technical Paper 428, 2002. ISSN 0429-9345.

[38] Data extracted from the FAO Fisheries Global Aquaculture Production Database for freshwater crustaceans. The most recent data sets are for 2003 and sometimes contain estimates. Retrieved June 28, 2005.

[39] Burkholder, J.M. and S.E. Shumway. 2011. Bivalve shellfish aquaculture and eutrophication. In, Shellfish Aquaculture and the Environment. Ed. S.E. Shumway. John Wiley & Sons.

[40] "Abalone Farming Information". Archived from the original on 13 November 2007. Retrieved 2007-11-08.

[41] "Abalone Farming on a Boat". Wired. 25 January 2002. Archived from the original on 4 January 2007. Retrieved 2007-01-27.

[42] World Wildlife Fund. "Sustainable Seafood, Farmed Seafood". Retrieved May 30, 2013.

[43] Ess, Charlie. "Wild product's versatility could push price beyond $2 for Alaska dive fleet". National Fisherman. Retrieved 2008-08-01.

[44] FAO (2014) The State of World Fisheries and Aquaculture 2014 (SOFIA)

[45] $86 thousand million

[46] Blumenthal, Les (August 2, 2010). "Company says FDA is nearing decision on genetically engineered Atlantic salmon" . Washington Post. Retrieved August 2010.

[47] "Wired 12.05: The Bluewater Revolution" . *wired.com*.

[48] Eilperin, Juliet (2005-01-24). "Fish Farming's Bounty Isn't Without Barbs" . *The Washington Post*.

[49] "The State of World Fisheries and Aquaculture" . *fao.org*.

[50] "Fisheries and aquaculture have good future". *Herald Globe*. Retrieved 27 May 2014.

[51] "FAO Fisheries & Aquaculture - FI fact sheet search" . *www.fao.org*. Retrieved 2015-06-08.

[52] "Aquaculture - U.S. Aquaculture Legislation Timeline" . *www.oceaneconomics.org*. Retrieved 2015-06-08.

[53] "Commerce and NOAA release national aquaculture policies to increase domestic seafood production, create sustainable jobs, and restore marine habitats" . *www.noaanews. noaa.gov*. Retrieved 2015-06-08.

[54] "Bill Summary & Status - 112th Congress (2011 - 2012) - H.R.2373 - THOMAS (Library of Congress)". *thomas.loc.gov*. Retrieved 2015-06-08.

[55] "Output of Aquatic Products" . *China Statistics*. Retrieved 2011-04-23.

[56] Pearson, Helen (2001). "China caught out as model shows net fall in fish" . *Nature* **414** (6863): 477. doi:10.1038/35107216.

[57] Heilprin, John (2001) Chinese Misreporting Masks Dramatic Decline In Ocean Fish Catches *Associated Press*, 29 November 2001.

[58] Reville, William (2002) Something fishy about the figures *The Irish Times*, 14 March 2002

[59] China disputes claim it over reports fish catch *Associated Press*, 17 December 2002.

[60] FAO (2006) The State of World Fisheries and Aquaculture (SOPHIA), Page 5.

[61] "FAO Fisheries Department - FISHERY STATISTICS: RELIABILITY AND POLICY IMPLICATIONS" . *fao.org*.

[62] Chopin T, Buschmann AH, Halling C, Troell M, Kautsky N, Neori A, Kraemer GP, Zertuche-Gonzalez JA, Yarish C and Neefus C. 2001. Integrating seaweeds into marine aquaculture systems: a key toward sustainability. Journal of Phycology 37: 975-986.

[63] Chopin T. 2006. Integrated multi-trophic aquaculture. What it is, and why you should care ... and don't confuse it with polyculture. Northern Aquaculture, Vol. 12, No. 4, July/August 2006, pg. 4.

[64] Neori A, Chopin T, Troell M, Buschmann AH, Kraemer GP, Halling C, Shpigel M and Yarish C. 2004. Integrated aquaculture: rationale, evolution and state of the art emphasizing seaweed biofiltration in modern mariculture. Aquaculture 231: 361-391.

[65] Offshore Aquaculture in the United States: Economic considerations, implications, and opportunities, U.S. Department of Commerce, National Oceanic & Atmospheric Administration, July 2008, p. 53

[66] Braithwaite, RA; McEvoy, LA (2005). "Marine biofouling on fish farms and its remediation" . *Advances in marine biology* **47**: 215–52. doi:10.1016/S0065-2881(04)47003-5. PMID 15596168.

[67] "Commercial and research fish farming and aquaculture netting and supplies" . Sterlingnets.com. Archived from the original on 26 July 2010. Retrieved 2010-06-16.

[68] "Aquaculture Netting by Industrial Netting" . Industrialnetting.com. Archived from the original on 29 May 2010. Retrieved 2010-06-16.

[69] Southern Regional Aquaculture Center at http://aquanic. org/publicat/usda_rac/efs/srac/162fs.pdf

[70] Diamond, Jared, *Collapse: How societies choose to fail or succeed,* Viking Press, 2005, pp. 479–485

[71] Costa-Pierce, B.A., 2002, *Ecological Aquaculture,* Blackwell Science, Oxford, UK.

[72] Thacker P, (June 2008) *Fish Farms Harm Local Food Supply,* Environmental Science and Technology, V. 40, Issue 11, pp 3445–3446

[73] FAO: Aquaculture Production Trends Analysis (2000)

[74] FAO: World Review of Fisheries and Aquaculture 2008: Highlights of Special Studies Rome.

[75] Tacon & Metian (2008): Global overview on the use of fish meal and fish oil in industrially compounded aquafeeds: Trends and future prospects. *Aquaculture* 285:146-158.

[76] OECD-FAO Agricultural Outlook 2014

[77] Torrissen et al. (2011) Atlantic Salmon (Salmo salar): The "Super-Chicken" of the Sea? *Reviews in Fisheries Science* 19:3

[78] USDA Trout-Grains Project

[79] NOAA/USDA: The Future of Aquafeeds (2011)

[80] "Oceans" . *davidsuzuki.org*.

[81] "Aquaculture's growth continuing: improved management techniques can reduce environmental effects of the practice.(UPDATE)." Resource: Engineering & Technology for a Sustainable World 16.5 (2009): 20-22. Gale Expanded Academic ASAP. Web. 1 October 2009.

[82] Azevedo-Santos, V. M. D.; Rigolin-Sá, O.; Pelicice, F. M. (2011). "Growing, losing or introducing? Cage aquaculture as a vector for the introduction of non-native fish in Furnas Reservoir, Minas Gerais, Brazil". *Neotropical Ichthyology* **9** (4): 915. doi:10.1590/S1679-62252011000400024.

[83] Azevedo-Santos, V.M.; Pelicice, F.M.; Lima-Junior, D.P.; Magalhães, A.L.B.; Orsi,M.L.; Vitule, J. R. S. & A.A. Agostinho, 2015. How to avoid fish introductions in Brazil: education and information as alternatives. **Natureza & Conservação**, in press.

[84] Nickerson, DJ (1999). "Trade-offs of mangrove area development in the Philippines". *Ecol. Econ.* **28** (2): 279–298. doi:10.1016/S0921-8009(98)00044-5.

[85] Gunawardena1, M; Rowan, JS (2005). "Economic Valuation of a Mangrove Ecosystem Threatened by Shrimp Aquaculture in Sri Lanka". *Journal of Environmental Management* **36** (4): 535–550. doi:10.1007/s00267-003-0286-9.

[86] Hinrichsen D (1998) *Coastal Waters of the World: Trends, Threats, and Strategies* Island Press. ISBN 978-1-55963-383-3

[87] Meat and Fish AAAS Atlas of Population and Environment. Retrieved 4 January 2010.

[88] FAO: Cultured Aquatic Species Information Programme: *Oncorhynchus kisutch* (Walbaum, 1792) Rome. Retrieved 8 May 2009.

[89] Mcleod C, J Grice, H Campbell and T Herleth (2006) Super Salmon: The Industrialisation of Fish Farming and the Drive Towards GM Technologies in Salmon Production CSaFe, Discussion paper 5, University of Otago.

[90] Robynne Boyd, Would you eat AquAdvantage salmon if approved? *Scientific American* online, 26 April 2013.

[91] FDA: AquAdvantage Salmon

[92] Hastein, T., Scarfe, A.D. and Lund, V.L. (2005) Science-based assessment of welfare: Aquatic animals. Rev. Sci. Tech. Off. Int. Epiz 24 (2) 529-547

[93] Chandroo, K.P., Duncan, I.J.H. and Moccia, R.D. (2004) "Can fish suffer?: Perspectives on sentience, pain, fear and stress." *Applied Animal Behaviour Science* 86 (3,4) 225-250

[94] Conte, F.S. (2004). "Stress and the welfare of cultured fish". *Applied Animal Behaviour Science* **86** (3-4): 205–223. doi:10.1016/j.applanim.2004.02.003.

[95] Huntingford, F. A.; Adams, C.; Braithwaite, V. A.; Kadri, S.; Pottinger, T. G.; Sandoe, P.; Turnbull, J. F. (2006). "Current issues in fish welfare" (PDF). *Journal of Fish Biology* **68** (2): 332–372. doi:10.1111/j.0022-1112.2006.001046.x.

[96] Ashley, P.J. (2006) Fish welfare: Current issues in aquaculture. Applied Animal Behaviour Science, doi:10.1016/j.applanim.2006.09.001

[97] Baras E. And Jobling (2002). "Dynamics of intracohort cannibalism in cultured fish". *Aquaculture Research* **33** (7): 461–479. doi:10.1046/j.1365-2109.2002.00732.x.

[98] Greaves K., Tuene S. (2001). "The form and context of aggressive behaviour in farmed Atlantic halibut (Hippoglossus hippoglossus L.)". *Aquaculture* **193** (1–2): 139–147. doi:10.1016/S0044-8486(00)00476-2.

[99] Ellis T., North B., Scott A.P., Bromage N.R., Porter M., Gadd D. (2002). "The relationships between stocking density and welfare in farmed rainbow trout". *Journal of Fish Biology* **61** (3): 493–531. doi:10.1111/j.1095-8649.2002.tb00893.x.

[100] Remen M., Imsland A.K., Steffansson S.O., Jonassen T.M., Foss A. (2008). "Interactive effects of ammonia and oxygen on growth and physiological status of juvenile Atlantic cod (*Gadus morhua*)". *Aquaculture* **274** (2–4): 292–299. doi:10.1016/j.aquaculture.2007.11.032.

[101] Paperna I (1991). "Diseases caused by parasites in the aquaculture of warm water fish". *Annual Review of Fish Diseases* **1**: 155–194. doi:10.1016/0959-8030(91)90028-I.

[102] Johnson S.C., Treasurer J.W., Bravo S., Nagasawa K., Kabata Z. (2004). "A review of the impact of parasitic copepods on marine aquaculture". *Zoological Studies* **43** (2): 229–243.

[103] Johansen L.H., Jensen I., Mikkelsen H., Bjorn P.A., Jansen P.A., Bergh O. (2011). "Disease interaction and pathogens exchange between wild and farmed fish populations with special reference to Norway". *Aquaculture* **315** (3–4): 167–186. doi:10.1016/j.aquaculture.2011.02.014.

[104] "Aquaculture Development". *google.be*.

[105] Tietenberg TH (2006) *Environmental and Natural Resource Economics: A Contemporary Approach*. Page 28. Pearson/Addison Wesley. ISBN 978-0-321-30504-6

[106] Knapp G, Roheim CA and Anderson JL (2007) *The Great Salmon Run: Competition Between Wild And Farmed Salmon* World Wildlife Fund. ISBN 978-0-89164-175-9

[107] Eilperin, Juliet; Kaufman, Marc (2007-12-14). "Salmon Farming May Doom Wild Populations, Study Says". *The Washington Post*.

[108] OSTROUMOV S. A. (2005). "Some aspects of water filtering activity of filter-feeders". *Hydrobiologia* **542**: 400. doi:10.1007/s10750-004-1875-1. Retrieved September 26, 2009.

[109] Rice, M.A. (2008). "Environmental impacts of shellfish aquaculture" (PDF). Retrieved 2009-10-08.

[110] "Aquaculture: Issues and Opportunities for Sustainable Production and Trade". ITCSD. July 2006.

[111] "Pew Oceans Commission report on Aquaculture"

[112] "Growing Premium Seafood-Inland!". USDA Agricultural Research Service. February 2009.

[113] "Stabilizing Climate" in Lester R. Brown, *Plan B 2.0 Rescuing a Planet Under Stress and a Civilization in Trouble* (NY: W.W. Norton & Co., 2006), p. 199.

2.1.13   References

- Corpron, K.E., Armstrong, D.A., 1983. Removal of nitrogen by an aquatic plant, *Elodea densa*, in recirculating *Macrobrachium* culture systems. Aquaculture 32, 347-360.

- Duarte, Carlos M; Marbá, Nùria and Holmer, Marianne (2007) *Rapid Domestication of Marine Species.* Science. Vol 316, no 5823, pp 382–383. podcast

- J. G. Ferreira, A.J.S. Hawkins, S.B. Bricker, 2007. Management of productivity, environmental effects and profitability of shellfish aquaculture – The Farm Aquaculture Resource Management (FARM) model. Aquaculture, 264, 160-174.

- GESAMP (2008) *Assessment and communication of environmental risks in coastal aquaculture* FAO Reports and Studies No 76. ISBN 978-92-5-105947-0

- Hepburn, J. 2002. *Taking Aquaculture Seriously.* Organic Farming, Winter 2002 © Soil Association.

- Kinsey, Darin, 2006 "'Seeding the water as the earth' : epicentre and peripheries of a global aquacultural revolution. Environmental History 11, 3: 527-66

- Naylor, R.L., S.L. Williams, and D.R. Strong. 2001. *Aquaculture – A Gateway For Exotic Species.* Science, 294: 1655-6.

- The Scottish Association for Marine Science and Napier University. 2002. Review and synthesis of the environmental impacts of aquaculture

- Higginbotham James *Piscinae: Artificial Fishponds in Roman Italy* University of North Carolina Press (June 1997)

- Wyban, Carol Araki (1992) *Tide and Current: Fishponds of Hawai'I* University of Hawaii Press:: ISBN 978-0-8248-1396-3

- Timmons, M.B., Ebeling, J.M., Wheaton, F.W., Summerfelt, S.T., Vinci, B.J., 2002. Recirculating Aquaculture Systems: 2nd edition. Cayuga Aqua Ventures.

- Piedrahita, R.H., 2003. Reducing the potential environmental impacts of tank aquaculture effluents through intensification and recirculation. Aquaculture 226, 35-44.

- Klas, S., Mozes, N., Lahav, O., 2006. Development of a single-sludge denitrification method for nitrate removal from RAS effluents: Lab-scale results vs. model prediction. Aquaculture 259, 342-353.

2.1.14   Further reading

- William McClarney (2013). *Freshwater Aquaculture.* Echo Point Books & Media, LLC. ISBN 1-62654-990-7.

- *AquaLingua* ISBN 978-82-529-2389-6

- *Rice–Fish Culture in China* (1995), ISBN 978-0-88936-776-0, OCLC 35883297

- Stickney, Robert (2009) *Aquaculture: An Introductory Text* CABI. ISBN 978-1-84593-589-4.

- Nash, Colin (2011) *The History of Aquaculture* John Wiley and Sons. ISBN 978-0-8138-2163-4.

- Birt, B., Rodwell, L., & Richards, J. (2009). "Investigation into the sustainability of organic aquaculture of Atlantic cod (*Gadus morhua*)". *Sustainability: Science, Practice & Policy* **5** (2): 4–14.

- Wilkey, Ryan; Myers, Mackenzie; Rintoul, Lyla; Robinson, Torie; Spina, Michelle (1 June 2011). "Fiji Aquaculture/Rice Farming Analysis" . *Digital Commons at Cal Poly.* Retrieved June 2011.

2.1.15   External links

- "Aquaculture Factsheet" . Waitt Institute. Retrieved 2015-06-08.

- Aquaculture at DMOZ

- Aquaculture science at DMOZ

- The Coastal Resources Center

- NOAA aquaculture

- The University of Hawaii's AquacultureHub

2.2   Beluga caviar

Beluga caviar is caviar consisting of the roe (or eggs) of the beluga sturgeon *Huso huso*. It is found primarily in the Caspian Sea, the world's largest salt-water lake, which is bordered by Iran and the CIS countries of Azerbaijan, Kazakhstan, Russia, and Turkmenistan. It can also be found in the Black Sea basin and occasionally in the Adriatic Sea.

Black Beluga caviar

Beluga caviar is the most expensive type of caviar,[1] with present market prices ranging from $7,000 to $10,000/kg ($3,200 to $4,500/lb).[2][3]

2.2.1 Harvesting

The Beluga sturgeon is currently considered to be critically endangered, causing the United States Fish and Wildlife Service to ban in 2005 the importation of Beluga caviar which originated in the Caspian Sea and Black Sea basin. In 2006, the Convention on International Trade in Endangered Species (CITES) suspended all trade made with the traditional caviar-producing regions of the Caspian and Black Seas (Beluga, Ossetra and Sevruga), (Azerbaijan, Bulgaria, China, Iran, Kazakhstan, Romania, Russia, Serbia and Montenegro, Turkmenistan, and Ukraine) due to the producing countries' failure to apply international regulations and recommendations.[4] Caviar from Iran is exempted from the ban. Iran is considered by CITES to practice effective conservation and policing of its fisheries.[5] In January 2007, this ban was partly lifted, allowing the sale of 96 tons of caviar, 15 percent below the official 2005 level.[6]

CITES maintained the 2007 quotas for 2008, drawing criticism for doing little to protect the declining sturgeon population.[7]

The Beluga sturgeon can take up to 20 years to reach maturity. The fish harvested for caviar are often nearly 900 kg (2,000 lb). The eggs themselves are the largest of the commonly used roes, and range in color from dark gray (almost black) to light gray, with the lighter colors coming from older fish, and being the most valued. A pearly white variety, called *Almas* (Persian for *diamond*), taken from a centennial female sturgeon, is the rarest type of Beluga available, with an extremely small production and prices reaching almost £25,000 per kilogram.[8]

Any additions by producers diminish the value of the roe, and the caviar usually reaches the market without any additions or processing whatsoever.

2.2.2 Service

Any fine caviar, especially Beluga, is to be enjoyed with as little embellishment as possible. Many people will simply dollop a (mother of pearl or another non-metallic) spoonful onto the back of their hand near the webbing between the thumb and forefinger and enjoy it that way, so others can use the spoon without "double dipping." A fine champagne or vodka to wash it down is usually all that a connoisseur will use. For a more filling caviar experience, one can serve blini, or perhaps cold, boiled potato halves, but fine caviar is almost never enjoyed with diced onions or eggs, as that would surely affect the subtle flavors and texture that makes Beluga and other fine caviar the delicacy that they are.

As with most caviars, Beluga is usually handled with a caviar spoon made of mother of pearl, bone, or other non-metallic material, as metal utensils tend to impart an unwelcome metallic taste to the delicate and expensive roe.[9] Beluga caviar is usually served by itself on toast, unlike other less expensive caviars that can be served in a variety of ways, including hollowed and cooked new potatoes, on a blini, or garnished with sour cream, crème fraîche, minced onion or minced hard boiled egg whites. These items can, however, be served with Beluga as palate cleansers.

2.2.3 References

[1] Expensive ingredients | Top 5 world's most expensive ingredients - Yahoo Lifestyle India

[2] Young, Mark C. (1999). *Guinness Book of World Records*. p. 94.

[3] Schmidt, Arno (2003). *Chef's Book of Formulas, Yields, and Sizes*. p. 48.

[4]   "BBC - International caviar trade banned, 2006" . BBC
      News. 2006-01-03. Retrieved 2012-10-22.

[5]   "The Nibble, "Caspian Caviar Update: News About The
      World's Favorite Roe" , 2006" . Thenibble.com. Retrieved
      2012-10-22.

[6]   "UN lifts embargo on caviar trade" . BBC News. 2007-
      01-02. Retrieved 2008-05-30.

[7]   "Beluga Sturgeon Threatened With Extinction, Yet Caviar
      Quotas Remain Unchanged" . 2008-03-06. Archived from
      the original on 19 September 2008. Retrieved 2008-09-15.

[8]   "Almas Beluga is the world's most expensive Caviar" .
      Luxury Launches. Retrieved February 1, 2013.

[9]   Fabricant, Florence (2003). *The New York Times Seafood
      Cookbook*. p. 287.

2.3   Black Sea

This article is about the body of water. For other uses, see
Black Sea (disambiguation).

The **Black Sea** is a sea between Southeastern Europe and

The port of the Black Sea in Yevpatoria, Crimea

The Black Sea in Batumi, Georgia

Swallow's Nest in Crimea

Western Asia. It is bounded by Europe, Anatolia and the
Caucasus, and drains through the Mediterranean into the
Atlantic Ocean, via the Aegean Sea and various straits. The
Bosphorus Strait connects it to the Sea of Marmara, and the
Strait of the Dardanelles connects that sea to the Aegean Sea
region of the Mediterranean. These waters separate eastern
Europe and western Asia. The Black Sea is also connected
to the Sea of Azov by the Strait of Kerch.

The Black Sea has an area of 436,400 km^2 (168,500 sq
mi) (not including the Sea of Azov),[1] a maximum depth
of 2,212 m (7,257 ft),[2] and a volume of 547,000 km^3
(131,000 cu mi).[3] The Black Sea forms in an east-west
trending elliptical depression which lies between Bulgaria,
Georgia, Romania, Russia, Turkey, and Ukraine.[4] It is
constrained by the Pontic Mountains to the south and by the

*Photo of the Black Sea near Gagra, Georgia, Russian Empire taken
in 1915*

Caucasus Mountains to the east, and features a wide shelf to
the northwest. The longest east-west extent is about 1,175
km (730 mi).

Important cities along the coast include Batumi, Burgas, Constanţa, Giresun, Hopa, Istanbul, Kerch, Mangalia, Năvodari, Novorossiysk, Odessa, Ordu, Poti, Rize, Sinop, Samsun, Sevastopol, Sochi, Sozopol, Sukhumi, Trabzon, Varna, Yalta and Zonguldak.

The Black Sea has a positive water balance; that is, a net outflow of water 300 km^3 (72 cu mi) per year through the Bosphorus and the Dardanelles into the Aegean Sea. Mediterranean water flows into the Black Sea as part of a two-way hydrological exchange. The Black Sea outflow is cooler and less saline, and floats over the warm, more saline Mediterranean inflow – as a result of differences in density caused by differences in salinity – leading to a significant anoxic layer well below the surface waters. The Black Sea also receives river water from large Eurasian fluvial systems to the north of the Sea, of which the Don, Dnieper and Danube are the most significant.

In the past, the water level has varied significantly. Due to these variations in the water level in the basin, the surrounding shelf and associated aprons have sometimes been land. At certain critical water levels it is possible for connections with surrounding water bodies to become established. It is through the most active of these connective routes, the Turkish Straits, that the Black Sea joins the world ocean. When this hydrological link is not present, the Black Sea is an endorheic basin, operating independently of the global ocean system, like the Caspian Sea for example. Currently the Black Sea water level is relatively high, thus water is being exchanged with the Mediterranean. The Turkish Straits connect the Black Sea with the Aegean Sea, and comprise the Bosphorus, the Sea of Marmara and the Dardanelles.

Sunset on the Black Sea at Laspi, Crimea

The estuary of the Veleka in the Black Sea. Longshore drift has deposited sediment along the shoreline which has led to the formation of a spit, Sinemorets, Bulgaria

2.3.1 Extent

The International Hydrographic Organization defines the limits of the Black Sea as follows:[*][5]

The Black Sea near Constanţa, Romania

On the Southwest. The Northeastern limit of the Sea of Marmara [A line joining Cape Rumili with Cape Anatoli (41°13'N)].

In the Kertch Strait. A line joining Cape Takil and Cape Panaghia (45°02'N).

2.3.2 Population

2.3.3 Name

Modern names

Current names of the sea are usually equivalents of the English name "Black Sea", including these given in the countries bordering the sea:[13]

- Abkhaz: *Amshyn Eikʷa* (Амшын Еикәа)

- Bulgarian: Cherno more (Черно море, IPA: [ˈtʃɛrno moˈrɛ])

- Georgian: Shavi zghva (შავი ზღვა)

- Laz: *Ucha zuğa* (უჩა ზუღა), or simply *Zuğa* "Sea"

- Romanian: *Marea Neagră* (pronounced [ˈmarea ˈne̯aɡrə])

- Russian: Chornoye morye (Чёрное море, IPA: [ˈtɕɵrnəjə ˈmorʲɪ])

- Turkish: *Karadeniz* (IPA: [kaˈɾadeniz])

- Ukrainian: Chorne more (Чорне море, IPA: [ˈtʃɔrnɛ ˈmɔrɛ])

Such names have not yet been shown conclusively to predate the 12th century, but there are indications that they may be considerably older.

In Greece, the historical name "Euxine Sea", which holds a different meaning (see below), is still widely used:

- Greek: Eúxeinos Póntos (Εὔξεινος Πόντος)

The Black Sea is one of four seas named in English after common colour terms—the others being the Red Sea, the White Sea and the Yellow Sea.

Historical names

Strabo's *Geographica* (1.2.10) reports that in antiquity, the Black Sea was often just called "the Sea" (ὁ πόντος *ho pontos*). For the most part, Graeco-Roman tradition refers to the Black Sea as the "Hospitable sea", Εὔξεινος Πόντος *Eúxeinos Póntos*. This is a euphemism replacing an earlier "Inhospitable Sea", Πόντος Ἄξεινος *Póntos Áxeinos*, first attested in Pindar (c. 475 BC).

Strabo (7.3.6) thinks that the Black Sea was called "inhospitable" before Greek colonization because it was difficult to navigate, and because its shores were inhabited by savage tribes. The name was changed to "hospitable" after the Milesians had colonized the southern shoreline, the Pontus, making it part of Greek civilization.

It is also possible that the epithet *Áxeinos* arose by popular etymology from a Scythian word *axšaina-* "unlit", "dark"; the designation "Black Sea" may thus date from antiquity.

A map of Asia dating to 1570, entitled "Asiae Nova Descriptio", from Abraham Ortelius's *Theatrum Orbis Terrarum*, labels the sea *Mar Maggior* ("Great Sea", cf. Latin *mare major*).

English-language writers of the 18th century often used the name "Euxine Sea" (/ˈjuːksɪn/ or /ˈjuːkˌsaɪn/) to refer to the Black Sea. Edward Gibbon, for instance, calls the sea by this name throughout *The History of the Decline and Fall of the Roman Empire*.[14]

2.3.4 Geology and bathymetry

The bay of Sudak, Crimea

The geological origins of the basin can be traced back to two distinct relict back-arc basins which were initiated by the splitting of an Albian volcanic arc and the subduction of both the Paleo- and Neo-Tethys Oceans, but the timings of these events remain controversial.[15][16] Since its initiation, compressional tectonic environments led to subsidence in the basin, interspersed with extensional phases resulting in large-scale volcanism and numerous orogenies, causing the uplift of the Greater Caucasus, Pontides, Southern Crimean Peninsula and Balkanides mountain ranges.[17]

The ongoing collision between the Eurasian and African plates and westward escape of the Anatolian block along the North Anatolian Fault and East Anatolian Faults dictates the current tectonic regime,[17] which features enhanced subsidence in the Black Sea basin and significant volcanic activity in the Anatolian region.[18] It is these geological mechanisms which, in the long term, have caused the periodic isolations of the Black Sea from the rest of the global ocean system.

The modern basin is divided into two sub-basins by a convexity extending south from the Crimean Peninsula. The large shelf to the north of the basin is up to 190 km (120 mi) wide, and features a shallow apron with gradients between 1:40 and 1:1000. The southern edge around Turkey and the eastern edge around Georgia, however, are typified by a narrow shelf that rarely exceeds 20 km (12 mi) in width and a steep apron that is typically 1:40 gradient with numerous submarine canyons and channel extensions. The Euxine abyssal plain in the centre of the Black Sea reaches a maximum depth of 2,212 metres (7,257.22 feet) just south of Yalta on the Crimean Peninsula.[19]

The littoral zone of the Black Sea is often referred to as the **Pontic littoral** or **Pontic zone**.[20]

The area surrounding the Black Sea is commonly referred to as the *Black Sea Region*. Its northern part lies within the *Chernozem belt* (black soil belt) which goes from eastern Croatia (Slavonia), along the Danube (northern Serbia, northern Bulgaria (Danubian Plain) and southern Romania (Wallachian Plain)) to northeast Ukraine and further across the Central Black Earth Region and southern Russia into Siberia.[21]

2.3.5 Hydrology

This SeaWiFS view reveals the colourful interplay of currents on the sea's surface

The Black Sea is a marginal sea[22] and is the world's largest body of water with a meromictic basin.[23] The deep waters do not mix with the upper layers of water that receive oxygen from the atmosphere. As a result, over 90%

of the deeper Black Sea volume is anoxic water.[24] The Black Sea's circulation patterns are primarily controlled by basin topography and fluvial inputs, which result in a strongly stratified vertical structure. Because of the extreme stratification, it is classified as a salt wedge estuary.

The Black Sea only experiences water transfer with the Mediterranean Sea, so all inflow and outflow occurs in the Bosphorus and Dardanelles. Inflow from the Mediterranean has a higher salinity and density than the outflow, creating the classical estuarine circulation. This means that inflow of dense water from Mediterranean occurs at the bottom of the basin while outflow of fresher Black Sea surface-water into the Marmara Sea occurs near the surface. Fresher surface water is the product of the fluvial inputs, and this makes the Black Sea a positive sea. The net input of freshwater creates an outflow volume about twice that of the inflow. Evaporation and precipitation are roughly equal at about 300 cubic kilometres per year (72 cu mi/a).[22]

Because of the narrowness and shallowness of the Bosphorus and Dardanelles (their respective depths are only 33 and 70 meters), inflow and outflow current speeds are high and there is significant vertical shear. This allows for turbulent mixing of the two layers.[22] Surface water leaves the Black Sea with a salinity of 17 psu and reaches the Mediterranean with a salinity of 34 psu. Likewise, inflow of the Mediterranean with salinity 38.5 psu experiences a decrease to about 34 psu.[22]

Mean surface circulation is cyclonic and waters around the perimeter of the Black Sea circulate in a basin-wide shelf-break gyre known as the Rim Current. The Rim Current has a maximum velocity of about 50–100 cm/s. Within this feature, two smaller cyclonic gyres operate, occupying the eastern and western sectors of the basin.[22] The Eastern and Western Gyres are well-organized systems in the winter but dissipate into a series of interconnected eddies in the summer and autumn. Mesoscale activity in the peripheral flow becomes more pronounced during these warmer seasons and is subject to interannual variability .

Outside of the Rim Current, numerous quasi-permanent coastal eddies are formed as a result of upwelling around the coastal apron and "wind curl" mechanisms. The intra-annual strength of these features is controlled by seasonal atmospheric and fluvial variations. During the spring, the Batumi eddy forms in the southeastern corner of the sea.[25]

Beneath the surface waters—from about 50–100 meters—there exists a halocline that stops at the Cold Intermediate Layer (CIL). This layer is composed of cool, salty surface waters, which are the result of localized atmospheric cooling and decreased fluvial input during the winter months. It is the remnant of the winter surface mixed layer.[22] The base of the CIL is marked by a major pycnocline at about

100–200 metres (330–660 ft) and this density disparity is the major mechanism for isolation of the deep water.

Below the pycnocline is the Deep Water mass, where salinity increases to 22.3 psu and temperatures rise to around 8.9 °C.[*][22] The hydrochemical environment shifts from oxygenated to anoxic, as bacterial decomposition of sunken biomass utilizes all of the free oxygen. Weak geothermal heating and long residence time create a very thick convective bottom layer.[*][25]

2.3.6 Hydrochemistry

Organic matter, including anthropogenic artifacts such as boat hulls, are well preserved. During periods of high surface productivity, short-lived algal blooms form organic rich layers known as sapropels. Scientists have reported an annual phytoplankton bloom that can be seen in many NASA images of the region.[*][26] As a result of these characteristics the Black Sea has gained interest from the field of marine archaeology as ancient shipwrecks in excellent states of preservation have been discovered, such as the Byzantine wreck Sinop D, located in the anoxic layer off the coast of Sinop, Turkey.

Modelling shows the release of the hydrogen sulphide clouds in the event of an asteroid impact into the Black Sea would pose a threat to health—or even life—for people living on the Black Sea coast.[*][27]

There have been isolated reports of flares on the Black Sea occurring during thunderstorms, possibly caused by lighting igniting combustible gas seeping up from the lake depths.[*][28]

2.3.7 Ecology

See also: List of fish of the Black Sea
 The Black Sea supports an active and dynamic marine ecosystem, dominated by species suited to the brackish, nutrient-rich, conditions. As with all marine food webs, the Black Sea features a range of trophic groups, with autotrophic algae, including diatoms and dinoflagellates, acting as primary producers. The fluvial systems draining Eurasia and central Europe introduce large volumes of sediment and dissolved nutrients into the Black Sea, but distribution of these nutrients is controlled by the degree of physiochemical stratification, which is, in turn, dictated by seasonal physiographic development.[*][29]

During winter, strong wind promotes convective overturning and upwelling of nutrients, while high summer temperatures result in a marked vertical stratification and a warm, shallow mixed layer.[*][30] Day length and insolation intensity also controls the extent of the photic zone. Subsurface

The port of Poti, Georgia

productivity is limited by nutrient availability, as the anoxic bottom waters act as a sink for reduced nitrate, in the form of ammonia. The benthic zone also plays an important role in Black Sea nutrient cycling, as chemosynthetic organisms and anoxic geochemical pathways recycle nutrients which can be upwelled to the photic zone, enhancing productivity.[*][31]

Phytoplankton

Phytoplankton blooms and plumes of sediment form the bright blue swirls that ring the Black Sea in this 2004 image

The main phytoplankton groups present in the Black Sea are dinoflagellates, diatoms, coccolithophores and cyanobacteria. Generally, the annual cycle of phytoplankton development comprises significant diatom and dinoflagellate-dominated spring production, followed by a weaker mixed assemblage of community development below the seasonal thermocline during summer months and a surface-intensified autumn production.[*][30][*][32] This pattern of productivity is also augmented by an *Emiliania huxleyi* bloom during the late spring and summer months.

- Dinoflagellates

  Annual dinoflagellate distribution is defined by an extended bloom period in subsurface waters during the late spring and summer. In November, subsurface plankton production is combined with surface production, due to vertical mixing of water masses and nutrients such as nitrite.*[29] The major bloom-forming dinoflagellate species in the Black Sea is *Gymnodinium* sp.*[33] Estimates of dinoflagellate diversity in the Black Sea range from 193*[34] to 267 species.*[35] This level of species richness is relatively low in comparison to the Mediterranean Sea, which is attributable to the brackish conditions, low water transparency and presence of anoxic bottom waters. It is also possible that the low winter temperatures below 4 °C (39 °F) of the Black Sea prevent thermophilous species from becoming established. The relatively high organic matter content of Black Sea surface water favour the development of heterotrophic (an organism which uses organic carbon for growth) and mixotrophic dinoflagellates species (able to exploit different trophic pathways), relative to autotrophs. Despite its unique hydrographic setting, there are no confirmed endemic dinoflagellate species in the Black Sea.*[35]

- Diatoms

  The Black Sea is populated by many species of marine diatom, which commonly exist as colonies of unicellular, non-motile auto- and heterotrophic algae. The life-cycle of most diatoms can be described as 'boom and bust' and the Black Sea is no exception, with diatom blooms occurring in surface waters throughout the year, most reliably during March.*[29] In simple terms, the phase of rapid population growth in diatoms is caused by the inwash of silicon-bearing terrestrial sediments, and when the supply of silicon is exhausted, the diatoms begin to sink out of the photic zone and produce resting cysts. Additional factors such as predation by zooplankton and ammonium-based regenerated production also have a role to play in the annual diatom cycle.*[29]*[30] Typically, *Proboscia alata* blooms during spring and *Pseudosolenia calcar-avis* blooms during the autumn.*[33]

- Coccolithophores

  Coccolithophores are a type of motile, autotrophic phytoplankton that produce $CaCO_3$ plates, known as coccoliths, as part of their life cycle. In the Black Sea, the main period of coccolithophore growth occurs after the bulk of the dinoflagellate growth has taken place. In May, the dinoflagellates move below the seasonal thermocline, into deeper waters, where more nutrients are available. This permits coccolithophores to utilise the nutrients in the upper waters, and by the end of May, with favourable light and temperature conditions, growth rates reach their highest. The major bloom forming species is *Emiliania huxleyi*, which is also responsible for the release of dimethyl sulfide into the atmosphere. Overall, coccolithophore diversity is low in the Black Sea, and although recent sediments are dominated by *E. huxleyi*, *Braarudosphaera bigelowii*, Holocene sediments have also been shown to contain Helicopondosphaera and Discolithina species.

- Cyanobacteria

  Cyanobacteria are a phylum of picoplanktonic (plankton ranging in size from 0.2 to 2.0 μm) bacteria that obtain their energy via photosynthesis, and are present throughout the world's oceans. They exhibit a range of morphologiies, including filamentous colonies and biofilms. In the Black Sea, several species are present, and as an example, *Synechococcus* spp. can be found throughout the photic zone, although concentration decreases with increasing depth. Other factors which exert an influence on distribution include nutrient availability, predation and salinity.*[36]

Endemic animal species

- Zebra mussel

  The Black Sea along with the Caspian Sea is part of the Zebra mussel's native range. The mussel has been accidentally introduced around the world and become an invasive species where it has been introduced.

- Common Carp

The Common Carp's native range extends to The Black Sea along with the Caspian Sea and Aral Sea. Like the Zebra mussel the Common Carp is an invasive species when introduced to other habitats.

- Round Goby

Is another native fish that is also found in the Caspian Sea. It preys upon Zebra mussels. Like the mussels and common carp it has become invasive when introduced to other environments, like the Great Lakes.

Ecological effects of pollution

Since the 1960s, rapid industrial expansion along the Black Sea coast line and the construction of a major dam has significantly increased annual variability in the N:P:Si ratio in the basin. In coastal areas, the biological effect of these changes has been an increase in the frequency of monospecific phytoplankton blooms, with diatom bloom frequency increasing by a factor of 2.5 and non-diatom bloom frequency increasing by a factor of 6. The non-diatoms, such as the prymnesiophytes *Emiliania huxleyi* (coccolithophore), *Chromulina* sp., and the Euglenophyte *Eutreptia lanowii* are able to out-compete diatom species because of the limited availability of Si, a necessary constituent of diatom frustules.[*][37] As a consequence of these blooms, benthic macrophyte populations were deprived of light, while anoxia caused mass mortality in marine animals.[*][38][*][39]

The decline in macrophytes was further compounded by overfishing during the 1970s, while the invasive ctenophore *Mnemiopsis* reduced the biomass of copepods and other zooplankton in the late 1980s. Additionally, an alien species—the warty comb jelly (*Mnemiopsis leidyi*)—was able to establish itself in the basin, exploding from a few individuals to an estimated biomass of one billion metric tons.[*][40] The change in species composition in Black Sea waters also has consequences for hydrochemistry, as Ca-producing coccolithophores influence salinity and pH, although these ramifications have yet to be fully quantified. In central Black Sea waters, Si levels were also significantly reduced, due to a decrease in the flux of Si associated with advection across isopycnal surfaces. This phenomenon demonstrates the potential for localised alterations in Black Sea nutrient input to have basin-wide effects.

Pollution reduction and regulation efforts have led to a partial recovery of the Black Sea ecosystem during the 1990s, and an EU monitoring exercise, 'EROS21', revealed decreased N and P values, relative to the 1989 peak.[*][41] Recently, scientists have noted signs of ecological recovery, in part due to the construction of new sewage treatment plants in Slovakia, Hungary, Romania, and Bulgaria in connection with membership in the European Union. *Mnemiopsis leidyi* populations have been checked with the arrival of another alien species which feeds on them.[*][42]

- Jellyfish
- Actinia
- Actinia
- Goby
- Stingray
- Goat fish
- Hermit crab, *Diogenes pugilator*
- Blue sponge
- Spiny dogfish (Black Sea Sharks at Risk)
- Seahorse

2.3.8 Climate

The ice on the Gulf of Odessa

Short-term climatic variation in the Black Sea region is significantly influenced by the operation of the North Atlantic Oscillation, the climatic mechanisms resulting from the interaction between the north Atlantic and mid-latitude air masses.[*][43] While the exact mechanisms causing the North Atlantic Oscillation remain unclear,[*][44] it is thought the climate conditions established in western Europe mediate the heat and precipitation fluxes reaching Central Europe and Eurasia, regulating the formation of winter cyclones, which are largely responsible for regional precipitation inputs[*][45] and influence Mediterranean Sea Surface Temperatures (SST's).[*][46]

The relative strength of these systems also limits the amount of cold air arriving from northern regions during winter.[*][47] Other influencing factors include the regional topography, as depressions and storms systems arriving from the Mediterranean are funneled through the low land around the Bosphorus, Pontic and Caucasus mountain ranges acting as wave guides, limiting the speed and paths of cyclones passing through the region[*][48]

2.3.9 History

Mediterranean connection during the Holocene

The Bosphorus, taken from the International Space Station

The Black Sea is connected to the World Ocean by a chain of two shallow straits, the Dardanelles and the Bosphorus. The Dardanelles is 55 m (180 ft) deep and the Bosphorus is as shallow as 36 m (118 ft). By comparison, at the height of the last ice age, sea levels were more than 100 m (330 ft) lower than they are now.

There is also evidence that water levels in the Black Sea were considerably lower at some point during the post-glacial period. Thus, for example, archaeologists found fresh-water snail shells and man-made structures in roughly 100 m (330 ft) of water off the Black Sea coast of modern Turkey. Therefore, it is agreed that the Black Sea had been a landlocked freshwater lake (at least in upper layers)

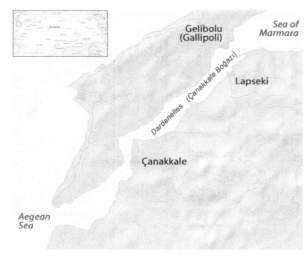

Map of the Dardanelles

during the last glaciation and for some time after.

In the aftermath of the last glacial period, water levels in the Black Sea and the Aegean Sea rose independently until they were high enough to exchange water. The exact timeline of this development is still subject to debate. One possibility is that the Black Sea filled first, with excess fresh water flowing over the Bosphorus sill and eventually into the Mediterranean Sea. There are also catastrophic scenarios, such as the "Black Sea deluge theory" put forward by William Ryan, Walter Pitman and Petko Dimitrov.

Deluge hypothesis Main article: Black Sea deluge hypothesis

The **Black Sea deluge** is a hypothesized catastrophic rise in the level of the Black Sea circa 5600 BC due to waters from the Mediterranean Sea breaching a sill in the Bosporus Strait. The hypothesis was headlined when *The New York Times* published it in December 1996, shortly before it was published in an academic journal.[*][49] While it is agreed that the sequence of events described did occur, there is debate over the suddenness, dating and magnitude of the events. Relevant to the hypothesis is that its description has led some to connect this catastrophe with prehistoric flood myths.[*][50]

Recorded history

The Black Sea was a busy waterway on the crossroads of the ancient world: the Balkans to the west, the Eurasian steppes to the north, Caucasus and Central Asia to the east, Asia Minor and Mesopotamia to the south, and Greece to the south-west.

A medieval map of the Black Sea by Diogo Homem.

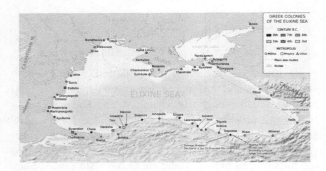

Greek colonies (8th-3rd century BCE) of the Black Sea (Euxine Sea)

The oldest processed gold in the world was found in Varna, and the Black Sea was supposedly sailed by the Argonauts. The land at the eastern end of the Black Sea, Colchis, (now Georgia), marked for the Greeks the edge of the known world.

The steppes to the north of the Black Sea have been suggested as the original homeland (*Urheimat*) of the speakers of the Proto-Indo-European language, (PIE) the progenitor of the Indo-European language family, by some scholars such as Marija Gimbutas; others move the heartland further east towards the Caspian Sea, yet others to Anatolia. Numerous ancient ports, some older than the Egyptian pyramids, line the Black Sea's coasts.

The Black Sea became an Ottoman Navy lake within five years of Genoa losing the Crimea in 1479, after which the only Western merchant vessels to sail its waters were those of Venice's old rival Ragusa. This restriction was gradually changed by the Russian Navy from 1783 until the relaxation of export controls in 1789 because of the French Revolution.[51][52]

The Black Sea was a significant naval theatre of World War I and saw both naval and land battles during World War II.

Archaeology

Ivan Aivazovsky. Black Sea Fleet in the Bay of Theodosia, *just before the Crimean War*

Ancient trade routes in the region are currently being extensively studied by scientists, as the Black Sea was sailed by Hittites, Carians, Thracians, Greeks, Persians, Cimmerians, Scythians, Romans, Byzantines, Goths, Huns, Avars, Bulgars, Slavs, Varangians, Crusaders, Venetians, Genoese, Lithuanians, Georgians, Poles, Tatars, Ottomans, and Russians.

Perhaps the most promising areas in deepwater archaeology are the quest for submerged prehistoric settlements in the continental shelf and for ancient shipwrecks in the anoxic zone, which are expected to be exceptionally well preserved due to the absence of oxygen. This concentration of historical powers, combined with the preservative qualities of the deep anoxic waters of the Black Sea, has attracted increased interest from marine archaeologists who have begun to discover a large number of ancient ships and organic remains in a high state of preservation.

2.3.10   Modern use

Yalta, Crimea

Black Sea coast with subtropical flora in Gagra, Georgia

Amasra, Turkey, is located on a small island in the Black Sea

Ordzhonikidze health resort in Sochi, Russia

Commercial and civic use

According to NATO, the Black sea is a strategic corridor that provides smuggling channels for moving legal and illegal goods including drugs, radioactive materials, and coun-

terfeit goods that can be used to finance terrorism.[53]

Navigation

Ports and ferry terminals According to the International Transport Workers' Federation 2013 study, there were at least 30 operating merchant seaports in the Black Sea (including at least 12 in Ukraine).[54]

Merchant fleet and traffic According to the International Transport Workers' Federation 2013 study, there were around 2,400 commercial vessels operating in the Black Sea.[54]

Fishing Anchovy: the Turkish commercial fishing fleet catches around 300,000 tons per year on average, and fishery carried out mainly in winter and the highest portion of the stock is caught between November and December.[55]

Hydrocarbons exploration Since the 1980s, the Soviet Union started offshore drilling for petroleum in the sea's western portion (adjoining Ukraine's coast). The independent Ukraine continued and intensified that effort within its Exclusive Economic Zone, inviting major international oil companies for exploration. Discovery of the new, massive oilfields in the area stimulated an influx of foreign investments. It also provoked a short-term peaceful territorial dispute with Romania which was resolved in 2011 by an international court redefining the Exclusive Economic Zones between the two countries.

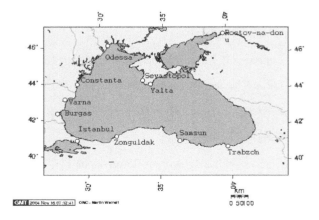

Cities of the Black Sea

Holiday resorts and spas In the years following the end of the Cold War, the popularity of the Black Sea as a tourist destination steadily increased. Tourism at Black Sea resorts became one of the region's growth industries.[56] The following is a list of well-known Black Sea resorts:

- 2 Mai (Romania)
- Agigea (Romania)
- Ahtopol (Bulgaria)
- Amasra (Turkey)
- Anaklia (Georgia)
- Anapa (Russia)
- Albena (Bulgaria)
- Alupka (Crimea, Russia/Ukraine (disputed))
- Alushta (Crimea, Russia/Ukraine (disputed))
- Balchik (Bulgaria)
- Batumi (Georgia)
- Burgas (Bulgaria)
- Byala (Bulgaria)
- Cap Aurora (Romania)
- Chakvi (Georgia)
- Constantine and Helena (Bulgaria)
- Constanța (Romania)
- Corbu (Romania)
- Costineşti (Romania)
- Eforie (Romania)
- Emona (Bulgaria)
- Eupatoria (Crimea, Russia/Ukraine (disputed))
- Foros (Crimea, Russia/Ukraine (disputed))
- Feodosiya (Crimea, Russia/Ukraine (disputed))
- Giresun (Turkey)
- Gagra (Abkhazia, Georgia[lower-alpha 1])
- Gelendzhik (Russia)
- Golden Sands (Bulgaria)
- Gonio (Georgia)
- Gurzuf (Crimea, Russia/Ukraine (disputed))
- Hopa (Artvin, Turkey)
- Istanbul (Turkey)
- Jupiter (Romania)
- Kamchia (Bulgaria)
- Kavarna (Bulgaria)
- Kiten (Bulgaria)
- Kobuleti (Georgia)
- Koktebel (Crimea, Russia/Ukraine (disputed))
- Lozenetz (Bulgaria)
- Mamaia (Romania)
- Mangalia (Romania)
- Năvodari (Romania)
- Neptun (Romania)
- Nesebar (Bulgaria)
- Novorossiysk (Russia)
- Ordu (Turkey)
- Obzor (Bulgaria)
- Odessa (Ukraine)
- Olimp (Romania)
- Pitsunda (Abkhazia, Georgia[lower-alpha 1])
- Pomorie (Bulgaria)
- Primorsko (Bulgaria)
- Rize (Turkey)
- Rusalka (Bulgaria)
- Samsun (Turkey)
- Saturn (Romania)
- Sinop (Turkey)
- Sochi (Russia)
- Sozopol (Bulgaria)
- Sudak (Crimea, Russia/Ukraine (disputed))
- Skadovsk (Ukraine)
- Sulina (Romania)
- Sunny Beach (Bulgaria)
- Şile (Turkey)

- Sveti Vlas (Bulgaria)

- Trabzon (Turkey)

- Tsikhisdziri (Georgia)

- Tuapse (Russia)

- Ureki (Georgia)

- Vama Veche (Romania)

- Varna (Bulgaria)

- Venus (Romania)

- Yalta (Crimea, Russia/Ukraine (disputed))

- Zonguldak (Turkey)

Soviet frigate Bezzavetny *(right) bumping the USS* Yorktown *during the 1988 Black Sea bumping incident.*

Ukrainian Navy artillery boat U170 in the Bay of Sevastopol

Modern military use

International and military use of the Straits   The 1936 Montreux Convention provides for a free passage of civilian ships between the international waters of the Black and the Mediterranean Seas. However, a single country (Turkey) has a complete control over the straits connecting the two seas. The 1982 amendments to the Montreux Convention allow Turkey to close the Straits at its discretion in both wartime and peacetime.*[57]

The 1936 Montreux Convention governs the passage of vessels between the Black and the Mediterranean Seas and the presence of military vessels belonging to non-littoral states in the Black Sea waters.*[58]

2.3.11   Trans-sea cooperation

Main articles: Black Sea Euroregion, Superior Prut and Lower Danube, Black Sea Games and Organization of the Black Sea Economic Cooperation

2.3.12   See also

- 1927 Crimean earthquakes

- Ancient Black Sea shipwrecks

- Anoxic event

- Bulgarian Black Sea Coast

- Caucasian Riviera

- Internationalization of the Danube River

- Karadeniz Technical University

- Kuma–Manych Depression

- Romanian Black Sea resorts

2.3.13   Notes

[1] Abkhazia has been a *de facto* independent republic since 1992, although remains a *de jure* autonomous republic of Georgia.

2.3.14   References

[1] Surface Area— "Black Sea Geography". *University of Delaware College of Marine Studies.* 2003. Retrieved April 3, 2014.

[2] Maximum Depth— "Europa – Gateway of the European Union Website". *Environment and Enlargement – The Black Sea: Facts and Figures.*

[3] "Unexpected changes in the oxic/anoxic interface in the Black Sea". *Nature Publishing Group.* March 30, 1989. Retrieved December 2, 2006.

[4] UNEP/GRID-Arendal Maps and Graphics Library (2001). "Socio-economic indicators for the countries of the Black Sea basin". Retrieved December 11, 2010.

[5] "Limits of Oceans and Seas, 3rd edition" (PDF). International Hydrographic Organization. 1953. Retrieved February 7, 2010.

[6] "Turkish Statistical Institute". Rapor.tuik.gov.tr. Retrieved January 14, 2014.

[7] "Turkish Statistical Institute". Rapor.tuik.gov.tr. Retrieved January 14, 2014.

[8] This place is located on the Crimean Peninsula, most of which is the subject of a territorial dispute between Russia and Ukraine. According to the political division of Russia, located on the peninsula are the federal subjects of the Russian Federation (the Republic of Crimea and the federal city of Sevastopol). According to the administrative-territorial division of Ukraine, located on the peninsula are the Ukrainian divisions (the Autonomous Republic of Crimea and the city with special status of Sevastopol).

[9] "Turkish Statistical Institute". Rapor.tuik.gov.tr. Retrieved January 14, 2014.

[10] Stiati.ca. "Cele mai mari orase din Romania". Stiati.ca. Retrieved January 14, 2014.

[11] "Turkish Statistical Institute". Rapor.tuik.gov.tr. Retrieved January 14, 2014.

[12] "Batumi City Hall website". http://www.batumi.ge. Retrieved 2012.

[13] Özhan Öztürk (2005). *Karadeniz Ansiklopedik Sözlük.* İstanbul: Heyamola Yayınları. pp. 617–620.

[14] Gibbon, Edward. *The History of the Decline and Fall of the Roman Empire.* Everyman's Library, 1910; reprinted 1993. ISBN 0-679-42308-7. Passim.

[15] McKenzie, DP (1970). "Plate tectonics of the Mediterranean region". *Nature* **226** (5242): 239–43. Bibcode:1970Natur.226..239M.   doi:10.1038/226239a0. PMID 16057188.

[16] McClusky, S., S. Balassanian; et al.   (2000). "Global Positioning System constraints on plate kinematics and dynamics in the eastern Mediterranean and Caucasus" (PDF). *Journal of Geophysical Research* **105** (B3): 5695–5719. Bibcode:2000JGR...105.5695M. doi:10.1029/1999JB900351.

[17] Shillington, Donna J.; White, Nicky; Minshull, Timothy A.; Edwards, Glyn R.H.; Jones, Stephen M.; Edwards, Rosemary A.; Scott, Caroline L. (2008). "Cenozoic evolution of the eastern Black Sea: A test of depth-dependent stretching models". *Earth and Planetary Science Letters* **265** (3–4): 360–378. Bibcode:2008E&PSL.265..360S. doi:10.1016/j.epsl.2007.10.033.

[18] Nikishin, A (2003).   "The Black Sea basin: tectonic history and Neogene–Quaternary rapid subsidence modelling".   *Sedimentary Geology* **156**: 149–168. Bibcode:2003SedG..156..149N.   doi:10.1016/S0037-0738(02)00286-5.

[19] *Remote Sensing of the European Seas.* 2008. p. 17. ISBN 1-4020-6771-2.

[20] Prothero, G.W. (1920). *Anatolia.* London: H.M. Stationery Office.

[21] "Agriculture in the Black Sea Region". Bs-agro.com. Retrieved January 14, 2014.

[22] Descriptive Physical Oceanography.   Talley, Pickard, Emery, Swift.

[23] "Meromictic". Merriam-webster.com. Retrieved January 14, 2014.

[24] "Exploring Ancient Mysteries: A Black Sea Journey". Ceoe.udel.edu. Retrieved January 14, 2014.

[25] Korotaev, G. (2003).   "Seasonal, interannual, and mesoscale variability of the Black Sea upper layer circulation derived from altimeter data". *Journal of Geophysical Research* **108**.   Bibcode:2003JGRC..108.3122K. doi:10.1029/2002JC001508.

[26] Black Sea Becomes Turquoise earthobservatory.nasa.gov. Retrieved December 2, 2006. Archived July 13, 2010 at the Wayback Machine

[27] Schuiling, Roelof Dirk; Cathcart, Richard B.; Badescu, Viorel; Isvoranu, Dragos; Pelinovsky, Efim (2006). "Asteroid impact in the Black Sea. Death by drowning or asphyxiation?". *Natural Hazards* **40** (2): 327–338. doi:10.1007/s11069-006-0017-7.

[28] http://www.cosis.net/abstracts/EGU2007/01654/ EGU2007-J-01654.pdf

[29] Oguz, T., H. W. Ducklow; et al. (1999).   "A physical-biochemical model of plankton productivity and nitrogen cycling in the Black Sea" (PDF). *Deep Sea Research Part I:* **46** (4): 597–636. Bibcode:1999DSRI...46..597O. doi:10.1016/S0967-0637(98)00074-0.

[30] Oguz, T. and A. Merico (2006).   "Factors controlling the summer Emiliania huxleyi bloom in the Black Sea: A modeling study" (PDF). *Journal of Marine Systems* **59** (3–4): 173–188. Bibcode:2006JMS....59..173O. doi:10.1016/j.jmarsys.2005.08.002.

[31] Friedrich, J., C. Dinkel; et al. (2002). "Benthic Nutrient Cycling and Diagenetic Pathways in the North-western Black Sea" (PDF). *Estuarine, Coastal and Shelf Science* **54** (3): 369–383. Bibcode:2002ECSS...54..369F. doi:10.1006/ecss.2000.0653. Archived from the original (PDF) on 15 April 2012.

[32] Eker, E., L. Georgieva; et al. (1999). "Phytoplankton distribution in the western and eastern Black Sea in spring and autumn 1995" (PDF). *ICES Journal of Marine Science* **56**: 15–22. doi:10.1006/jmsc.1999.0604.

[33] Eker-Develi, E (2003). "Distribution of phytoplankton in the southern Black Sea in summer 1996, spring and autumn 1998". *Journal of Marine Systems* **39** (3–4): 203–211. Bibcode:2003JMS....39..203E. doi:10.1016/S0924-7963(03)00031-9.

[34] Krakhmalny, A. F. (1994). "Dinophyta of the Black Sea (Brief history of investigations and species diversity)." Algologiya 4: 99–107.

[35] Gomez, F. and L. Boicenco (2004). "An annotated checklist of dinoflagellates in the Black Sea" (PDF). *Hydrobiologia* **517** (1): 43–59. doi:10.1023/B:HYDR.0000027336.05452.07.

[36] Uysal, Z (2006). "Vertical distribution of marine cyanobacteria Synechococcus spp. in the Black, Marmara, Aegean, and eastern Mediterranean seas". *Deep Sea Research Part II: Topical Studies in Oceanography* **53** (17–19): 1976–1987. Bibcode:2006DSR....53.1976U. doi:10.1016/j.dsr2.2006.03.016.

[37] Humborg, Christoph; Ittekkot, Venugopalan; Cociasu, Adriana; Bodungen, Bodo v. (1997). "Effect of Danube River dam on Black Sea biogeochemistry and ecosystem structure". *Nature* **386** (6623): 385–388. Bibcode:1997Natur.386..385H. doi:10.1038/386385a0.

[38] Sburlea, A., L. Boicenco; et al. (2006). "Aspects of eutrophication as a chemical pollution with implications on marine biota at the Romanian Black Sea shore". *Chemicals as Intentional and Accidental Global Environmental Threats*. NATO Security through Science Series: 357–360. doi:10.1007/978-1-4020-5098-5_28. ISBN 978-1-4020-5096-1.

[39] Gregoire, M., C. Raick; et al. (2008). "Numerical modeling of the central Black Sea ecosystem functioning during the eutrophication phase". *Progress in Oceanography* **76** (3): 286–333. Bibcode:2008PrOce..76..286G. doi:10.1016/j.pocean.2008.01.002.

[40] Colin Woodard (February 11, 2001). *Ocean's end: travels through endangered seas*. Basic Books. pp. 1–28. ISBN 978-0-465-01571-9. Retrieved August 1, 2011.

[41] Lancelot, C (2002). "Modelling the Danube-influenced North-western Continental Shelf of the Black Sea. II: Ecosystem Response to Changes in Nutrient Delivery by the Danube River after its Damming in 1972" (PDF). *Estuarine, Coastal and Shelf Science* **54** (3): 473–499. Bibcode:2002ECSS...54..473L. doi:10.1006/ecss.2000.0659.

[42] Woodard, Colin, "The Black Sea's Cautionary Tale," *Congressional Quarterly Global Researcher*, October 2007, pp. 244–245

[43] Hurrell, J. W. (1995). "Decadal Trends in the North Atlantic Oscillation: Regional Temperatures and Precipitation". *Science* **269** (5224): 676–679. Bibcode:1995Sci...269..676H. doi:10.1126/science.269.5224.676. PMID 17758812.

[44] Lamy, F., Arz, H. W., Bond, G. C., Barh, A. and Pätzold, J. (2006). "Multicentennial-scale hydrological changes in the Black Sea and northern Red Sea during the Holocene and the Arctic/North Atlantic Oscillation" (PDF). *Paleoceanography* **21**. Bibcode:2006PalOc..21.1008L. doi:10.1029/2005PA001184. Archived from the original (PDF) on 10 June 2015.

[45] "Spatial and temporal analysis of annual rainfall variations in Turkey". Bibcode:1996IJCli..16.1057T. doi:10.1002/(SICI)1097-0088(199609)16:9<1057::AID-JOC75>3.3.CO;2-4.

[46] Cullen, H. M., A. Kaplan; et al. (2002). "Impact of the North Atlantic Oscillation on Middle Eastern climate and streamflow" (PDF). *Climatic Change* **55** (3): 315–338. doi:10.1023/A:1020518305517.

[47] Ozsoy, E. and U. Unluata (1997). "Oceanography of the Black Sea: A review of some recent results". *Earth-Science Reviews* **42** (4): 231–272. Bibcode:1997ESRv...42..231O. doi:10.1016/S0012-8252(97)81859-4.

[48] Brody, L. R., Nestor, M.J.R. (1980). Regional Forecasting Aids for the Mediterranean Basin. Handbook for Forecasters in the Mediterranean, Naval Research Laboratory. Part 2.

[49] Wilford, John Noble (17 December 1996). "Geologists Link Black Sea Deluge To Farming's Rise". *The New York Times*. Retrieved 17 June 2013.

[50] William Ryan and Walter Pitman (1998). *Noah's Flood: The New Scientific Discoveries About the Event That Changed History*. New York: Simon & Schuster Paperbacks. ISBN 0-684-85920-3.

[51] David Nicolle (1989). *The Venetian Empire 1200-1670*. Osprey Publishing. p. 17. ISBN 978-0-85045-899-2.

[52] Bruce McGowan. *Economic Life in Ottoman Europe: Taxation, Trade and the Struggle for Land, 1600-1800, Studies in Modern Capitalism*. p. 134. ISBN 978-0-521-13536-8.

[53] "Black Sea Security". *NATO Advanced Research Workshop*. NATO. 2010. Retrieved 2010.

[54] "Черное море признано одним из самых неблагоприятных мест для моряков". *International Transport Workers' Federation*. BlackSeaNews. May 27, 2013. Retrieved September 20, 2013.

[55] Turkish Black Sea Acoustic Surveys: Winter distribution of anchovy along the Turkish coast Serdar SAKINAN. Middle East Technical University - Institute of Marine Sciences

[56] "Bulgarian Sea Resorts". Retrieved February 2, 2007.

[57] "Montreaux and The Bosphorus Problem" (in Turkish).

[58] "Montreaux Convention and Turkey (pdf)" (PDF).

2.3.15 Bibliography

- Stella Ghervas, "Odessa et les confins de l'Europe: un éclairage historique", in Stella Ghervas et François Rosset (ed), *Lieux d'Europe. Mythes et limites*, Paris, Editions de la Maison des sciences de l'homme, 2008. ISBN 978-2-7351-1182-4

- Charles King, *The Black Sea: A History*, 2004, ISBN 0-19-924161-9

- William Ryan and Walter Pitman, *Noah's Flood*, 1999, ISBN 0-684-85920-3

- Neal Ascherson, *Black Sea* (Vintage 1996), ISBN 0-09-959371-8

- Özhan Öztürk. Karadeniz: Ansiklopedik Sözlük (Black Sea: Encyclopedic Dictionary). 2 Cilt (2 Volumes). Heyamola Publishing. Istanbul.2005 ISBN 975-6121-00-9.

- Rüdiger Schmitt, "Considerations on the Name of the Black Sea", in: *Hellas und der griechische Osten* (Saarbrücken 1996), pp. 219–224

- West, Stephanie (2003). 'The Most Marvellous of All Seas' : the Greek Encounter with the Euxine **50** (2). *Greece & Rome*. pp. 151–167.

- Petko Dimitrov, Dimitar Dimitrov (2004. ISBN 954-579-335-X, 91p.). *THE BLACK SEA, THE FLOOD AND THE ANCIENT MYTHS*. Varna. Check date values in: |date= (help)

- Dimitrov, D (2010). *Geology and Non-traditional resources of the Black Sea*. LAP Lambert Academic Publishing. p. 244. ISBN 978-3-8383-8639-3.

2.3.16 External links

- Space Monitoring of the Black Sea Coastline and Waters

- Pictures of the Black sea coast all along the Crimean peninsula

- China: China wants to build a "Black Sea" highway Agriculture in the Black Sea Region (BS-AGRO.COM)

- Black Sea Environmental Internet Node

- Black Sea Organization for Integration and Sustainable Development

- Black Sea-Mediterranean Corridor during the last 30 ky: UNESCO IGCP 521 WG12

2.4 Caspian Sea

The **Caspian Sea** (Russian: Каспийское мо́ре, tr. *Kaspiyskoye more*; IPA: [kɐ'spʲijskəjə 'morʲə], Azerbaijani: *Xəzər dənizi*, Kazakh: Каспий теңізі *Kaspiy teñizi*, Persian: دریای کاسپین خزرXazar Daryⵏ-e, Kⵏspiyan Daryⵏ-e, Turkmen: *Hazar deñizi*) is the largest enclosed inland body of water on Earth by area, variously classed as the world's largest lake or a full-fledged sea.[2][3] The sea has a surface area of 371,000 km^2 (143,200 sq mi) (not including Garabogazköl Aylagy) and a volume of 78,200 km^3 (18,800 cu mi).[4] It is in an endorheic basin (it has no outflows) and located between Europe and Asia.[5] It is bounded to the northeast by Kazakhstan, to the northwest by Russia, to the west by Azerbaijan, to the south by Iran, and to the southeast by Turkmenistan. The Caspian Sea lies to the east of the Caucasus Mountains and to the west of the vast steppe of Central Asia. Its northern part, the Caspian Depression, is one of the lowest points on Earth.

The ancient inhabitants of its coast perceived the Caspian Sea as an ocean, probably because of its saltiness and large size. It has a salinity of approximately 1.2% (12 g/l), about a third of the salinity of most seawater.

2.4.1 Etymology

The word Caspian is derived from the name of the Caspi (Aramaic: Kspy, Greek: Kaspioi, Persian: کاسپی), ancient people who lived to the south-west of the sea in Transcaucasia.[6] Strabo wrote that "to the country of the Albanians belongs also the territory called Caspiane, which was named after the Caspian tribe, as was also the sea; but the tribe has now disappeared".[7] Moreover, the Caspi

Gates, which is the name of a region in Tehran province of Iran, possibly indicates that they migrated to the south of the sea. The Iranian city Qazvin shares the root of its name with that of the sea. In fact, the traditional Arabic name for the sea itself is Bahr al-Qazwin (Sea of Qazvin).[*][8]

In classical antiquity among Greeks and Persians it was called the *Hyrcanian Ocean*.[*][9] In Persian antiquity, as well as in modern Iran, it is known as the *Mazandaran Sea* (Persian: دریای مازندران). In Iran, it is also referred to as Daryā-i Xazar sometimes.[*][10] In Turkic-speaking countries it is known as the *Khazar Sea*. Old Russian sources call it the Khvalyn or Khvalis Sea (Хвалынское море / Хвалисское море) after the name of Khwarezmia.[*][11] Ancient Arabic sources refer to it as *Baḥr Gīlān* (بحر گیلان) meaning "the Gilan Sea".

Turkic languages use a consistent nomenclature that is different from the Indo-European languages above. For instance, in Turkmen, the name is *Hazar deňizi*, in Azeri, it is *Xəzər dənizi*, and in modern Turkish, it is *Hazar denizi*. In all these cases, the second word simply means "sea", and the first word refers to the historical Khazars who had a large empire based to the north of the Caspian Sea between the 7th and 10th centuries.

2.4.2 Physical characteristics

Formation

The Caspian Sea, like the Aral Sea, Black Sea, and Lake Urmia, is a remnant of the ancient Paratethys Sea. It became landlocked about 5.5 million years ago due to tectonic uplift and a fall in sea level. During warm and dry climatic periods, the landlocked sea almost dried up, depositing evaporitic sediments like halite that were covered by wind-blown deposits and were sealed off as an evaporite sink[*][12] when cool, wet climates refilled the basin.[*][13] Due to the current inflow of fresh water, the Caspian Sea is a freshwater lake in its northern portions. It is more saline on the Iranian shore, where the catchment basin contributes little flow. Currently, the mean salinity of the Caspian is one third that of Earth's oceans. The Garabogazköl embayment, which dried up when water flow from the main body of the Caspian was blocked in the 1980s but has since been restored, routinely exceeds oceanic salinity by a factor of 10.[*][2]

Geography

The Caspian Sea is the largest inland body of water in the world and accounts for 40 to 44% of the total lacustrine waters of the world.[*][14] The coastlines of the Caspian are shared by Azerbaijan, Iran, Kazakhstan, Russia, and

Map of the Caspian Sea, yellow shading indicates Caspian drainage basin. (Since this map was drawn, the adjacent Aral Sea has greatly decreased in size)

Turkmenistan. The Caspian is divided into three distinct physical regions: the Northern, Middle, and Southern Caspian.[*][15] The Northern–Middle boundary is the Mangyshlak Threshold, which runs through Chechen Island and Cape Tiub-Karagan. The Middle–Southern boundary is the Apsheron Threshold, a sill of tectonic origin between the Eurasian continent and an oceanic remnant,[*][16] that runs through Zhiloi Island and Cape Kuuli.[*][17] The Garabogazköl Bay is the saline eastern inlet of the Caspian, which is part of Turkmenistan and at times has been a lake in its own right due to the isthmus that cuts it off from the Caspian.

Differences between the three regions are dramatic. The Northern Caspian only includes the Caspian shelf,[*][18] and is very shallow; it accounts for less than 1% of the total water volume with an average depth of only 5–6 metres (16–20 ft). The sea noticeably drops off towards the Middle Caspian, where the average depth is 190 metres (620 ft).[*][17] The Southern Caspian is the deepest, with oceanic depths of over 1,000 metres (3,300 ft). The Middle and Southern Caspian account for 33% and 66% of the total water volume, respectively.[*][15] The northern portion of the Caspian Sea typically freezes in the winter, and in the coldest winters ice forms in the south as well.[*][19]

Over 130 rivers provide inflow to the Caspian, with the Volga River being the largest. A second affluent, the Ural River, flows in from the north, and the Kura River flows into the sea from the west. In the past, the Amu Darya (Oxus) of Central Asia in the east often changed course to empty into the Caspian through a now-desiccated riverbed called the Uzboy River, as did the Syr Darya farther north. The Caspian also has several small islands; they are primarily located in the north and have a collective land area of roughly 2,000 km² (770 sq mi). Adjacent to the North Caspian is the Caspian Depression, a low-lying region 27 metres (89 ft) below sea level. The Central Asian steppes stretch across the northeast coast, while the Caucasus mountains hug the western shore. The biomes to both the north and east are characterized by cold, continental deserts. Conversely, the climate to the southwest and south are generally warm with uneven elevation due to a mix of highlands and mountain ranges; the drastic changes in climate alongside the Caspian have led to a great deal of biodiversity in the region.*[2]

The Caspian Sea has numerous islands throughout, all of them near the coasts; none in the deeper parts of the sea. Ogurja Ada is the largest island. The island is 37 km (23 mi) long, with gazelles roaming freely on it. In the North Caspian, the majority of the islands are small and uninhabited, like the Tyuleniy Archipelago, an Important Bird Area (IBA), although some of them have human settlements.

Hydrology

Caspian Sea near Aktau, Mangistau region, Kazakhstan.

The Caspian has characteristics common to both seas and lakes. It is often listed as the world's largest lake, although it is not a freshwater lake. It contains about 3.5 times more water, by volume, than all five of North America's Great Lakes combined. The Caspian was once part of the Tethys Ocean, but became landlocked about 5.5 million years ago due to plate tectonics.*[14] The Volga River (about 80% of the inflow) and the Ural River discharge into the Caspian Sea, but it has no natural outflow other than by evaporation. Thus the Caspian ecosystem is a closed basin, with its own sea level history that is independent of the eustatic level of the world's oceans. The level of the Caspian has fallen and risen, often rapidly, many times over the centuries.

Some Russian historians claim that a medieval rising of the Caspian, perhaps caused by the Amu Darya changing its inflow to the Caspian from the 13th century to the 16th century, caused the coastal towns of Khazaria, such as Atil, to flood. In 2004, the water level was 28 m (92 ft) below sea level.

Over the centuries, Caspian Sea levels have changed in synchrony with the estimated discharge of the Volga, which in turn depends on rainfall levels in its vast catchment basin. Precipitation is related to variations in the amount of North Atlantic depressions that reach the interior, and they in turn are affected by cycles of the North Atlantic Oscillation. Thus levels in the Caspian Sea relate to atmospheric conditions in the North Atlantic thousands of miles to the northwest.

The last short-term sea-level cycle started with a sea-level fall of 3 m (9.84 ft) from 1929 to 1977, followed by a rise of 3 m (9.84 ft) from 1977 until 1995. Since then smaller oscillations have taken place.*[20]

Environmental degradation

The Volga River, the largest in Europe, drains 20% of the European land area and is the source of 80% of the Caspian's inflow. Its lower reaches are heavily developed with numerous unregulated releases of chemical and biological pollutants. Although existing data are sparse and of questionable quality, there is ample evidence to suggest that the Volga is one of the principal sources of transboundary contaminants into the Caspian. The magnitude of fossil fuel extraction and transport activity constitute risks to water quality. Underwater oil and gas pipelines have been constructed or proposed, increasing potential environmental threats.*[21]

Vulf, Azerbaijan has been affected by ecological damage because of the petrochemical industry. This has significantly decreased species of marine birds in the area.

2.4.3 Nature

Fauna

Sturgeons, including the beluga sturgeon, the largest freshwater fish in the world, inhabit the Caspian Sea in great numbers and yield roe (eggs) that are processed into caviar. Overfishing has depleted a number of the historic fisheries including the economic exhaustion of the tuna fishery.*[22] In recent years overfishing has threatened the sturgeon population to the point that environmentalists advocate banning sturgeon fishing completely until the population recovers. However, the high price of sturgeon caviar allows fisher-

Illustration of two Caspian tigers, extinct since the 1970s.

Iran's northern Caspian Hyrcanian mixed forests are maintained by moisture captured from the Caspian Sea by the Alborz mountain range of Gilan, Iran.

man to afford bribes to ensure the authorities look the other way, making regulations in many locations ineffective.[23] Caviar harvesting further endangers the fish stocks, since it targets reproductive females.

Reptiles native to the sea include spur-thighed tortoise (*Testudo graeca buxtoni*) and Horsfield's tortoise. Although Caspian turtles (*Mauremys caspica*) distribute in nearby areas, this species is completely adapted for freshwaters.

The zebra mussel and the common carp are native to the Caspian and Black Seas, but have become invasive species elsewhere, when introduced.

The area has given its name to several species, including the Caspian gull and the Caspian tern. The Caspian seal (*Pusa caspica*) is the only aquatic mammal and is endemic to the Caspian Sea, being one of very few seal species that live in inland waters, but is different from those inhabiting freshwaters due to hydrological environment of Caspian

Sea. There are several species and subspecies of fish endemic to the Caspian Sea, including the kutum (also known as the Caspian white fish), Caspian marine shad, Caspian roach, Caspian bream (some report that the bream occurring in the Aral Sea is the same subspecies), and a Caspian "salmon" (a subspecies of trout, *Salmo trutta caspiensis*), which is critically endangered.[23]

Archeological studies of Gobustan petroglyphs indicate that there once had been dolphins and porpoises[24][25] likely being present in Caspian Sea at least until Quaternary period.[26] although the rock art on Kichikdash Mountain assumed to be of a dolphin,[27] might instead represent the famous beluga sturgeon due to its shape with multiple fins and size (430 cm in length), but fossil records suggest certain ancestors of modern dolphins and whales, such as *Macrokentriodon morani* (bottlenose dolphins) and *Balaenoptera sibbaldina* (blue whales) were presumably larger than their present descendants.

Flora

Many rare and endemic plant species of Russia are associated with the tidal areas of the Volga delta and riparian forests of the Samur River delta. The shoreline is also a unique refuge for plants adapted to the loose sands of the Central Asian Deserts. The principal limiting factors to successful establishment of plant species are hydrological imbalances within the surrounding deltas, water pollution, and various land reclamation activities. The water level change within the Caspian Sea is an indirect reason for which plants may not get established. This affects aquatic plants of the Volga delta, such as *Aldrovanda vesiculosa* and the native *Nelumbo caspica*. About 11 plant species are found in the Samur River delta, including the unique liana forests that date back to the Tertiary period.

The rising level of the Caspian Sea between 1994–96 reduced the number of habitats for rare species of aquatic vegetation. This has been attributed to a general lack of seeding material in newly formed coastal lagoons and water bodies.

2.4.4 History

The earliest hominid remains found around the Caspian Sea are from Dmanisi dating back to around 1.8 Ma and yielded a number of skeletal remains of Homo erectus or Homo ergaster. More later evidence for human occupation of the region come from a number of caves in Georgia and Azerbaijan such as Kudaro and Azykh Caves. There is evidence for Lower Palaeolithic human occupation south of the Caspian from western Alburz. These are Ganj Par and Darband Cave sites. Neanderthal remains also have been

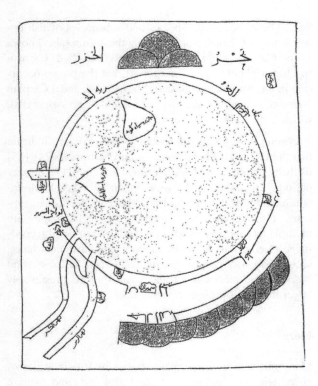

Caspian Sea (Bahr ul-Khazar). Ibn Hawqal

Caspian Sea map from 1747

The 17th-century Cossack rebel and pirate Stenka Razin, on a raid in the Caspian (Vasily Surikov, 1906)

discovered at a cave site in Georgia. Discoveries in the Huto cave and the adjacent Kamarband cave, near the town of Behshahr, Mazandaran south of the Caspian in Iran, suggest human habitation of the area as early as 11,000 years ago.[*][28][*][29]

The Caspian area is rich in energy resources. Wells were being dug in the region as early as the 10th century.[*][30] By the 16th century, Europeans were aware of the rich oil and gas deposits around the area. English traders Thomas Bannister and Jeffrey Duckett described the area around Baku as "a strange thing to behold, for there issueth out of the ground a marvelous quantity of oil, which serveth all the country to burn in their houses. This oil is black and is called nefte. There is also by the town of Baku, another kind of oil which is white and very precious (i.e., petroleum)."[*][31]

In the 18th century, during the rule of Peter I the Great, Fedor I. Soimonov, hydrographer and pioneering explorer of the Caspian Sea charted the until then little known body of water. Soimonov drew a set of four maps and wrote the 'Pilot of the Caspian Sea', the first report and modern maps of the Caspian, that were published in 1720 by the Russian Academy of Sciences.[*][32]

Today, oil and gas platforms are abounding along the edges of the sea.[*][33]

Cities

Ancient

- Hyrcania, ancient state in the north of Iran

- Anzali, Gilan Province of Iran

- Astara, Gilan Province of Iran

- Astarabad, Mazandaran Province of Iran

- Tamisheh, Mazandaran Province of Iran

Baku, the capital of Azerbaijan is the largest city by the Caspian Sea.

- Atil, Khazaria

- Khazaran

- Baku, Azerbaijan

- Derbent, Dagestan, Russia

- Xacitarxan, modern-day Astrakhan

Modern

2.4.5 Oil extraction

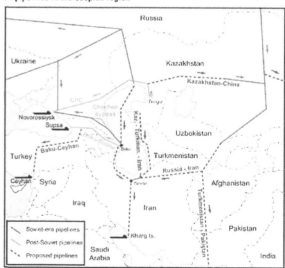

Oil pipelines in the Caspian region. September 2002.

The world's first offshore wells and machine-drilled wells were made in Bibi-Heybat Bay, near Baku, Azerbaijan. In 1873, exploration and development of oil began in some of the largest fields known to exist in the world at that time on the Absheron peninsula near the villages of Balakhanli,

Caspian region oil and natural gas infrastructure. August 2013.

Sabunchi, Ramana and Bibi Heybat. Total recoverable reserves were more than 500 million tons. By 1900, Baku had more than 3,000 oil wells, 2,000 of which were producing at industrial levels. By the end of the 19th century, Baku became known as the "black gold capital", and many skilled workers and specialists flocked to the city.

By the turn of the 20th century, Baku was the center of international oil industry. In 1920, when the Bolsheviks captured Azerbaijan, all private property – including oil wells and factories – was confiscated. Afterwards, the republic's entire oil industry came under the control of the Soviet Union. By 1941, Azerbaijan was producing a record 23.5 million tons of oil, and the Baku region supplied nearly 72% of all oil extracted in the entire USSR.*[30]

In 1994, the "Contract of the Century" was signed, signaling the start of major international development of the Baku oil fields. The Baku–Tbilisi–Ceyhan pipeline, a major pipeline allowing Azerbaijan oil to flow straight to the Turkish Mediterranean port of Ceyhan, opened in 2006.

Political issues

Many of the islands along the Azerbaijani coast continue to hold significant geopolitical and economic importance because of the potential oil reserves found nearby. Bulla Island, Pirallahı Island, and Nargin, which was used as a former Soviet base and is the largest island in the Baku bay, all hold oil reserves.

The collapse of the USSR and subsequent opening of the region has led to an intense investment and development scramble by international oil companies. In 1998, Dick Cheney commented that "I can't think of a time when we've had a region emerge as suddenly to become as strategically significant as the Caspian." [34]

A key problem to further development in the region is the status of the Caspian Sea and the establishment of the water boundaries among the five littoral states. The current disputes along Azerbaijan's maritime borders with Turkmenistan and Iran could potentially affect future development plans.

Much controversy currently exists over the proposed Trans-Caspian oil and gas pipelines. These projects would allow Western markets easier access to Kazakh oil and, potentially, Uzbek and Turkmen gas as well. Russia officially opposes the project on environmental grounds. However, analysts note that the pipelines would bypass Russia completely, thereby denying the country valuable transit fees, as well as destroying its current monopoly on westward-bound hydrocarbon exports from the region.[35] Recently, both Kazakhstan and Turkmenistan have expressed their support for the Trans-Caspian Pipeline.[36]

U.S. diplomatic cables disclosed by WikiLeaks revealed that BP covered up a gas leak and blowout incident in September 2008 at an operating gas field in the Azeri-Chirag-Guneshi area of the Azerbaijan Caspian Sea.[37][38]

2.4.6 Territorial status

Southern Caspian Energy Prospects (portion of Iran). Country Profile 2004.

Caspian Sea, Azerbaijan

As of 2000, negotiations related to the demarcation of the Caspian Sea had been going on for nearly a decade among the states bordering the Caspian – Azerbaijan, Russia, Kazakhstan, Turkmenistan, and Iran. The status of the Caspian Sea[39] is the key problem. Access to mineral resources (oil and natural gas), access for fishing, and access to international waters (through Russia's Volga river and the canals connecting it to the Black Sea and Baltic Sea) all depend upon the outcomes of negotiations. Access to the Volga River is particularly important for the landlocked states of Azerbaijan, Kazakhstan, and Turkmenistan. This concerns Russia, because the potential traffic would utilise its inland waterways. If a body of water is labeled as a sea, then there would be some precedents and international treaties obliging the granting of access permits to foreign vessels. If a body of water is labeled merely as a lake, then there are no such obligations. Environmental issues are also somewhat connected to the status and borders issue.

All five Caspian littoral states maintain naval forces on the sea.[40]

According to a treaty signed between Iran and the Soviet Union, the Caspian Sea is technically a lake and was divided into two sectors (Iranian and Soviet), but the resources (then mainly fish) were commonly shared. The line between the two sectors was considered an international border in a common lake, like Lake Albert. The Soviet sector was subdivided into the four littoral republics' administrative sectors.

Russia, Kazakhstan, and Azerbaijan have bilateral agreements with each other based on median lines. Because of their use by the three nations, median lines seem to be the most likely method of delineating territory in future agreements. However, Iran insists on a single, multilateral agreement between the five nations (as this is the only way for it to achieve a one-fifth share of the sea). Azerbaijan is at odds with Iran over some oil fields that both states claim. Occasionally, Iranian patrol boats have fired at vessels sent by

Azerbaijan for exploration into the disputed region. There are similar tensions between Azerbaijan and Turkmenistan (the latter claims that the former has pumped more oil than agreed from a field, recognized by both parties as shared).

The Caspian littoral states' meeting in 2007 signed an agreement that bars any ship not flying the national flag of a littoral state from entering the sea.*[41]

Cross-border inflow

UNECE recognizes several rivers that cross international borders which flow into the Caspian Sea.*[42] These are:

2.4.7 Transport

Although the Caspian Sea is endorheic, its main tributary, the Volga, is connected by important shipping canals with the Don River (and thus the Black Sea) and with the Baltic Sea, with branch canals to Northern Dvina and to the White Sea.

Another Caspian tributary, the Kuma River, is connected by an irrigation canal with the Don basin as well.

Several scheduled ferry services (including train ferries) operate on the Caspian Sea, including:

- a line between Türkmenbaşy, Turkmenistan (formerly Krasnovodsk) and Baku.

- a line between Baku and Aktau.

- several lines between cities in Iran and Russia.

The ferries are mostly used for cargo, only the Baku – Aktau and Baku – Türkmenbaşy routes accept passengers.

Canals

As an endorheic basin, the Caspian Sea basin has no natural connection with the ocean. Since the medieval period, traders reached the Caspian via a number of portages that connected the Volga and its tributaries with the Don (which flows into the Sea of Azov) and various rivers that flow into the Baltic. Primitive canals connecting the Volga Basin with the Baltic have been constructed as early as the early 18th century; since then, a number of canal projects have been completed. The two modern canal systems connecting the Volga basin with the ocean are the Volga–Baltic Waterway and the Volga–Don Canal.

The proposed Pechora-Kama Canal was a project that was widely discussed between the 1930s and 1980s. Shipping was a secondary consideration; its main goal was to redirect some of the water of the Pechora River (which flows into the Arctic Ocean) via the Kama into the Volga. The goals were both irrigation and stabilizing the water level in the Caspian, which was thought to be falling dangerously fast at the time. In 1971 some construction experiments were conducted using nuclear explosions.

In June 2007, in order to boost his oil-rich country's access to markets, Kazakhstan's President Nursultan Nazarbaev proposed a 700-kilometre (435-mile) link between the Caspian and Black seas. It is hoped that the "Eurasia Canal" (Manych Ship Canal) would transform landlocked Kazakhstan and other Central Asian countries into maritime states, enabling them to significantly increase trade volume. Although the canal would traverse Russian territory, it would benefit Kazakhstan through its Caspian Sea ports. The most likely route for the canal, the officials at the Committee on Water Resources at Kazakhstan's Agriculture Ministry say, would follow the Kuma-Manych Depression, where currently a chain of rivers and lakes is already connected by an irrigation canal (Kuma-Manych Canal). Upgrading the Volga–Don Canal would be another option.*[43]

2.4.8 See also

- Baku Oil Fields

- Caspian people

- Ekranoplan, a ground effect plane which was developed on the Caspian Sea.

- Epoch of Extremal Inundations

- Framework Convention for the Protection of the Marine Environment of the Caspian Sea

- Shah Deniz gas field

- South Caucasus pipeline

- Southern Gas Corridor

- Tengiz Field

- Trans-Caspian Gas Pipeline

- Trans-Caspian Oil Pipeline

2.4.9 References

[1] van der Leeden, Troise, and Todd, eds., *The Water Encyclopedia*. Second Edition. Chelsea F.C., MI: Lewis Publishers, 1990, p. 196.

[2] "Caspian Sea – Background". Caspian Environment Programme. 2009. Retrieved 11 September 2012.

[3] "ESA: Observing the Earth – Earth from Space: The southern Caspian Sea". ESA.int. Retrieved 2007-05-25.

[4] Lake Profile: Caspian Sea. *LakeNet.*

[5] "Caspian Sea".

[6] Caspian Sea in Encyclopædia Britannica.

[7] "Strabo. Geography. 11.3.1". Perseus.tufts.edu. Retrieved 2011-04-14.

[8] *Iran* (5th ed., 2008), by Andrew Burke and Mark Elliott, p. 28, Lonely Planet Publications, ISBN 978-1-74104-293-1

[9] Hyrcania. www.livius.org. Retrieved 2012-05-20.

[10] Drainage Basins – Caspian Sea. Briancoad.com. Retrieved 2012-05-20.

[11] Max Vasmer, *Etimologicheskii slovar' russkogo yazyka*, Vol. IV (Moscow: Progress, 1973), p. 229.

[12] In system dynamics, a sink is a place where a flow of materials ends its journey, removed from the system.

[13] Comparable evaporite beds underlie the Mediterranean.

[14] "Caspian Sea". *Iran Gazette.* Archived from the original on 2009-01-22. Retrieved 2010-05-17.

[15] Hooshang Amirahmadi (10 June 2000). *The Caspian Region at a Crossroad: Challenges of a New Frontier of Energy and Development.* Palgrave Macmillan. pp. 112–. ISBN 978-0-312-22351-9. Retrieved 20 May 2012.

[16] Khain V. E. Gadjiev A. N. Kengerli T. N (2007). "Tectonic origin of the Apsheron Threshold in the Caspian Sea". *Doklady Earth Sciences* **414**: 552–556. doi:10.1134/S1028334X07040149.

[17] Henri J. Dumont; Tamara A. Shiganova; Ulrich Niermann (20 July 2004). *Aquatic Invasions in the Black, Caspian, and Mediterranean Seas.* Springer. ISBN 978-1-4020-1869-5. Retrieved 20 May 2012.

[18] A. G. Kostianoi and A. Kosarev (16 December 2005). *The Caspian Sea Environment.* Birkhäuser. ISBN 978-3-540-28281-5. Retrieved 20 May 2012.

[19] "News Azerbaijan". *ann.az.* Retrieved 9 October 2015.

[20] "Welcome to the Caspian Sea Level Project Site". Caspage.citg.tudelft.nl. Archived from the original on 2011-07-24. Retrieved 2010-05-17.

[21] "Caspian Environment Programme". caspianenvironment.org. Retrieved 30 October 2012.

[22] C. Michael Hogan *Overfishing.* Encyclopedia of Earth. eds. Sidney Draggan and Cutler Cleveland. National Council for Science and the Environment, Washington DC

[23] Fishing Prospects at the Wayback Machine (archived September 5, 2008). iran-daily.com (2007-01-14)

[24] "The Caspian Sea". *All The Sea.* Retrieved 2015-01-16.

[25] "Masuleh". Retrieved 2015-01-16.

[26] "Gobustan Petroglyphs – Methods & Chronology". The Smithsonian Institution. Retrieved 2015-01-19.

[27] "Gobustan Petroglyphs – Subject Matter". The Smithsonian Institution. Retrieved 2015-01-19.

[28] "Major Monuments". Iranair.com. Retrieved 2012-05-20.

[29] Safeguarding Caspian Interests at the Wayback Machine (archived June 3, 2009). iran-daily.com (2006-11-26)

[30] The Development of the Oil and Gas Industry in Azerbaijan SOCAR

[31] Back to the Future: Britain, Baku Oil and the Cycle of History SOCAR

[32] "Fedor I. Soimonov". *Encyclopedia Britannica.* Retrieved 9 October 2015.

[33] "Caspian Sea".

[34] The Great Gas Game, *Christian Science Monitor*, (2001-10-25)

[35] Sergei Blagov, Russia Tries to Scuttle Proposed Trans-Caspian Pipeline, Eurasianet, (2006-03-27)

[36] Russia Seeking To Keep Kazakhstan Happy, Eurasianet, (2007-12-10)

[37] Tim Webb (2010-12-15). "WikiLeaks cables: BP suffered blowout on Azerbaijan gas platform". The Guardian (London). Retrieved 2013-03-26.

[38] Walt, Vivienne (2010-12-18). "WikiLeaks Reveals BP's 'Other' Offshore Drilling Disaster". Time. Retrieved 2013-03-26.

[39] Khoshbakht B. Yusifzade. "8.3 The Status of the Caspian Sea – Dividing Natural Resources Between Five Countries". Azer.com. Retrieved 2010-05-17.

[40] "The great Caspian arms race", *Foreign Policy*, June 2012

[41] Russia Gets Way in Caspian Meet at the Wayback Machine (archived January 20, 2008)

[42] "Drainage basing of the Caspian Sea" (PDF). unece.org.

[43] Caspian Canal Could Boost Kazakh Trade Business Week (2007-07-09)

2.4.10 External links

- Names of the Caspian Sea
- Caspian Sea Region
- Target: Caspian Sea Oil John Robb, 2004
- Dating Caspian sea level changes
- Caspian Sea Is Dying

2.5   Caviar spoon

Mother of pearl caviar spoon

Mother of pearl caviar spoon 5.5 inch with engraved sterling silver handle

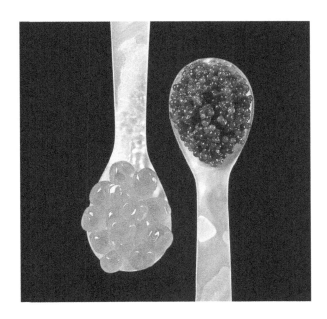

Caviar spoons with assorted caviar

Caviar spoons are traditionally made of inert materials, such as mother of pearl,*[1] gold, animal horn, and wood.*[2]

There is a custom that caviar should not be served with a metal spoon, because metal may impart an undesirable flavour.*[3] Some food experts point out that caviar is stored and sold in metal tins, and therefore any effect of metal on caviar flavour is a misconception;*[4] however, others point out that silver is reactive, and may affect caviar flavour.*[5]

Caviar spoons range in length from 3 to 5 inches, and have a small shallow bowl that may be either oval or paddle shaped.

2.5.1   References

[1] Wolke, Robert L. (2002). *What Einstein Told His Cook: Kitchen Science Explained* (1st ed.). New York: W.W. Norton. p. 163. ISBN 0393011836.

[2] "Eating Utensils: History of Cutlery: History of the Spoon". Retrieved 25 April 2014.

[3] Tesauro, Jason and Phineas Mollod (2002). *The Modern Gentleman* (2nd ed.). [Berkeley, Calif.]: Ten Speed Press. p. 48. ISBN 9781607740063.

[4] About.com. "Gourmet Food - Storing and Serving Caviar". Retrieved 1 April 2012.

[5] Burnside, Margaret Word (Jan–Feb 2010). "Ask Margaret: Why can't caviar be served with metal spoons?". *Tampa Bay Magazine* **25** (1). Retrieved 14 November 2012.

2.5.2   External links

- Images of caviar spoons at Jordanas.com

2.6   Coregonus

Coregonus is a diverse genus of fish in the salmon family (Salmonidae). The type species is *Coregonus lavaretus*. The *Coregonus* species are known as **whitefishes**. The genus contains at least 68 described extant taxa, but the true number of species is a matter of debate.

Several species, including the Arctic cisco (*C. autumnalis*), the Bering cisco (*C. laurettae*), and the least cisco (*C. sardinella*) are anadromous, moving between salt water and fresh water.

The genus was previously subdivided into two subgenera *Coregonus* ("true whitefishes") and *Leucichthys* ("ciscoes"), *Coregonus* comprising taxa with sub-terminal mouth and usually a benthic feeding habit, *Leucichthys* those with terminal or supra-terminal mouth and usually a pelagic plankton-feeding habit. This classification is not natural however: based on molecular data, ciscoes comprise two distinct lineages within the genus. Moreover, the genus *Stenodus* is not phylogenetically distinct from *Coregonus*.*[1]

Many whitefish species or ecotypes, especially from the Great Lakes and the Alpine lakes of Europe, have gone extinct over the past century or are endangered. All *Coregonus* species are protected under appendix III of the Bern Convention.

2.6.1   Species diversity

There is much uncertainty and confusion in the classification of the many of species of this genus. Particularly, one extreme view of diversity recognises just two main species in Northern and Central Europe, the common whitefish *C. lavaretus* and the vendace *C. albula*, whereas others would divide these into numerous, often narrowly distributed species. In North America, the ciscoes of the *Coregonus artedi* complex in the Great Lakes area comprise several, often co-occurring forms or ecotypes, whose taxonomic status remains controversial.

In 2012, FishBase listed 78 extant and recently extinct species in this genus (extinct species are marked with a dagger, "†"):[*][2]

- *Coregonus albellus* Fatio, 1890 (autumn brienzlig)

- *Coregonus albula* Linnaeus, 1758 (vendace)

- †*Coregonus alpenae* (Koelz, 1924) (longjaw cisco)

- *Coregonus alpinus* Fatio, 1885 (kropfer)

- *Coregonus anaulorum* Chereshnev, 1996

- *Coregonus arenicolus* Kottelat, 1997

- *Coregonus artedi* Lesueur, 1818 (northern cisco or lake herring)

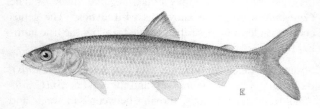

Cisco or lake herring, Coregonus artedi

- *Coregonus atterensis* Kottelat, 1997

- *Coregonus austriacus* C. C. Vogt, 1909

- *Coregonus autumnalis* (Pallas, 1776) (Arctic cisco)

- *Coregonus baerii* Kessler, 1864

- *Coregonus baicalensis* Dybowski, 1874

- *Coregonus baunti* Mukhomediyarov, 1948

- *Coregonus bavaricus* Hofer, 1909

- *Coregonus bezola* Fatio, 1888 (bezoule)

- *Coregonus candidus* Goll, 1883

- *Coregonus chadary* Dybowski, 1869 (Khadary whitefish)

- *Coregonus clupeaformis* (Mitchill, 1818) (lake whitefish)

- *Coregonus clupeoides* Lacépède, 1803 (powan)

- *Coregonus confusus* Fatio, 1885

- *Coregonus danneri* C. C. Vogt, 1908

- *Coregonus duplex* Fatio, 1890

- *Coregonus fatioi* Kottelat, 1997

- †*Coregonus fera* Jurine, 1825 (fera)

- *Coregonus fontanae* M. Schulz & Freyhof, 2003 (Stechlin cisco)

- †*Coregonus gutturosus* (C. C. Gmelin (de), 1818)

- *Coregonus heglingus* Schinz, 1822

- †*Coregonus hiemalis* Jurine, 1825 (gravenche)

- *Coregonus hoferi* L. S. Berg, 1932

- *Coregonus holsata* Thienemann, 1916

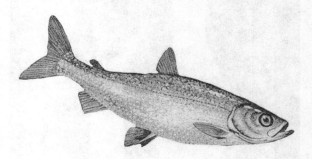

Bloater, Coregonus hoyi

- *Coregonus hoyi* (Milner, 1874) (bloater)

- *Coregonus huntsmani* W. B. Scott, 1987 (Atlantic whitefish)

- †*Coregonus johannae* (G. Wagner, 1910) (deepwater cisco)

- *Coregonus kiletz* Michailovsky, 1903

- *Coregonus kiyi* (Koelz, 1921) (kiyi)

- *Coregonus ladogae* Pravdin, Golubev & Belyaeva, 1938

Common whitefish, Coregonus lavaretus *(sensu lato)*

- *Coregonus laurettae* T. H. Bean, 1881 (Bering cisco)

- *Coregonus lavaretus* Linnaeus, 1758 (common white-fish, European whitefish; lavaret)

- *Coregonus lucinensis* Thienemann, 1933

- *Coregonus lutokka* Kottelat, Bogutskaya & Freyhof, 2005

- *Coregonus macrophthalmus* Nüsslin, 1882

- *Coregonus maraena* (Bloch, 1779) (maraena whitefish)

- *Coregonus maraenoides* L. S. Berg, 1916

- *Coregonus maxillaris* Günther, 1866

- *Coregonus megalops* Widegren, 1863 (lacustrine fluvial whitefish)

- *Coregonus migratorius* (Georgi, 1775) (omul)

- *Coregonus muksun* (Pallas, 1814) (muksun)

- *Coregonus nasus* (Pallas, 1776) (broad whitefish)

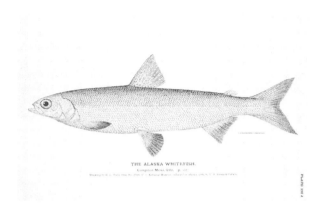

Coregonus nelsonii

- *Coregonus nelsonii* T. H. Bean, 1884 (Alaska whitefish)

- *Coregonus nigripinnis* (Milner, 1874) (blackfin cisco)

- *Coregonus nilssoni* Valenciennes, 1848

- *Coregonus nipigon* (Koelz, 1925)

- *Coregonus nobilis* Haack, 1882

- †*Coregonus oxyrinchus* Linnaeus, 1758 (houting)

- *Coregonus palaea* G. Cuvier, 1829

- *Coregonus pallasii* Valenciennes, 1848

- *Coregonus peled* (J. F. Gmelin, 1789) (peled)

- *Coregonus pennantii* Valenciennes, 1848 (gwyniad)

Coregonus pidschian

- *Coregonus pidschian* (J. F. Gmelin, 1789) (humpback whitefish)

- *Coregonus pollan* W. Thompson, 1835 (Irish pollan)

- *Coregonus pravdinellus* Dulkeit, 1949

- *Coregonus reighardi* (Koelz, 1924) (shortnose cisco)

- *Coregonus renke* (Schrank, 1783)

- *Coregonus restrictus* Fatio, 1885

- *Coregonus sardinella* Valenciennes, 1848 (Sardine cisco)

- *Coregonus stigmaticus* Regan, 1908 (schelly)

- *Coregonus subautumnalis* Kaganowsky, 1932

- *Coregonus suidteri* Fatio, 1885

- *Coregonus trybomi* Svärdson (sv), 1979

- *Coregonus tugun* (Pallas, 1814)

- *Coregonus ussuriensis* L. S. Berg, 1906 (Amur whitefish)

- *Coregonus vandesius* J. Richardson, 1836 (vendace)

- *Coregonus vessicus* Dryagin, 1932

- *Coregonus wartmanni* (Bloch, 1784)

- *Coregonus widegreni* Malmgren, 1863 (Valaam white-fish)

- *Coregonus zenithicus* (D. S. Jordan & Evermann, 1909) (shortjaw cisco)

- *Coregonus zuerichensis* Nüsslin, 1882

- *Coregonus zugensis* Nüsslin, 1882

2.6.2   References

[1] Bernatchez L, Colombani F, Dodson JJ (1991) Phylogenetic relationships among the subfamily Coregoninae as revealed by mitochondrial DNA restriction analysis *Journal of Fish Biology* 39 (Suppl A):283-290.

[2] Froese, Rainer, and Daniel Pauly, eds. (2012). Species of *Coregonus* in FishBase. February 2012 version.

- "Coregonus". Integrated Taxonomic Information System. Retrieved 12 December 2004.

- Division of Endangered Species, U.S. Fish and Wildlife Service. "Extinct Species List". U.S. Fish and Wildlife Service. Retrieved 12 December 2004.

2.6.3   External links

- Media related to Coregonus at Wikimedia Commons

- Data related to Coregonus at Wikispecies

2.7   Cristoforo di Messisbugo

Cristoforo di Messisbugo or **Cristoforo da Messisbugo** (15th century – 1548) was a steward of the House of Este in Ferrara and an Italian cook of the Renaissance.

2.7.1   Biography

From 1524 to 1548, he served at the courts of Alfonso I and his son Ercole II in Ferrara, where he organized many lavish banquets. Greatly appreciated as a master of ceremonies, he was made count palatine on 20 January 1533 by the Holy Roman Emperor Charles V.

His cookbook *Banchetti, composizioni di vivande e apparecchio generale*, which was published posthumously in 1549, is addressed to those preparing princely feasts and provides detailed descriptions of the menus for his official banquets at the Este court. As well as listing recipes, it also discusses logistics, decor, and cooking equipment. *Libro novo nel*

Fig. 119.—Interior of Italian Kitchen.—Fac-simile of a Woodcut in the Book on Cookery of Christoforo di Messisbugo, "Banchetti composizioni di Vivande," 4to., Ferrara, 1549.

Illustration to Messisbugo's cookbook on how to prepare a banquet, Banchetti composizioni di vivande e apparecchio generale

qual si insegna a far d'ogni sorte di vivanda, attributed to him and published in Venice in 1564, well after his death, is largely a repetition of his recipes in *Banchetti*. Some of the dishes he described survive today in the Ferrara area.

Beluga sturgeon abounded in the Po River in the 16th century and they were a frequent capture. The first known reference to the preparation of sturgeon caviar in Italy is in Messisbugo's books. He described how to prepare the caviar both to be consumed fresh and to be preserved.

He is buried in the church of the monastery of Sant'Antonio in Polesine.

2.7.2   See also

- Bartolomeo Scappi

2.7.3   Notes

2.7.4   References

- Alberto Capatti, Massimo Montanari, *Italian Cuisine: A Cultural History*, 2003.

2.7.5 Bibliography

- Cristoforo da Messisbugo, *Banchetti, composizioni di vivande e apparecchio generale*, Ferrare, 1549

- Cristoforo da Messisbugo, *Libro novo nel qual si insegna a far d'ogni sorte di vivanda*, Venezia, 1564

2.7.6 External links

- Photos de la Bibliothèque Casanatense

- Banchetti, composizioni di vivande e apparecchio generale

- Libro novo nel qual si insegna a far d'ogni sorte di vivanda

2.8 God Loves Caviar

God Loves Caviar (Greek: Ο Θεός αγαπάει το χαβιάρι, translit. O Theós agapáei to chaviári) is a 2012 Greek drama film directed by Yannis Smaragdis.[1][2]

2.8.1 Plot

The film is based upon the true story of Ioannis Varvakis, a Greek caviar merchant and eventual benefactor from Psara who was formerly a pirate. He was born in Psara, and from an early age he learned to navigate the seas, an occupation revered and steeped in tradition on the island where he grew up. At the age of 17 he built his own ship, which he would later offer to the Russians during the Orlov Revolt. Ultimately, his ship was destroyed, and he turned to Saint Petersburg to ask for an audience with Catherine the Great. He was given compensation for the loss of his ship and granted authorization to fish freely in the Caspian Sea. Lending to his superb navigational skills and excellent seamanship abilities, he dominated the Caspian Sea and soon became substantially wealthy. When he initially discovered the superior caviar of the Beluga Sturgeon, he quickly discerned that there could be an incredible market trading for this product. From the caviar trade he eventually became a millionaire and later donated part of his fortune for important works that improved the life of Russians and Greeks on the Black Sea coasts. In his later years, he became a member of the Filiki Eteria, which would contribute to the overthrow of the Ottoman rule of Greece. He passed away in 1825 in Zante, during the Greek War of Independence. After his death, his entire estate went to the Ioannis Varvakis Foundation which would offer up important grants throughout Greece. The script follows the entire life of Varvakis, but the film's narration begins with his final moments in Zante.[3][4]

2.8.2 Cast

- Sebastian Koch as Ioannis Varvakis

- Evgeniy Stychkin as Ivan

- Juan Diego Botto as Lefentarios

- Olga Sutulova as Helena

- John Cleese as McCormick

- Catherine Deneuve as Empress Catherine II of Russia

- Akis Sakellariou as Kimon

- Alexandra Sakelaropoulou as Varvakis' Mother

- Fotini Baxevani

- Lakis Lazopoulos as Fisherman of God

- Pavlos Kontoyannidis

- Alexandros Mylonas as Temporary Prime Minister

- Yannis Vouros as Businessman A

2.8.3 Reception

The film was one of the official selections that debuted in 2012 Toronto Film Festival.[5] In 2013 the film was the highest grossing film in Greece.[6]

2.8.4 References

[1] "God Loves Caviar". *TIFF*. Retrieved 2012-10-12.

[2] "N.Y.Times Review of God Loves Caviar". *The New York Times*. Retrieved 20 October 2012.

[3] "God Loves Caviar" by Iannis Smaragdis / Toronto 2012 review". flix.gr. Retrieved 2 January 2015.

[4] "Ο Βαρβάκης". godlovescaviar.gr. Retrieved 2 January 2015.

[5] "Παγκόσμια Πρεμιέρα της ταινίας "Ο Θεός αγαπάει το Χαβιάρι" στο Διεθνές Φεστιβάλ Κινηματογράφου του Τορόντο." . godlovescaviar.gr. Retrieved 2 January 2015.

[6] "God Loves Caviar serves up a hero in Greece's hour of need". theguardian.com. Retrieved 2 January 2015.

2.8.5 External links

- *God Loves Caviar* at the Internet Movie Database

2.9 Ioannis Varvakis

Ioannis Varvakis (Greek: Ιωάννης Βαρβάκης; 1745–1825), also known as **Ivan Andreevich Varvatsi** (Russian: Иван Андреевич Варваци), was a Greek distinguished member of the Russian and Greek communities, national hero, member of the Filiki Eteria and benefactor of the places where he lived.

2.9.1 Origins, early life

Ioannis was born on the Greek island of Psara, son to Andreas Leontis and Maria Moros. His mother later cloistered herself in a monastery on the island of Khios, where she died during the Chios Massacre in 1822. His real name was **Ioannis Leontides** (Ιωάννης Λεοντίδης); *Varvakis* was the nickname that he received during his childhood due to his imposing eyes, which were similar to the eyes of a bird of prey which lives on the island of Psara and is known as *varvaki* (βαρβάκι, "Eleonora's falcon").

2.9.2 Hero of the war for independence

Varvakis was a Greek Orthodox Christian who became a skilful sailor at the age of 17 and built a ship, the *St. Andrew*, which he later offered (with his crew) to the Russian forces during the Russo-Turkish War, 1768-1774. He spent his entire fortune to equip the ship and to arm it with cannons and showed extraordinary courage during the Battle of Chesma (Turkish: Çeşme) in July 1770. His xebec was transformed into a fire ship, packed with combustibles, set on fire and steered into a large Turkish ship. But the war did not give independence to Greece, as the Ottoman sultan signed peace by the Treaty of Kuçuk Kainarji in 1774, which granted Russia the northern part of the Black Sea. On the other hand, this war created a mass exodus of Greeks to Russia.

2.9.3 At service of Catherine the Great

Without any money in his pocket, Ioannis Varvakis decided to seek an audience with Catherine II of Russia ("Catherine the Great"). He went to Saint Petersburg, where he met with Grigori Alexandrovich Potemkin, Russian general-field marshal, statesman, and favorite of Catherine II the

Varvakis Coat of Arms.

Great, who arranged the audience with the Empress of Russia. Catherine II the Great was particularly generous giving Varvakis 1,000 golden roubles as a gift and an authorisation for unlimited and duty-free fishery in the Caspian Sea and the right to choose a place to settle in Russia. He also received an official patent signed by Catherine the Great, proving that Ivan Andreevich Varvatsi (his new Russian name) was named first lieutenant of the Russian Navy on October 21, 1772.

2.9.4 Varvakis in Astrakhan

From Saint Petersburg, he left for Astrakhan to develop a fishery, though he had no experience. In the northern Caspian Sea his fishery enterprise made him a millionaire. The boats of Varvakis caught sturgeon, white salmon and other valuable fish. Knowing the passion of Greeks for caviar, he tried to arrange exporting caviar to Europe. He invented a solution to preserve the freshness of the caviar eggs while being transported by ship. He produced timber boxes, which did not cause alterations in the precious eggs, were absolutely waterproof and thus were maintained in very good condition. Until then the caviar had been preserved in caves. Varvakis shipped caviar from Astrakhan to Greece by camel or by boat through the Volga river. In 1788, the business of Varvakis employed more than 3,000 workers.

In 1810-1817, Ioannis Varvakis financed the delayed construction of the channel linking river Volga to its arm Kutum. The channel, which was initially built as "Astrakhansky" was renamed by the decree of December 31, 1817 as "Varvatsievski". After Russian revolution, it was renamed to "The May 1st Channel".

Astrakhan,"The May 1st Channel"

2.9.5 Varvakis in Taganrog

The Greek Monastery in Taganrog, where the burial service for Alexander I of Russia was chanted in 1825.

In 1810, Varvakis was granted the title of hereditary nobleman with a family coat of arms by Alexander I of Russia, who also made him Court Counsel and decorated with a diamond Order of St. Anne awarded for exceptional services and the Order of St. Vladimir.

In 1812, he moved to the city of Taganrog, populated by Greek colonists who, like the Greeks of classical times, took refuge from poverty or tyranny in townships around the northern Black Sea and the Sea of Azov. In 1813, Ivan Varvatsi spent 600,000 rubles for construction of Greek Jerusalem Monastery (Иерусалимский греческий монастырь) in Taganrog. When Alexander I died in Taganrog in 1825, the funeral service for the Russian Tsar was chanted in this monastery.

The Mansion of Ivan Varvatsi in Taganrog.

Varvatsi's mansion in Taganrog suffered extensive damage during Siege of Taganrog in Crimean War. The walls were filled with cannonballs and rifle bullets, and were left in that condition. The building was nicknamed "house with bullets"(дом с пулями).

2.9.6 Return to Greece

Ioannis Varvakis actively assisted the Greeks during the Greek Revolution, especially his home island of Psara. After the destruction of the island by the Turkish Fleet, he returned to Greece himself in 1824 to aid the refugees, and died on Zakynthos on January 10, 1825. Varvakis desired to promote education for the new Greek state, and in his will he left 1 million rubles for the building of a high school, which was named Varvakeio (Βαρβάκειον Λύκειον) in his honor. Varvakis also financed the building of Athens' closed market, the *Varvakeios Agora.*[1][2]

2.9.7 Descendants

The descendance of Varvakis' noble name was continued through the female line. His first daughter, Maria Varvakis who was born in 1770, married Greek merchant Nikolay Ivanovich Komnino. Since he had no sons, and willing to honor the name for the future generations, Ioannis Varvakis addressed to his patron, Catherine the Great, a request to permit his daughter Maria have a Double-barrelled name, that is the family name of Varvakis, her father, and that of her husband, Komnino. Catherine II granted his appeal, creating the noble family of Komnino-Varvatsi (Комнино-Варваци). All sons of Maria and Nikolay Komnino-Varvatsi (Ivan, Yegor, Mark, Kozma and Andrey) were granted noble titles by the Yekaterinoslav Government decree of April 25, 1821, paying tribute to achievements and contributions made by their grandfather, Ioannis Varvakis. Their descendants were later married into other Greek-Russian families, including the Sarandinaki family at Taganrog.

The graves of Maria and Nadezhda Komnino-Varvatsi are located at the Taganrog Old Cemetery near The All-Saints Church in Taganrog.

2.9.8 Legacy

The Varvakeio school in 1867.

In the 19th century, one of the streets in Taganrog was named after Varvatsi (Варвациевский переулок). In the 1920s it was renamed after poet Mikhail Lermontov.

In 2012 a monument dedicated to Varvakis was inaugurated in the city of Astrakhan.*[3]

Director Yannis Smaragdis directed a film (*God Loves Caviar*) dedicated to the life of Ioannis Varvakis and his invention for transportation of caviar eggs. German actor Sebastian Koch portrayed Ioannis Varvakis. The film, a co-production of Greece, Russia, and Spain was released in 2012.*[4]*[5] The film, however, contains significant historical inaccuracies, such as showing Emperor Paul I ruling at the time of Greek revolution in 1821. (In reality, he had been assassinated 20 years before these events).

2.9.9 References

[1] Βαρβάκειο Πειραματικό Γυμνάσιο

[2] "Photos from Varvakios Agora market in Athens" .

[3] Про астраханского пирата

[4] God Loves Caviar (2012) at IMDB

[5] God Loves Caviar - New Film, Tue, 01/02/2011

2.9.10 Sources

• Энциклопедия Таганрога. Таганрог: Антон, 1998. —624 с. —ISBN 5-88040-017-4.

2.10 Ossetra

Wild Iranian Ossetra Caviar, ready to serve with mother-of-pearl spoons (which look suspiciously plastic) and Champagne.

Ossetra (also Oscietra, Osetra, or Asetra) caviar, is one of the most prized and expensive types of caviar,*[1] (eclipsed in price only by Beluga caviar). It is obtained from Ossetra sturgeon which weighs 50-400 pounds and can live up to 50 years.

Ossetra caviar varies in color, from deep brown to gold. Lighter varieties are more sought after, as they have the richest flavor and come from the oldest of sturgeon. Golden Ossetra is a rare form of Ossetra caviar, and is golden-yellow in color with a very rich flavor.*[2]

The word Ossetra is the transcription of the Russian word "осётр" ("осетр") which translates into English as sturgeon. At one time the term "ossetra" simply referred to Russian sturgeon species harvested for this type of caviar.

2.10.1 Source animals

In Russian, there are different names for the species of sturgeon that live in various territories such as *Beluga* (Huso Huso), Sevruga (*Acipenser stellatus*) and Sterlet (*Acipenser ruthenus*). The name Ossetra corresponds to the species *Acipenser gueldenstaedtii*, which is much smaller than Beluga sturgeon (Huso huso), and has a firmer texture. In the territory of the Russian Federation dwells another type of sturgeon, *Siberian sturgeon* (Acipenser Baerii), which is farmed all over the world because it can adapt to a wider range of habitats. It begins to produce caviar faster than Acipenser gueldenstaedtii.

2.10.2 History

Throughout the entire history of black caviar consumption, reference to Ossetra was made only to the fish that was caught first in Imperial Russia, then the USSR, and now in the Russian Federation.

2.10.3 Production

Today, Caspian Ossetra is facing extinction in its native habitat. Farming sturgeon is the only way to continue the production of high quality caviar. Israel is currently the leader in the production of Russian Ossetra Caviar Acipenser gueldenstaedtii. Branded as "Karat Caviar" recent exports are now available in the United States in order to meet the demand for caviar since there has been no 2009 issue for wild Caspian Caviar production. A group of companies referred to as Russian Caviar House, sell and distribute Siberian Ossetra Caviar (Acipenser baerii) due to their affiliation with DIANA Fish Trading, LLC, which manufactures 80% of all legal sturgeon caviar in Russia.[3] On July 17th, Black Caviar Company partnered with Russian Caviar House, following a decade long halt prohibiting the import of Russian caviar - the partnership enables Black Caviar Company to sell Russian black caviar within the United States.[4]

As with other caviars, ossetra is traditionally served on blinis with crème fraiche. Lower-grade varieties of caviar are used as stuffing in many seafood dishes, and some meat dishes. Caviar is often added to salads as well.

2.10.4 References

[1] Prices for Ossetra caviar

[2] Ossetra caviar

[3] http://russian-caviar-house.com.ua/engl/en/russkiy-ikornyi-dom-o-kompanii.html

[4] http://www.wkrg.com/story/26044640/black-caviar-company-begins-exclusive-distribution-of-authentic-russian-oset

2.10.5 External links

- World Sturgeon Conservation Society

- Osetra Caviar

2.11 Ovary

For ovary as part of plants, see Ovary (botany).

"Ovaria" redirects here. This is also a proposed section and a synonym of Solanum.

As a component of names, see Overy.

The **ovary** (From Latin: *ovarium*, literally "egg" or "nut") is an ovum-producing reproductive organ, often found in pairs as part of the vertebrate female reproductive system. Birds have only one functional ovary (left), while the other remains vestigial. Ovaries in female are analogous to testes in male, in that they are both gonads and endocrine glands. Although ovaries occur in a wide variety of animals, both vertebrate and invertebrate, this article is primarily about human ovaries.

2.11.1 Structure

In the case of human ovaries, each one is whitish in color and located alongside the lateral wall of the uterus in a region called the ovarian fossa. The fossa usually lies beneath the external iliac artery and in front of the ureter and the internal iliac artery. It is about 4 cm x 3 cm x 2 cm in size.[1]

Usually, ovulation occurs in one of the two ovaries (at random) releasing a fertilizable egg each menstrual cycle; however, if there was a case where one ovary was absent or dysfunctional then the other ovary would continue providing eggs to be released without any changes in cycle length or frequency.

Ligaments

In humans the paired ovaries lie within the pelvic cavity, on either side of the uterus, to which they are attached via a fibrous cord called the ovarian ligament. The ovaries are uncovered in the peritoneal cavity but are tethered to the body wall via the suspensory ligament of the ovary. The part of the broad ligament of the uterus that covers the ovary is known as the mesovarium. The ovary is thus considered an intraperitoneal organ.

Extremities

There are two extremities to the ovary:

- The end to which the fallopian tube attaches is called the *tubal extremity* and ovary is connected to it by infundibulopelvic ligament.*[1]

- The other extremity is called the *uterine extremity*. It points downward, and it is attached to the uterus via the ovarian ligament.

Histology

- Follicular cells flat epithelial cells that originate from surface epithelium covering the ovary

- Granulosa cells - surrounding follicular cells have changed from flat to cuboidal and proliferated to produce a stratified epithelium

- Gametes*[2]

- The outermost layer is called the germinal epithelium.

- The *ovarian cortex* consists of ovarian follicles and stroma in between them. Included in the follicles are the cumulus oophorus, membrana granulosa (and the granulosa cells inside it), corona radiata, zona pellucida, and primary oocyte. The zona pellucida, theca of follicle, antrum and liquor folliculi are also contained in the follicle. Also in the cortex is the corpus luteum derived from the follicles.

- The innermost layer is the *ovarian medulla*. It can be hard to distinguish between the cortex and medulla, but follicles are usually not found in the medulla.

The ovary also contains blood vessels and lymphatics.*[3]

2.11.2   Function

Gamete production

Main article: Oogenesis

The ovaries are the site of production and periodical release of egg cells, the female gametes. In the ovaries, the developing egg cell (or oocyte) grows within the environment provided by follicles. Follicles are composed of different types and number of cells according to the stage of their maturation, and their size is indicative of the stage of oocyte development.*[4]*:833

When the oocyte finishes its maturation in the ovary, a surge of luteinizing hormone secreted by the pituitary gland stimulates the release of the oocyte through the rupture of the follicle, a process called ovulation.*[5] The follicle remains functional and reorganizes into a corpus luteum, which secretes progesterone in order to prepare the uterus for an eventual implantation of the embryo.*[4]*:839

Endocrine function

Ovaries secrete estrogen, testosterone*[6]*[7] and progesterone. In women, fifty percent of testosterone is produced by the ovaries and adrenal glands and released directly into the blood stream.*[8] Estrogen is responsible for the appearance of secondary sex characteristics for females at puberty and for the maturation and maintenance of the reproductive organs in their mature functional state. Progesterone prepares the uterus for pregnancy, and the mammary glands for lactation. Progesterone functions with estrogen by promoting menstrual cycle changes in the endometrium.

Ovarian aging

As women age, they experience a decline in reproductive performance leading to menopause. This decline is tied to a decline in the number of ovarian follicles. Although about 1 million oocytes are present at birth in the human ovary, only about 500 (about 0.05%) of these ovulate, and the rest are wasted. The decline in ovarian reserve appears to occur at a constantly increasing rate with age,*[9] and leads to nearly complete exhaustion of the reserve by about age 52. As ovarian reserve and fertility decline with age, there is also a parallel increase in pregnancy failure and meiotic errors resulting in chromosomally abnormal conceptions.

Women with an inherited mutation in the DNA repair gene BRCA1 undergo menopause prematurely,*[10] suggesting that naturally occurring DNA damages in oocytes are repaired less efficiently in these women, and this inefficiency leads to early reproductive failure. The BRCA1 protein plays a key role in a type of DNA repair termed homologous recombinational repair that is the only known cellular process that can accurately repair DNA double-strand breaks. Titus et al.*[11] showed that DNA double-strand breaks accumulate with age in humans and mice in primordial follicles. Primordial follicles contain oocytes that are at an intermediate (prophase I) stage of meiosis. Meiosis is the general process in eukaryotic organisms by which germ cells are formed, and it is likely an adaptation for removing DNA damages, especially double-strand breaks, from germ line DNA.[*][12] (see Meiosis and Origin and function of meiosis). Homologous recombinational repair is especially promoted during meiosis. Titus et al.[*][11] also found that expression of 4 key genes necessary for homologous recombinational repair of DNA double-strand breaks (BRCA1, MRE11, RAD51 and ATM) decline with age in the oocytes of humans and mice. They hypothesized that DNA double-strand break repair is vital for the maintenance of oocyte reserve and that a decline in efficiency of repair with age plays a key role in ovarian aging.

2.11.3   Clinical significance

Ovarian diseases can be classified as endocrine disorders or as a disorders of the reproductive system.

If the egg fails to release from the follicle in the ovary an ovarian cyst may form. Small ovarian cysts are common in healthy women. Some women have more follicles than usual (polycystic ovary syndrome), which inhibits the follicles to grow normally and this will cause cycle irregularities.

Other conditions include:

- Ovarian neoplasms, including Ovarian cancer

- Luteoma

- Hypogonadism

- Hyperthecosis

- Ovarian torsion

- Ovarian apoplexy (rupture)

- Premature Ovarian failure

- Anovulation

- Ovarian Cysts: Follicular cyst, Corpus Luteum cyst, Theca-lutein cyst, Chocolate cyst

- Ovarian germ cell tumors: Dysgerminoma, Choriocarcinoma, Yolk sac tumor, Teratoma

- Ovarian non-germ cell tumors

  - Serous cystadenoma

  - Serous cystadenocarcinoma

  - Mucinous cystadenoma

  - Mucinous cystadenocarcinoma

  - Brenner tumor

  - Granulosa cell tumor

  - Krukenberg tumor

2.11.4   Society and culture

Cryopreservation

Cryopreservation of ovarian tissue, often called *ovarian tissue cryopreservation*, is of interest to women who want to preserve their reproductive function beyond the natural limit, or whose reproductive potential is threatened by cancer therapy,[*][13] for example in hematologic malignancies or breast cancer.[*][14] The procedure is to take a part of the ovary and carry out slow freezing before storing it in liquid nitrogen whilst therapy is undertaken. Tissue can then be thawed and implanted near the fallopian, either orthotopic (on the natural location) or heterotopic (on the abdominal wall),[*][14] where it starts to produce new eggs, allowing normal conception to take place.[*][15] A study of 60 procedures concluded that ovarian tissue harvesting appears to be safe.[*][14] The ovarian tissue may also be transplanted into mice that are immunocompromised (SCID mice) to avoid graft rejection, and tissue can be harvested later when mature follicles have developed.[*][16]

2.11.5   Other animals

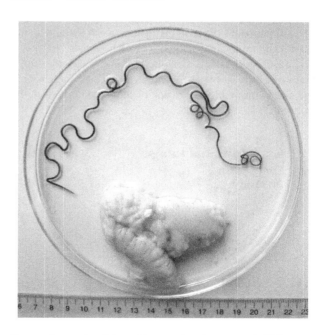

Ovary of a marine fish and its parasite, the nematode Philometra fasciati

Ovaries of some kind are found in the female reproductive system of many animals that employ sexual reproduction, including invertebrates. However, they develop in a very different way in most invertebrates than they do in vertebrates, and are not truly homologous.[*][17]

Many of the features found in human ovaries are common to

all vertebrates, including the presence of follicular cells, tunica albuginea, and so on. However, many species produce a far greater number of eggs during their lifetime than do humans, so that, in fish and amphibians, there may be hundreds, or even millions of fertile eggs present in the ovary at any given time. In these species, fresh eggs may be developing from the germinal epithelium throughout life. Corpora lutea are found only in mammals, and in some elasmobranch fish; in other species, the remnants of the follicle are quickly resorbed by the ovary. In birds, reptiles, and monotremes, the egg is relatively large, filling the follicle, and distorting the shape of the ovary at maturity.*[17]

Amphibians and reptiles have no ovarian medulla; the central part of the ovary is a hollow, lymph-filled space.

The ovary of teleosts is also often hollow, but in this case, the eggs are shed into the cavity, which opens into the oviduct.*[17] Certain nematodes of the genus *Philometra* are parasitic in the ovary of marine fishes and can be spectacular, with females as long as 40 cm, coiled in the ovary of a fish half this length.*[18] These nematodes never parasitize humans.

Although most normal female vertebrates have two ovaries, this is not the case in all species. In most birds and in platypuses, the right ovary never matures, so that only the left is functional. (Exceptions include the Kiwi and some, but not all raptors, in which both ovaries persist.*[19]*[20]) In some elasmobranchs, only the right ovary develops fully. In the primitive jawless fish, and some teleosts, there is only one ovary, formed by the fusion of the paired organs in the embryo.*[17]

2.11.6 Additional images

- Left Ovary
- Ovaries
- Uterus

2.11.7 See also

- Ovarian reserve
- Folliculogenesis
- Oophorectomy

2.11.8 References

[1] Daftary, Shirish; Chakravarti, Sudip (2011). Manual of Obstetrics, 3rd Edition. Elsevier. pp. 1-16. ISBN 9788131225561.

[2] Langman's Medical Embryology, Lippincott Williams & Wilkins, 10th ed, 2006

[3] Brown, H. M.; Russell, D. L. (2013). "Blood and lymphatic vasculature in the ovary: Development, function and disease". *Human Reproduction Update* **20**: 29. doi:10.1093/humupd/dmt049.

[4] Ross M, Pawlina W (2011). *Histology: A Text and Atlas* (6th ed.). Lippincott Williams & Wilkins. ISBN 978-0-7817-7200-6.

[5] Melmed, S; Polonsky, KS; Larsen, PR; Kronenberg, HM (2011). *Williams Textbook of Endocrinology* (12th ed.). Saunders. p. 595. ISBN 978-1437703245.

[6] Normal Testosterone and Estrogen Levels in Women

[7] Testosterone: MedlinePlus Medical Encyclopedia

[8] Androgens in women

[9] Hansen KR, Knowlton NS, Thyer AC, Charleston JS, Soules MR, Klein NA. (2008). A new model of reproductive aging: the decline in ovarian non-growing follicle number from birth to menopause. Hum Reprod 23(3):699-708. doi: 10.1093/humrep/dem408. PMID 18192670

[10] Rzepka-Górska I, Tarnowski B, Chudecka-Głaz A, Górski B, Zielińska D, Tołoczko-Grabarek A. (2006). Premature menopause in patients with BRCA1 gene mutation. Breast Cancer Res Treat 100(1):59-63. PMID 16773440

[11] Titus S, Li F, Stobezki R, Akula K, Unsal E, Jeong K, Dickler M, Robson M, Moy F, Goswami S, Oktay K. (2013). Impairment of BRCA1-related DNA double-strand break repair leads to ovarian aging in mice and humans. Sci Transl Med 5(172):172ra21. doi: 10.1126/scitranslmed.3004925. PMID 23408054

[12] Harris Bernstein, Carol Bernstein and Richard E. Michod (2011). Meiosis as an Evolutionary Adaptation for DNA Repair. Chapter 19 in DNA Repair. Inna Kruman editor. InTech Open Publisher. DOI: 10.5772/25117 http://www.intechopen.com/books/dna-repair/meiosis-as-an-evolutionary-adaptation-for-dna-repair

[13] Isachenko V, Lapidus I, Isachenko E, et al. (2009). "Human ovarian tissue vitrification versus conventional freezing: morphological, endocrinological, and molecular biological evaluation.". *Reproduction* **138** (2): 319–27. doi:10.1530/REP-09-0039. PMID 19439559.

[14] Oktay K, Oktem O (November 2008). "Ovarian cryopreservation and transplantation for fertility preservation for medical indications: report of an ongoing experience". *Fertil. Steril.* **93** (3): 762–8. doi:10.1016/j.fertnstert.2008.10.006. PMID 19013568.

[15] Livebirth after orthotopic transplantation of cryopreserved ovarian tissue The Lancet, Sep 24, 2004

[16] Lan C, Xiao W, Xiao-Hui D, Chun-Yan H, Hong-Ling Y (December 2008). "Tissue culture before transplantation of frozen-thawed human fetal ovarian tissue into immunodeficient mice". *Fertil. Steril.* **93** (3): 913–9. doi:10.1016/j.fertnstert.2008.10.020. PMID 19108826.

[17] Romer, Alfred Sherwood; Parsons, Thomas S. (1977). *The Vertebrate Body*. Philadelphia, PA: Holt-Saunders International. pp. 383–385. ISBN 0-03-910284-X.

[18] Moravec, František; Justine, Jean-Lou (2014). "Philometrids (Nematoda: Philometridae) in carangid and serranid fishes off New Caledonia, including three new species". *Parasite* **21**: 21. doi:10.1051/parasite/2014022. ISSN 1776-1042. PMC 4023622. PMID 24836940.

[19] Fitzpatrick, F. L. 1934. Unilateral and bilateral ovaries in raptorial birds. The Wilson Bulletin 46 (1): 19-22.

[20] Kinsky, F. C. 1971. The consistent presence of paired ovaries in the Kiwi(Apteryx) with some discussion of this condition in other birds. Journal of Ornithology 112 (3): 334–357.

2.11.9 External links

- From the American Medical Association

- Merck Online Medical Library: Female Reproductive System

2.12 Pasteurization

"Pasteurized" redirects here. For the racehorse, see Pasteurized (horse).

Pasteurization (American English) or **pasteurisation**

Cream pasteurizing and cooling coils at Murgon Butter Factory, 1939

(British English) is a process invented by French scientist Louis Pasteur during the nineteenth century. In 1864, Pasteur discovered that heating beer and wine was enough to kill most of the bacteria that caused spoilage, preventing these beverages from turning sour. This was achieved by eliminating pathogenic microbes and lowering microbial numbers to prolong the quality of the beverage. Today, the process of pasteurisation is used widely in the dairy and food industries for microbial control and preservation of the food consumed.[1]

Unlike sterilization, pasteurization is not intended to kill all micro-organisms in the food. Instead, it aims to reduce the number of viable pathogens so they are unlikely to cause disease (assuming the pasteurized product is stored as indicated and is consumed before its expiration date). Commercial-scale sterilization of food is not common because it adversely affects the taste and quality of the product. Certain foods, such as dairy products, may be superheated to ensure pathogenic microbes are destroyed.[2]

2.12.1 Alcoholic beverages

The process of heating wine for preservation purposes has been known in China since 1117,[3] and was documented in Japan in the diary *Tamonin-nikki*, written by a series of monks between 1478 and 1618.

Much later, in 1768, an Italian priest and scientist Lazzaro Spallanzani proved experimentally that heat killed bacteria, and that they do not re-appear if the product is hermetically sealed.[4] In 1795, a Parisian chef and confectioner named Nicolas Appert began experimenting with ways to preserve foodstuffs, succeeding with soups, vegetables, juices, dairy products, jellies, jams, and syrups. He placed the food in glass jars, sealed them with cork and sealing wax and placed them in boiling water.[5] In that same year, the French military offered a cash prize of 12,000 francs for a new method to preserve food. After some 14 or 15 years of experimenting, Appert submitted his invention and won the prize in January 1810. Later that year,[6] Appert published *L'Art de conserver les substances animales et végétales* (or *The Art of Preserving Animal and Vegetable Substances*). This was the first cookbook of its kind on modern food preservation methods.[7][8]

La Maison Appert (English: The House of Appert), in the town of Massy, near Paris, became the first food-bottling factory in the world,[5] preserving a variety of food in sealed bottles. Appert's method was to fill thick, large-mouthed glass bottles with produce of every description, ranging from beef and fowl to eggs, milk and prepared dishes. His greatest success for publicity was an entire sheep. He left air space at the top of the bottle, and the cork would then be sealed firmly in the jar by using a vise. The bottle was then wrapped in canvas to protect it, while it was dunked into boiling water and then boiled for as much time as Appert deemed appropriate for cooking the contents thoroughly. Appert patented his method, sometimes called in his honor "appertisation".

Appert's method was so simple and workable that it quickly became widespread. In 1810, British inventor and merchant Peter Durand, also of French origin, patented his own method, but this time in a tin can, so creating the modern-day process of canning foods. In 1812, Englishmen Bryan Donkin and John Hall purchased both patents and began producing preserves. Just a decade later, Appert's method of canning had made its way to America.[9] Tin can production was, however, not common until the beginning of the 20th century, partly because a hammer and chisel were needed to open cans until the invention of a can opener by an inventor named Yates in 1855.[5]

Appert's preservation by boiling involved heating the food to an unnecessarily high temperature, and for an unnecessarily long time, which could destroy some of the flavor of the preserved food.

A less aggressive method was developed by the French chemist Louis Pasteur during an 1864[4] summer holiday in Arbois. To remedy the frequent acidity of the local wines, he found out experimentally that it is sufficient to heat a young wine to only about 50–60 °C (122–140 °F) for a brief time to kill the microbes, and that the wine could subsequently be aged without sacrificing the final quality.[4] In honour of Pasteur, the process became known as "pasteurization"[10] Pasteurization was originally used as a way of preventing wine and beer from souring,[11] and it would be many years before milk was pasteurized. In the United States in the 1870s, it was common for milk to contain contaminants to mask spoilage before milk was regulated.[12]

2.12.2 Milk

Milk is an excellent medium for microbial growth,[13] and when stored at ambient temperature bacteria and other pathogens soon proliferate.[14]

The US Centers for Disease Control (CDC) says improperly handled raw milk is responsible for nearly three times more hospitalizations than any other food-borne disease outbreak, making it one of the world's most dangerous food products.[15][16] Diseases prevented by pasteurization can include tuberculosis, brucellosis, diphtheria, scarlet fever, and Q-fever; it also kills the harmful bacteria Salmonella, Listeria, Yersinia, Campylobacter, Staphylococcus aureus, and Escherichia coli O157:H7,[17][18] among others.

Pasteurization is the reason for milk's extended shelf life.

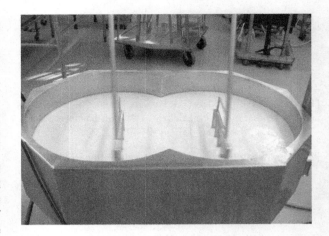

400 lbs of milk in cheese vat

High-temperature, short-time (HTST) pasteurized milk typically has a refrigerated shelf life of two to three weeks, whereas ultra-pasteurized milk can last much longer, sometimes two to three months. When ultra-heat treatment (UHT) is combined with sterile handling and container technology (such as aseptic packaging), it can even be stored unrefrigerated for up to 9 months.

History

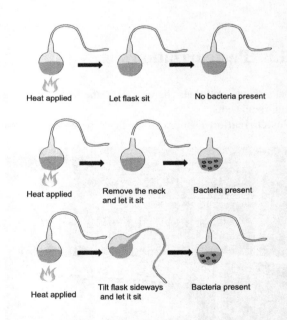

Louis Pasteur's pasteurization experiment illustrates the fact that the spoilage of liquid was caused by particles in the air rather than the air itself. These experiments were important pieces of evidence supporting the idea of Germ Theory of Disease.

Before the widespread urban growth caused by industrialization, people kept dairy cows even in urban areas and the short time period between production and consumption minimised the disease risk of drinking raw milk.[*][19] However, as urban densities increased and supply chains lengthened to the distance from country to city, raw milk (often days old) began to be recognised as a source of disease. For example, between 1912 and 1937 some 65,000 people died of tuberculosis contracted from consuming milk in England and Wales alone.[*][20]

Developed countries adopted milk pasteurization to prevent such disease and loss of life, and as a result milk is now widely considered one of the safest foods.[*][19] A traditional form of pasteurization by scalding and straining of cream to increase the keeping qualities of butter was practiced in England before 1773 and was introduced to Boston in the USA by 1773,[*][21] although it was not widely practiced in the United States for the next 20 years. It was still being referred to as a "new" process in American newspapers as late as 1802.[*][22] Pasteurization of milk was suggested by Franz von Soxhlet in 1886.[*][23] In the early 20th century, Milton Joseph Rosenau, established the standards (i.e. low temperature, slow heating at 60 °C (140 °F) for 20 minutes) for the pasteurization of milk,[*][24][*][25] while at the United States Marine Hospital Service, notably in his publication of The Milk Question (1912).[*][26]

Process

Older pasteurization methods used temperatures below boiling, since at very high temperatures, micelles of the milk protein casein will irreversibly aggregate, or "curdle". Newer methods use higher temperature, but shorten the time. Among the pasteurization methods listed below, the two main types of pasteurization used today are high-temperature, short-time (HTST, also known as "flash") and extended shelf life (ESL):

- HTST milk is forced between metal plates or through pipes heated on the outside by hot water, and the milk is heated to 72 °C (161 °F) for 15 seconds.[*][27][*]:8 Milk simply labeled "pasteurized" is usually treated with the HTST method.

- UHT, also known as ultra-heat-treating, processing holds the milk at a temperature of 140 °C (284 °F) for four seconds.[*][28] During UHT processing milk is sterilized and not pasteurized. This process allows milk or juice to be stored several months without refrigeration. The process is achieved by spraying the milk or juice through a nozzle into a chamber that is filled with high-temperature steam under pressure. After the temperature reaches 140 °C the fluid is cooled instantly in a vacuum chamber, and packed in a presterilized airtight container.[*][28] Milk labeled

"ultra-pasteurized" or simply "UHT" has been treated with the UHT method.

- ESL milk has a microbial filtration step and lower temperatures than UHT milk.[*][29] Since 2007, it is no longer a legal requirement in European countries (for example in Germany) to declare ESL milk as ultra-heated; consequently, it is now often labeled as "fresh milk" and just advertised as having an "extended shelf life", making it increasingly difficult to distinguish ESL milk from traditionally pasteurized fresh milk.

- A less conventional, but US FDA-legal, alternative (typically for home pasteurization) is to heat milk at 63 °C (145 °F) for 30 minutes.[*][30]

Pasteurization methods are usually standardized and controlled by national food safety agencies (such as the USDA in the United States and the Food Standards Agency in the United Kingdom). These agencies require that milk be HTST pasteurized to qualify for the pasteurized label. Dairy product standards differ, depending on fat content and intended usage. For example, pasteurization standards for cream differ from standards for fluid milk, and standards for pasteurizing cheese are designed to preserve the enzyme phosphatase, which aids cutting. In Canada, all milk produced at a processor and intended for consumption must be pasteurized, which legally requires that it be heated to at least 72 °C for at least 16 seconds,[*][31] then cooling it to 4 °C to ensure any harmful bacteria are destroyed. The UK Dairy Products Hygiene Regulations 1995 requires that milk be heat treated for 15 seconds at 71.7 °C or other effective time/temperature combination.[*][32]

A process similar to pasteurization is thermization, which uses lower temperatures to kill bacteria in milk. It allows a milk product, such as cheese, to retain more of the original taste, but thermized foods are not considered pasteurized by food regulators.[*][30]

Microwave volumetric heating

Microwave volumetric heating (MVH) is the newest available pasteurization technology. It uses microwaves to heat liquids, suspensions, or semi-solids in a continuous flow. Because MVH delivers energy evenly and deeply into the whole body of a flowing product, it allows for gentler and shorter heating, so that almost all heat-sensitive substances in the milk are preserved.[*][33]

Efficiency

The HTST pasteurization standard was designed to achieve a five-log reduction, killing 99.999% of the number of viable micro-organisms in milk.[*][34] This is considered adequate for destroying almost all yeasts, molds, and common spoilage bacteria and also to ensure adequate destruction of common pathogenic, heat-resistant organisms (including *Mycobacterium tuberculosis*, which causes tuberculosis, but not *Coxiella burnetii*, which causes Q fever).[*][34] As a precaution, modern equipment tests and identifies bacteria in milk being processed. HTST pasteurization processes must be designed so the milk is heated evenly, and no part of the milk is subject to a shorter time or a lower temperature.

Even pasteurization without quality control can be effective, though this is generally not permitted for human consumption; a study of farms feeding calves on pasteurized waste milk using a mixture of pasteurization technologies (none of which were routinely monitored for performance) found the resulting pasteurized milk to meet safety requirements at least 92% of the time.[*][35]

An effect of the heating of pasteurization is that some vitamin, mineral, and beneficial (or probiotic) bacteria is lost. Soluble calcium and phosphorus levels decrease by 5%, thiamine (vitamin B_1) and vitamin B_{12} (cobalamin) levels by 10%, and vitamin C levels by 20%.[*][20][*][36] However, these losses are not significant nutritionally.[*][37]

Verification

Direct microbiological techniques are the ultimate measurement of pathogen contamination but these are costly and time consuming (24–48 hours), which means that products are able to spoil by the time pasteurization is verified.

As a result of the unsuitability of microbiological techniques, milk pasteurization efficacy is typically monitored by checking for the presence of alkaline phosphatase, which is denatured by pasteurization. B. tuberculosis, the bacterium requiring the highest temperature to be killed of all milk pathogens is killed at similar ranges of temperature and time as those which denature alkaline phosphatase. For this reason, presence of alkaline phosphatase is deemed to be an ideal diagnostic tool for pasteurization efficacy.[*][38][*][39]

Phosphatase denaturing was originally monitored using a phenol-phosphate substrate. When hydrolysed by the enzyme these compounds liberate phenols, which were then reacted with dibromoquinonechlorimide to give a colour change, which itself was measured by checking absorption at 610 nm (spectrophotometry). Some of the phenols used were inherently coloured (phenolpthalein, nitrophenol) and were simply assayed unreacted.[*][32] Spectrophotometric analysis is satisfactory but is of relatively low accuracy because many natural products are coloured. For this reason, modern systems (since 1990) use fluorometry which is able to detect much lower levels of raw milk contamination.[*][32]

Unpasteurized milk

For more details on this topic, see Raw milk.

According to the United States Centers for Disease Control between 1998 and 2011 79% of the dairy related outbreaks were due to raw milk or cheese products.[*][40] They report 148 outbreaks, 2,384 illnesses (284 requiring hospitalizations) as well as 2 deaths due to raw milk or cheese products during the same time period.[*][40]

2.12.3 Consumer acceptance

As pasteurization is a very old and traditional way of preservation, it is well known and accepted by consumers. Nearly every label of milk products contains the word "pasteurization" and it is associated by consumers with good quality attributes and safety. In the consumer studies of Hightech Europe consumers mentioned more positive than negative associations for this technology showing that these products are well accepted.[*][41]

2.12.4 Products that are commonly pasteurized

- Beer
- Canned food
- Dairy products
- Milk
- Juices
- Low alcoholic beverages
- Syrups
- Vinegar
- Water
- Wines

2.12.5 See also

- Food irradiation
- Flash pasteurization
- Pascalization

- Homogenization

- Pasteurized eggs

- Solar water disinfection

- Thermoduric bacteria

- Food preservation

- Food storage

- Food microbiology

- Sterilization

- Thermization

- Louis Pasteur

2.12.6 References

[1] "What is pasteurisation?".

[2] Montville, T. J., and K. R. Matthews: "food microbiology an introduction", page 30. American Society for Microbiology Press, 2005.

[3] Hornsey, Ian Spencer and George Bacon (2003). *A History of Beer and Brewing*. Royal Society of Chemistry. p. 30. ISBN 0-85404-630-5. [⋯] sake is pasteurized and it is interesting to note that a pasteurization technique was first mentioned in 1568 in the _Tamonin-nikki_, the diary of a Buddhist monk, indicating that it was practiced in Japan some 300 years before Pasteur. In China, the first country in East Asia to develop a form of pasteurization, the earliest record of the process is said to date from 1117.

[4] Vallery-Radot, René (2003-03-01). *Life of Pasteur 1928*. pp. 113–114. ISBN 978-0-7661-4352-4.

[5] Lance Day, Ian McNeil, ed. (1996). *Biographical Dictionary of the History of Technology*. Routledge. ISBN 0-415-19399-0.

[6] Gordon L. Robertson (1998). *Food Packaging: Principles End Practice*. Marcel Dekker. p. 187. ISBN 978-0-8247-0175-8.

[7] ""The First Book on Modern Food Preservation Methods (1810)"". Historyofscience.com. 2009-09-29. Retrieved 2014-03-19.

[8] Wiley, R. C (1994). *Minimally processed refrigerated fruits and vegetables*. p. 66. ISBN 978-0-412-05571-3. Nicolas Appert in 1810 was probably the first person [⋯]

[9] Alvin Toffler, "Future Shock".

[10] "BBC - History - Louis Pasteur".

[11] Carlisle, Rodney (2004). *Scientific American Inventions and Discoveries*, p.357. John Wiley & Songs, Inc., new Jersey. ISBN 0-471-24410-4.

[12] Hwang, Andy; Huang, Lihan (31 January 2009). *Ready-to-Eat Foods: Microbial Concerns and Control Measures*. CRC Press. p. 88. ISBN 978-1-4200-6862-7. Retrieved 19 April 2011.

[13] "Harold Eddleman, "Making Milk Media", Indiana Biolab". Disknet.com. Retrieved 2014-03-19.

[14] "Frank O'Mahony, "Rural dairy technology: Experiences in Ethiopia", International Livestock Centre for Africa". Ilri.org. Retrieved 2014-03-19.

[15] "Food safety of raw milk". Foodsmart.govt.nz. Retrieved 2014-03-19.

[16] Langer, Adam J.; Ayers, Tracy; Grass, Julian; Lynch, Michael; Angulo, Frederick; Mahon, Barbara. "Nonpasteurized Dairy Products, Disease Outbreaks, and State Laws—United States, 1993–2006" (PDF). *http://www.cdc.gov/foodsafety/rawmilk/raw-milk-questions-and-answers.html*. Retrieved 11 February 2015.

[17] "Milk Pasteurization: Guarding against disease", Michigan State University Extension

[18] Smith, P. W., (August 1981), "Milk Pasteurization" Fact Sheet Number 57, U.S. Department of Agriculture Research Service, Washington, D.C.

[19] Hotchkiss, Joseph H. (2001), "Lambasting Louis: Lessons from Pasteurization" (PDF), *National Agricultural Biotechnology Council Report* **13**: 61

[20] Wilson, G. S. (1943), "The Pasteurization of Milk", *British Medical Journal* **1** (4286): 261, doi:10.1136/bmj.1.4286.261, PMC 2282302, PMID 20784713

[21] News article, *[Boston] Independent Ledger*, 16 June 1783

[22] News article, *Western Constellation*, 19 July 1802

[23] Franz Soxhlet (1886) "Über Kindermilch und Säuglings-Ernährung" (On milk for babies and infant nutrition), *Münchener medizinische Wochenschrift* (Munich Medical Weekly), vol. 33, pages 253, 276.

[24] url = http://jewishcurrents.org/january-1-pasteurization-34519

[25] url=http://www.cdc.gov/mmwr/preview/mmwrhtml/mm4840b1.htm

[26] url= http://www.biodiversitylibrary.org/bibliography/27504#/summary

[27] "Grade A Pasteurized Milk Ordinance 2009 Revision". US Department of Health and Human Services.

[28] Tortora, Gerard (2010). Microbiology: An Introduction, p.191. Pearson Benjamin Cummings, San Francisco. ISBN 0-321-55007-2.

[29] Koel, Jaan (2001). "Paving the Way for ESL". *Dairy Foods*.

[30] Rich, Robert (5 September 2003). "Keeping it raw". *The Mountain View Voice* (Embarcadero Publishing Company). Retrieved 23 October 2010.

[31] Canadian Food Inspection System – Dairy Production and Processing Regulations (Fourth Edition) – 2005

[32] Langridge, E W. *The Determination of Phosphatase Activity*. Quality Management Ltd. Retrieved 2013-12-20.

[33] "Gentle pasteurization of milk – with microwaves". *ScienceDaily*.

[34] Stabel, J. R.; Lambertz, A. (2004), "Efficacy of Pasteurization Conditions for the Inactivation of *Mycobacterium avium* subsp. *paratuberculosis* in Milk", *Journal of Food Protection* **67** (12): 2719

[35] "Penn State Study Finds Calf Milk Pasteurization Effective, but Variable ―Dairy ―Penn State Extension". Extension.psu.edu. 2010-12-14. Retrieved 2014-03-19.

[36] Krauss, W. E., Erb, J. H. and Washburn, R.G., "Studies on the nutritive value of milk, II. The effect of pasteurization on some of the nutritive properties of milk," Ohio Agricultural Experiment Station Bulletin 518, page 30, January, 1933.

[37] Claeys, Wendy L.; Sabine Cardoen, Georges Daube, Jan De Block, Koen Dewettinck, Katelijne Dierick, Lieven De Zutter, André Huyghebaert, Hein Imberechts, Pierre Thiange, Yvan Vandenplas, Lieve Herman (May 2013). "Raw or heated cow milk consumption: Review of risks and benefits". *Food Control* **31** (1): 251–262. doi:10.1016/j.foodcont.2012.09.035.

[38] Kay, H. (1935). "Some Results of the Application of a Simple Test for Efficiency of Pasteurisation". *The Lancet* **225** (5835): 1516–1518. doi:10.1016/S0140-6736(01)12532-8.

[39] Hoy, W. A.; Neave, F. K. (1937). "The Phosphatase Test for Efficient Pasteurisation". *The Lancet* **230** (5949): 595. doi:10.1016/S0140-6736(00)83378-4.

[40] "CDC - Raw Milk Questions and Answers - Food Safety". Cdc.gov. 2014-03-07. Retrieved 2014-03-19.

[41] "Documents". Hightecheurope.eu. Retrieved 2014-03-19.

2.12.7 Further reading

- Raw milk expert testimony dated: April 25, 2008 Case: ORGANIC PASTURES DAIRY COMPANY, LLC, and CLARAVALE FARM, INC., Plaintiffs, vs. No. CU-07-00204 STATE OF CALIFORNIA and A.G. KAWAMURA, SECRETARY OF CALIFORNIA DEPARTMENT OF FOOD AND AGRICULTURE, Defendants. - Expert Witnesses: Dr. Theodore Beals & Dr. Ronald Hull

2.12.8 External links

- Online forum on modern day pasteurization equipment

- Extended Shelf Life

- Unraveling the mysteries of extended shelf life

2.13 Roe

For other uses, see Roe (disambiguation).
Roe (/roʊ/) or **hard roe** is the fully ripe internal egg masses

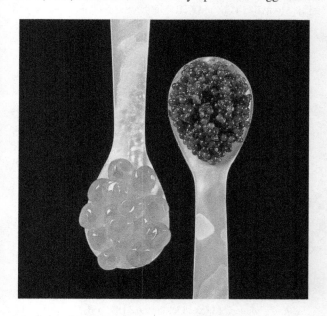

Salmon roe (left) and sturgeon roe (caviar) (right)

in the ovaries, or the released external egg masses of fish and certain marine animals, such as shrimp, scallop and sea urchins. As a seafood, roe is used both as a cooked ingredient in many dishes and as a raw ingredient. The roe of marine animals, such as the roe of lumpsucker, hake and salmon, is an excellent source of omega-3 fatty acids.*[1] Roe from a sturgeon or sometimes other fishes is the raw base product from which caviar is made.

The term **soft roe** or **white roe** denotes fish milt.

Prawns skagen topped with cold-smoked salmon roe, on bread

2.13.1 Around the world

Africa

South Africa The large Indian population in KwaZulu Natal consumes fish roe in the form of slightly sour curry or battered and deep fried.

Americas

United States In the United States, several kinds of roe are produced: salmon from the Pacific coast, shad and herring species like the American shad and alewife, mullet, paddlefish, American bowfin, and some species of sturgeon. Shad, pike and other roe are sometimes pan-fried with bacon. Spot Prawn roe (hard to find) is also a delicacy from the North Pacific. Flounder roe, pan-fried and served with grits is popular on the Southeastern coast.

Canada In the province of New Brunswick, roe (caviare) of the Atlantic sturgeon is harvested from the Saint John river.

Roe from the cisco is harvested from the Great Lakes, primarily for overseas markets.

Roe is also extracted from herring, salmon, and sea urchins.

Chile In Chile, sea urchin roe is a traditional food known as an "erizo de mar". Chile is one of many countries that exports sea urchins to Japan in order to fulfill Japanese demand.

Peru In Peru, roe is served in many seafood restaurants sauteed, breaded and pan fried, and sometimes accompanied by a side of fresh onion salad. It is called Huevera Frita. Cojinova (Seriolella violacea) yields the best roe for this dish. Despite the fact that many people like it, it is hardly considered a delicacy. Upscale restaurants are not expected to offer it, but street vendors and smaller restaurants will make their first daily sales of it before they run out. Cojinova itself (considered a medium quality fish) is caught for its fish meal, not for its roe, which is considered a chance product. Sea urchin roe is considered a delicacy and it is used (at customer request) to add strength to ceviche.

Asia

Bangladesh Roe from the Ilish fish is considered a delicacy in Bangladesh. The roe is usually deep-fried, although other preparations such as **mashed roe** where the roe crushed along with oil, onion and pepper, or **curry of roe** can also be found.

China In many regions in China, crab and urchin roes are eaten as a delicacy. Crab roe are often used as topping in dishes such as "crab roe tofu" (蟹粉豆腐). Nanxiang Steamed Bun Restaurant serves "crab roe xiaolongbao" as their special. Shrimp roes are also eaten in certain places, especially around the downstream of Yangtze River, such as Wuhu, as toppings for noodle soup.

India Among the tribal populace of eastern India, roe that has been deeply roasted over an open fire is a delicacy. In this region, the roe of rohu is also considered a delicacy and is eaten fried or as a stuffing within a fried pointed gourd to make *potoler dolma*.

All along the Konkan coast and Northern Kerala, the roe of sardines, black mackerel and several other fish is considered a delicacy. The roe can be eaten fried (after being coated with red chilli paste) and also as a thick curry (gashi). In the state of Kerala, roe is deep fried in coconut oil, and is considered a delicacy. A common method of quick preparation is to wrap the roe in wet banana leaves and cook it over charcoal embers.

In Odisha and West Bengal, roe of several fresh-water fish, including hilsa, are eaten, the roe being cooked separately or along with the fish, the latter method being preferred for all but large fishes. Roe, either light or deep-fried are also eaten as snacks or appetizers before a major meal.

Iran In the Caspian provinces of Gilan and Mazandaran, several types of roe are used. Called *ashpal* or *ashbal*, roe is consumed grilled, cured, salted, or mixed with other ingredients. If salted or cured, it is consumed as a condiment. If used fresh, it is usually grilled, steamed, or mixed with eggs and fried to form a custard-like dish called "Ashpal Kuku".

Besides the much sought-after caviar, roe from kutum (also known as Caspian white fish or *Rutilus frisii kutum*), Caspian roach (called "kuli" in Gileki), bream (called "kulmeh" in Gileki), and Caspian salmon are highly prized. Roe from carp is less common and barbel roe is also occasionally used.

Israel Several sections of the Israeli cuisine include roe. In Modern Hebrew, roe is commonly referred to by its Russian name "ikra" (איקרה). When necessary, the color is also mentioned: white or pink, as appropriate. Israeli "white ikra" is commonly made of carp or herring eggs, while "red ikra" is made of flathead mullet eggs or, in rarer cases, salmon eggs. The term "caviar" is separate, and denotes only sturgeon eggs.

Ikra is served as a starter dish, to be eaten with pita or similar breads, particularly in Arab restaurants. It can also be purchased in stores, in standard-sized plastic packages. In home cooking it is similarly served as a starter dish.

In Judaism, roe from kosher fish--fish with fins and scales--is considered kosher. Like fish in general, it is considered pareve. Roe is considered kosher only if the fish from which it's harvested is kosher as well. This means that sturgeon roe is not considered kosher from an Orthodox Jewish perspective.

For most Orthodox Jewish consumers who keep kosher, roe or caviar must be processed under kosher supervision as well. The only exception to this rule is red roe, thanks to a widely accepted responsa by the Bais Yosef.*[2]

Ikuradon, *a bowl of rice topped with salmon roe*

Uncooked noodle made from shrimp roe

as bait, first-time sushi eaters who have experienced fishing may be taken aback when served ikura. It is a loan word from the Russian, "икра" (soft-shelled eggs, in this context caviar)

- Sujiko (すじこ/筋子) - Also salmon roe. The difference is that sujiko is still inside its sac when it is prepared. It also has a different color; sujiko is red to dark-red while ikura is lighter in color, sometimes almost orange. Sujiko is also sweeter in taste.

- Masago (真砂子)- Smelt roe, similar to Tobiko, but smaller.

- Kazunoko (数の子/鯑) - Herring roe, yellow or pinkish, having a firm, rubbery texture and appearance, usually pickled. The roe is in a single cohesive mass and so looks like a piece of fish.

- Mentaiko (明太子) - Alaska pollock roe, spiced with powdered red pepper and surrounded by a thin, elastic membrane. Mentaiko is usually pink to dark red.

Salmon roe at the Shiogama seafood market in Japan

Japan A variety of roe types are used in Japanese cuisine, including the following which are used raw in sushi:

- Ikura (イクラ) - Salmon roe. Large reddish-orange individual spheres. Since salmon eggs are also used

- Tarako (たらこ/鱈子) - Salted Alaska pollock roe, sometimes grilled.

- Tobiko (飛び子) - Flying fish roe, very crunchy, reddish orange in color.

Sea urchin roe.

- Uni (うに/雲丹) - Sea urchin roe, soft and melting. Color ranges from orange to pale yellow. Humans consume the reproductive organs ("roe") either raw or briefly cooked. Sea urchin roe is a popular food in Korean cuisine, and it is called "uni" in Japanese sushi cuisine. Apart from domestic consumption, a number of other countries export the sea urchin to Japan in order to meet its demand throughout the country. Traditionally considered an aphrodisiac, sea urchin roe has been found to contain the cannabinoid anandamide.*[3]

- Karasumi (カラスミ/鱲子) - is a specialty of Nagasaki and along with salt-pickled sea urchin roe and Konowata one of the three chinmi of Japan. It is made by desalinating salt pickled mullet roe and sundrying it.

Korea All kinds of fish roe are widely eaten in Korea including sea urchin, salmon, herring, flying fish, cod, among others. Myeongran jeot (⊠⊠⊠) refers to the jeotgal (salted fermented seafood) made with pollock roe seasoned with chili pepper powders. It is commonly consumed as banchan, small dish accompanied with cooked rice or ingredient for altang (⊠⊠), a kind of jjigae (Korean stew).

Lebanon Sea urchin roe, or toutia توتية as it is known locally, is eaten directly from the sea urchin shell fresh using a small spoon. Some people add a twist of lemon juice to the roe and eat it in Lebanese flat bread.

Malaysia Particularly in Sarawak, Malaysia, Toli Shad fish roe is a popular delicacy among locals and tourists. The roe is usually found in the street market in Sarawak's capital city of Kuching. The roe can be sold for up to 19 USD per 100 grams and is considered expensive among locals, but the price can reach up to 30 USD in other states of Malaysia.

The roe is usually salted before sale but fresh roe is also available. The salted roe is usually pan fried or steamed and eaten with steamed rice. The fish itself is also usually salted and served along with the roe.

New Zealand

The Maori people and other New Zealanders eat sea urchin roe, called "Kina".*[4] Kina is sold in fishshops, supermarkets, and alongside the road. Most commercial Kina is imported from the Chatham Islands.

Europe

All around the Mediterranean, botargo is an esteemed specialty made of the cured roe pouch of flathead mullet, tuna, or swordfish; it is called bottarga (Italian), poutargue or boutargue (French), botarga (Spanish), batarekh (Arabic) or avgotaraho (Greek αυγοτάραχο).

Denmark Lumpfish (*stenbider*) roe is used extensively in Danish cuisine, on top of halved or sliced hard-boiled eggs, on top of mounds of shrimp, or in combination with other fish or seafood. Another commonly eaten roe is that from the cod (*torsk*).

France Sea urchin roe (*oursin* in French) is eaten directly from the sea and in restaurants, where it is served both by itself and in seafood platters, usually spooned from the shell of the animal. Crab, shrimp and prawn roe still attached to those animals is also considered a delicacy.

Finland Common whitefish and especially vendace from the fresh water lakes in Finland are renowned for the excellent delicate taste of the roe. Roe is served as topping of toast or on blini with onion and smetana.

Greece Tarama is salted and cured carp or cod roe used to make taramosalata, a Greek and Turkish meze consisting of tarama mixed with lemon juice, bread crumbs, onions, and olive oil; it is eaten as a dip.

Avgotaraho (αυγοτάραχο) or botargo is the prepared roe of the flathead mullet.

Taramosalata, *salad made with* tarama

Romanian roe salad decorated with black olives

Italy   Bottarga is primary the salted and dried roe pouch of the Atlantic bluefin tuna; can be also prepared with the dried roe pouch of the flathead mullet, even if it is considered of low quality and less tasty. It is used minced for dressing pasta or in slice with olive oil and lemon (Fishermen style). The coastal town of Alghero, Sardinia, is also known for its "bogamarì" specialty (fresh sea urchin roe).

Netherlands   In the Netherlands fried roe of hering is eaten.

Norway   Norwegian caviar is most commonly made from cod, but caviar made from lumpsucker or capelin roe is also available.

In some areas it is also common to fry the roe from freshly caught fish, to be eaten on bread or with potatoes and flatbread.

Portugal   Codfish roe and sardine roe are sold in olive oil. The fresh roe of hake (pescada) is also consumed (a popular way of eating it is boiled with vegetables, and simply seasoned with olive oil and a dash of vinegar). In the South of Portugal, the "ouriço do mar" (sea urchin) is highly appreciated. In the Sines area (Alentejo), a layer of dried pine needles is placed on the ground and, on top of it, a layer of sea urchins. This layer is topped with a second layer of dried pine needles. The pile is set on fire. The roe is removed from the cooked sea urchins and eaten. Sea urchin is not consumed in May, June, July, and August.

Romania   Fish roe is very popular in Romania as a starter (like salată de icre) or sometimes served for breakfast on toasted bread. The most common roe is that of the European carp; pike, herring, cod are also popular. Fried soft roe is also a popular dish. Sturgeon roe is a delicacy normally served at functions.

The Russian Federation   In Russian, all types of fish roe are called "икра" (*ikra*, caviar), and there is no linguistic distinction between the English words "roe" and "caviar." Sturgeon roe, called "чёрная икра" (*chyornaya ikra*, "black caviar") is most prized. It is usually served lightly salted on buttered rye bread, or used as an ingredient in various *haute cuisine* sauces and dishes. It is followed in prestige by salmon roe, called "red caviar," which is less expensive, but still considered a delicacy. More common roes, such as cod, pollock, and herring are everyday dishes. Salted cod or pollock roe on buttered bread is common breakfast fare and herring roe is often eaten smoked or fried. The roe of freshwater fish is also popular but the commercial availability is lower. Soft roe of various fishes is also widely consumed, mostly fried, and is a popular cantina-style dish.

Roe found in dried vobla fish is considered delicious; though dried vobla roe is not produced separately as a stand-alone dish, roe-carrying vobla is prized.

Spain   Cod and hake roe is commonly consumed throughout the country in many different forms: sautéed, grilled, fried, marinated, pickled, boiled and with mayonnaise, or in salad. Tuna and ling dry brined roe is traditional in Andalusia and the Mediterranean coasts since antiquity. In all the Spanish coastal regions, sea urchin roe is considered a delicacy and consumed raw.

Sweden   Smoked and salted cod roe paste, commonly served as sandwich topping is popular in Sweden. The most famous brand is Kalles kaviar.

Lightly salted roe of the vendace is called Löjrom in Swedish. It is naturally orange in colour. The most sought after type is Kalix Löjrom from Kalix in the northern Baltic sea.

Most Löjrom consumed in Sweden is however imported frozen from North America.

Stenbitsrom, the roe of lumpfish is naturally a bleak unappetizing gray, but is coloured black (to emulate Black Caviar) or orange (to emulate Löjrom). Stenbitsrom sells in much larger volume than Löjrom, but it has two drawbacks: it tastes little more than its salt and artificial additives, and the colour additives tend to bleed into other parts of the food you serve it with (such as a boiled egg), or to discolour the porcelain dish.

There is also a trend to use more Laxrom (Salmon roe), which is a natural orange colour, and has large diameter.

United Kingdom Roe consumed within the UK is generally soft roe as opposed to hard roe. Though not popular, herring roe is sold within many British supermarkets. Battered cod roe can also be bought within many fish and chip shops. Various tinned roes are on sale in supermarkets e.g. soft cod roes, pressed cod roes and herring roes.

2.13.2 See also

- Smoked egg

2.13.3 References

[1] Roe of Marine Animals Is Best Natural Source of Omega-3 *Science Daily*, 11 December 2009.

[2] http://www.crcweb.org/kosher_articles/kosher_fish.php

[3] Bisogno; et al. (1997). "Occurrence and metabolism of anandamide and related acyl-ethanolamides in ovaries of the sea urchin Paracentrotus lividus" . *Biochim Biophys Acta* **1346** (3): 338–48. doi:10.1016/s0005-2760(97)00009-x. PMID 9150253.

[4] 2. Sea urchins - Starfish, sea urchins and other echinoderms - Te Ara Encyclopedia of New Zealand

2.14   Royal fish

Under the law of the United Kingdom, whales and sturgeons are **royal fish**, and when taken become the personal property of the monarch of the United Kingdom as part of his or her royal prerogative.

2.14.1   In England and Wales

According to William Blackstone's *Commentaries on the Laws of England*, the "superior excellence" of whale

*Sturgeons, along with whales, dolphins and porpoises, are **royal fish**.*

and sturgeon made them uniquely suited for the monarch's use.[1] Sir Matthew Hale added porpoise as one of the royal fish.[2] Near the English coast they belong to the monarch immediately upon being caught, while ownership is also transferred to the monarch when a catch from any location is cast up on the shores. The kings of Denmark and the dukes of Normandy enjoyed a similar prerogative.

The monarch's right to royal fish was recognized by a statute enacted during the reign of Edward II.[3] According to Henry de Bracton, *de balena vero sufficit . . . si rex habeat caput, et regina caudam*: the king owns the head of the whale, the queen owns the tail.[4] In *Moby-Dick*, Herman Melville quoted the speculations of jurist William Prynne, that the queen received the tail, in order to be supplied with whalebone for her corsets and stays[5] (although as Melville points out, "whalebone" is in fact baleen, from the *mouths* of certain whales). If Prynne's suggestion as to the purpose of the rule is followed, the situation may be reversed when a queen regnant is the Monarch; a definitive ruling has not yet been made.

Under current law, the Receiver of Wreck is the official appointed to take possession of royal fish when they arrive on English shores. The law of royal fish continues to excite some notice and occasional controversy, as evidenced when a fisherman caught and sold a sturgeon in Swansea Bay in 2004.[6]

2.14.2   In Scotland

In Scotland, the monarch's property right inheres in those whales too large to be pulled to land by a "wain pulled by six oxen"; in practice, this is interpreted as requiring the whales to be over 25 feet long.[7] Authority to collect them on behalf of the monarch is given to the Scottish Government

Marine Directorate.

2.14.3   In Ireland

In Ireland the Crown, as part of the Lordship of Ireland, also claimed the prerogative of taking royal fish, which extended to porpoises and dolphins. There is a record of a dispute between the Crown and Christopher St Lawrence, 2nd Baron Howth in about 1440 over ownership of an exceptionally large grampus (Risso's Dolphin) which had been stranded on Howth peninsula in Dublin Bay. The Crown claimed it as a royal fish, while Lord Howth claimed it on foot of the immemorial right of his family to possession of every grampus and porpoise taken on the peninsula.*[8]

2.14.4   See also

- Swan Upping

2.14.5   References

[1] William Blackstone, *Commentaries on the Laws of England*, book I, ch. 8 "Of the King's Revenue" , ss. X, p. *280

[2] Hale *De Jure Maris* c.7

[3] 17 Edw. II c. 11, *De prærogativa regis*.

[4] Bracton, *De Legibus et Consuetudinibus Angliæ*, book 3. c. 3

[5] Herman Melville, *Moby-Dick*, ch. XC.

[6] BBC News, "Police inquiry over sturgeon sale", June 3, 2004, accessed Oct. 26, 2007.

[7] *Royal Fish: Guidance in Dealing with Stranded Royal Fish*

[8] Ball, F. Elrington *History of Dublin* Vol.5 1917:Alexander Thom and Co. Dublin p.49

2.15   Sevruga

Sevruga is one of the highest priced varieties of caviar, eclipsed in cost only by the Beluga and Ossetra varieties. It is harvested from the Sevruga sturgeon (*Acipenser stellatus*) native to the Caspian Sea, and may be distinguished from its more expensive cousins by the size of the eggs, which are generally smaller.*[1]

Sevruga is the smallest of the caviar-producing sturgeons. It can grow as far as 150 lbs. in weight and 7 feet in length. It is native to the Black, Azov, Caspian and Aegean Sea basins.

Because the Stellate sturgeon is the most common and reproduces more quickly, this makes Sevruga caviar the most commonly found of the sturgeon caviars, and the most inexpensive of the three main types of sturgeon caviar - Beluga, Osetra and Sevruga.*[2] It's calculated that about half the caviar production comes from Sevruga. Sevruga caviar eggs are a pearlescent grey, and smaller in size than other sturgeon. The flavor is more pronounced than other varieties, often described as saltier, but it can vary depending on the origin of the fish. The caviar is packaged and sold in red tins.

2.15.1   Other types of Sevruga

A rare type of caviar known Imperial Caviar, from the Sterlet sturgeon (Acipenser ruthenus), a now nearly extinct species of sturgeon from the Caspian Sea,*[3] is sometimes incorrectly labeled as Sevruga, as well as the even rarer Golden Caviar from the albino Sterlet, the caviar being yellow in color. "Pressed sevruga caviar" can also be found, made of a blend of Osetra and Sevruga caviar that has been heated in a saline solution.*[4]

2.15.2   References

[1] "Sevruga Caviar" . Food Fancy. Retrieved 26 September 2012.

[2] "Types of Caviar Caviar" . Gourmet Food Store.

[3] http://www.cites.org/eng/com/ac/16/16-7-2a5.pdf

[4] "World Markets and Industry of Selected Commercially-Exploited Aquatic Species with an International Conservation Profile" . FOOD AND AGRICULTURE ORGANIZATION OF THE UNITED NATIONS.

2.16   Sterlet

The **sterlet** (*Acipenser ruthenus*) is a relatively small species of sturgeon from Eurasia native to large rivers that flow into the Black Sea, Azov Sea, and Caspian Sea, as well as rivers in Siberia as far east as Yenisei. Populations migrating between fresh and salt water (anadromous) have been extirpated.*[1]

Due to overfishing (for its flesh, caviar, and isinglass), pollution, and dams, the sterlet has declined throughout its native range and is considered vulnerable by the IUCN.*[1] Restocking projects are ongoing, and it has been introduced to some regions outside its native range, but the latter have generally not become self-sustaining.*[1] Today, the majority of the international trade involves sterlets from aquaculture.*[1]

2.16.1 Physical appearance

- The sterlet may reach 16 kg in weight and 100 to 125 cm in length, rarely exceeding a length of 3 ft.

- It is quite variable in coloration, but usually has a yellowish ventral side.

- It is distinguishable from other European species of sturgeons by the presence of a great number of whitish lateral scutes, fringed barbels, and an elongated and narrow snout, highly variable in length.

2.16.2 Feeding habits

The sterlet's main source of food is benthic organisms; they commonly feed on crustaceans, worms, and insect larvae.

On exhibition Subaqueous Vltava, Prague

2.16.3 Life history

The sterlet commonly reaches the age of 22 to 25 years. Males reach sexual maturity at 3–7 years old and females at 4–12 years old. Spawning occurs from the middle of April to the beginning of June. Females may lay from 15,000–44,000 eggs, at water temperatures preferably 12–17°C (54–63°F).

2.16.4 As pond fish

Sterlets require relatively large ponds with good water conditions, and may get entangled in plants such as blanketweed. They may require special food such as sterlet sticks, as they are unable to digest the vegetable proteins usually found in commercial fish foods.

2.16.5 As food

Sterlet with satsivi

In Russia, it is held in high esteem on account of its excellent flesh, contributing also to the best kinds of caviar and isinglass.

2.16.6 Sturgeon hybrids

- Sterlet x Beluga (*Huso huso*) = (Bester)

- Sterlet x Siberian [Russian (*Acipenser gueldenstaedtii*)]

- Sterlet x Diamondback

- Hybrids are hardier than their parents.

2.16.7 References

[1] Gesner, J., Freyhof, J. & Kottelat, M. (2010). "Acipenser ruthenus". *IUCN Red List of Threatened Species. Version 2012.2*. International Union for Conservation of Nature.

2.17 Sturgeon

For other uses, see Sturgeon (disambiguation).

Sturgeon is the common name for the 27 species of fish belonging to the family Acipenseridae. Their evolution

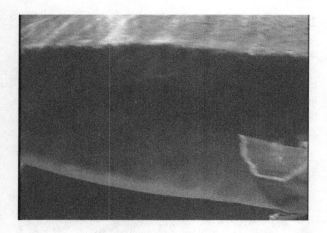

Beluga sturgeon in an aquarium.

dates back to the Triassic some 245 to 208 million years ago.[*][2] The family is grouped into four genera: *Acipenser*, *Huso*, *Scaphirhynchus* and *Pseudoscaphirhynchus*. Four species may now be extinct.[*][3] Two closely related species, *Polyodon spathula* (paddlefish) and *Psephurus gladius* (Chinese paddlefish, possibly extinct) are of the same order, Acipenseriformes, but are in the family Polyodontidae and are not considered to be "true" sturgeons. Both sturgeons and paddlefish have been referred to as "primitive fishes" because their morphological characteristics have remained relatively unchanged since the earliest fossil record.[*][4][*][5] Sturgeons are native to subtropical, temperate and sub-Arctic rivers, lakes and coastlines of Eurasia and North America.[*][6]

Sturgeons are long-lived, late-maturing fishes with distinctive characteristics, such as a heterocercal caudal fin similar to that of sharks, and an elongated spindle-like body that is smooth-skinned, scaleless and armored with 5 lateral rows of bony plates called scutes. Several species can grow quite large, typically ranging 7–12 feet (2–3½ m) in length. The largest sturgeon on record was a Beluga female captured in the Volga estuary in 1827, weighing 1,571 kg (3,463 lb) and 7.2 m (24 ft) long. Most sturgeons are anadromous bottom-feeders which migrate upstream to spawn but spend most of their lives feeding in river deltas and estuaries. Some species inhabit freshwater environments exclusively while others primarily inhabit marine environments near coastal areas, and are known to venture into open ocean.

Several species of sturgeon are harvested for their roe which is processed into caviar —a luxury food and the reason why caviar producing sturgeons are among the most valuable of all wildlife resources.[*][7] They are particularly vulnerable to overexploitation and other threats, including pollution and habitat fragmentation. Most species of sturgeon are considered to be at risk of extinction, making them more critically endangered than any other group of species.[*][8]

2.17.1   Evolution

Acipenseriform fishes appeared in the fossil record some 245 to 208 million years ago presumably near the end of the Triassic, making them among the most ancient of actinopterygian fishes. True sturgeons appear in the fossil record during the Upper Cretaceous. In that time, sturgeons have undergone remarkably little morphological change, indicating their evolution has been exceptionally slow and earning them informal status as living fossils.[*][9][*][10] This is explained in part by the long generation interval, tolerance for wide ranges of temperature and salinity, lack of predators due to size and bony plated armor, or scutes, and the abundance of prey items in the benthic environment. Although their evolution has been remarkably slow, they are a highly evolved living fossil, and do not closely resemble their ancestral chondrosteans. They do however still share several primitive characteristics, such as heterocercal tail, reduced squamation, more fin rays than supporting bony elements, and unique jaw suspension.[*][11]

Despite the existence of a fossil record, full classification and phylogeny of the sturgeon species has been difficult to determine, in part due to the high individual and ontogenic variation, including geographical clines in certain features, such as rostrum shape, number of scutes and body length. A further confounding factor is the peculiar ability of sturgeons to produce reproductively viable hybrids, even between species assigned to different genera. While ray-finned fishes have a long evolutionary history culminating in our most familiar fishes, past adaptive radiations have left only a few survivors, like sturgeons and garfish.[*][12]

The wide range of the acipenserids and their endangered status have made collection of systematic materials difficult. These factors have led researchers in the past to identify over 40 additional species that were rejected by later scientists.[*][13] It is still unclear whether the species in the *Acipenser* and *Huso* genera are monophyletic (descended from one ancestor) or paraphyletic (descended from many ancestors)—though it is clear that the morphologically motivated division between these two genera is not supported by the genetic evidence. There is an ongoing effort to resolve the taxonomic confusion using a continuing synthesis of systematic data and molecular techniques.[*][10][*][14]

2.17.2   Physical characteristics

Sturgeons retain several primitive characters among the bony fishes. Along with other members of the subclass Chondrostei, they are unique among bony fishes because the skeleton is almost entirely cartilaginous. Notably, however, the cartilagineous skeleton is not a primitive character, but a derived one: sturgeon ancestors had bony skele-

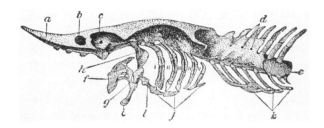

Sturgeon skull - a, Rostrum; b, nasal capsule; c eye-socket; d, foramina for spinal nerves; e, notochord; g, quadrate bone; h, hyomandibular bone; i, mandible; j. basibranchials; k, ribs; l, hyoid bone; I, II, III, IV, V, branchial arches.

tons.[11][15][16] They also lack vertebral centra, and are partially covered with bony plates called scutes rather than scales. They also have four barbels—sensory organs that precede their toothless, wide mouths. They navigate their riverine habitats traveling just off the bottom with their barbels dragging along gravel, or murky substrate. Sturgeon are recognizable for their elongated bodies, flattened rostra, distinctive scutes and barbels, and elongated upper tail lobes. The skeletal support for the paired fins of ray-finned fish is inside the body wall, although the ray-like structures in the webbing of the fins can be seen externally.

Sturgeon have been referred to as both the Leviathans and Methuselahs of freshwater fish. They are among the largest fish: some beluga (*Huso huso*) in the Caspian Sea reportedly attain over 5.5 m (18 ft) and 2000 kg[17] (4400 lb) while for kaluga (*H. dauricus*) in the Amur River, similar lengths and over 1000 kg (2200 lb) weights have been reported.[18] They are also among the longest-lived of the fishes, some living well over 100 years and attaining sexual maturity at 20 years or more.[19] The combination of slow growth and reproductive rates and the extremely high value placed on mature, egg-bearing females make sturgeon particularly vulnerable to overfishing.

Sturgeons are polyploid; some species have four, eight, or 16 sets of chromosomes.[20]

2.17.3 Life cycle

Sturgeons are long-lived, late maturing fishes. Their average lifespan is 50 to 60 years, and their first spawn does not occur until they are around 15 to 20 years old. Sturgeons are broadcast spawners, and do not spawn every year because they require specific conditions. Those requirements may or may not be met every year due to varying environmental conditions, such as the proper photoperiod in Spring, clear water with shallow rock or gravel substrate where the eggs can adhere, and proper water temperature and flow for oxygenation of the eggs. A single female may release 100,000 to 3 million eggs but not all will be fertilized. The

fertilized eggs become sticky and will adhere to the bottom substrate upon contact. It takes 8–15 days for the embryos to mature into larval fish. During that time, they are dependent on their yolk saks for nourishment.[21][22] River currents carry the larvae downstream into backwater areas, such as oxbows and sloughs where the free-swimming fry will spend their first year feeding on insect larvae and crustacea. During their first year of growth, they will reach 18 to 20 cm (7 to 8 inches) in length and migrate back into the swift-flowing currents in the main stem river.

2.17.4 Range and habitat

Sturgeon range from subtropical to subarctic waters in North America and Eurasia. In North America, they range along the Atlantic Coast from the Gulf of Mexico to Newfoundland, including the Great Lakes and the St. Lawrence, Missouri, and Mississippi Rivers, as well as along the West Coast in major rivers from California and Idaho to British Columbia. They occur along the European Atlantic coast, including the Mediterranean basin, especially in the Adriatic Sea and the rivers of North Italy;[23] in the rivers that flow into the Black, Azov, and Caspian Seas (Danube, Dnepr, Volga and Don); the north-flowing rivers of Russia that feed the Arctic Ocean (Ob, Yenisei, Lena, Kolyma); in the rivers of Central Asia (Amu Darya and Syr Darya) and Lake Baikal. In the Pacific Ocean, they are found in the Amur River along the Russian-Chinese border, on Sakhalin Island, and in the Yangtze and other rivers in northeast China.[19][24]

Throughout this extensive range, almost all species are highly threatened or vulnerable to extinction due to a combination of habitat destruction, overfishing, and pollution.[24]

No species are known to naturally occur south of the equator, though attempts at sturgeon aquaculture are being made in Uruguay, South Africa, and other places.[25]

Most species are at least partially anadromous, spawning in fresh water and feeding in nutrient-rich, brackish waters of estuaries or undergoing significant migrations along coastlines. However, some species have evolved purely freshwater existences, such as the lake sturgeon (*Acipenser fulvescens*) and the Baikal sturgeon (*A. baerii baicalensis*), or have been forced into them by anthropogenic or natural impoundment of their native rivers, as in the case of some subpopulations of white sturgeon (*A. transmontanus*) in the Columbia River[26] and Siberian sturgeon (*A. baerii*) in the Ob basin.[27]

The underside and mouth of a sturgeon

2.17.5 Behavior

Sturgeon are primarily benthic feeders, with a diet of shells, crustaceans and small fish. They feed by extending their syphon-like mouths to suck food from the benthos. Having no teeth, they are unable to seize prey, though larger individuals can swallow very large prey items, including whole salmon.[28] Sturgeons feed non-visually. They are believed to use a combination of sensors, including olfactory, tactile and chemosensory cues detected by the four barbels, and electroreception using their ampullae of Lorenzini.[29]

The sturgeons' electroreceptors are located on the head and are sensitive to weak electric fields generated by other animals or geoelectric sources.[30] The electroreceptors are thought to be used in various behaviors such as feeding, mating and migration.[29]

In 1731, an observer of leaping sturgeon wrote:

Many sturgeon leap completely out the water,[32] usually making a loud splash which can be heard half a mile away on the surface and probably further under water. It is not known why they do this, but suggested functions include group communication to maintain group cohesion, catching airborne prey, courtship display, or to help shed eggs during spawning. Other plausible explanations include escape from predators, shedding parasites, or to gulp or expel air.[33] Another explanation is that it "simply feels good" .[31] Leaping sturgeon are known to occasionally cause injuries to humans in boats;[34] in 2015, a 5-year-old girl died after a sturgeon leapt from the Suwannee River and struck her.[35]

2.17.6 Conservation status

Because of their long reproductive cycles, long migrations, and sensitivity to environmental conditions, many species are under severe threat from overfishing,[36] poaching, water pollution, and damming of rivers.[37] There is also a noticeable decline in sturgeon populations as the demand for caviar increases. According to the IUCN, over 85% of sturgeon species are classified as at risk of extinction, making them more critically endangered than any other group of species.[8][38]

A 2013 study on the critically endangered sturgeon populations in the Danube River Basin determined that ongoing illegal fishing activity and caviar trade is threatening the future of Danube sturgeons.[39] Jutta Jahrl, a conservation expert with the World Wildlife Federation stated that "Romania and Bulgaria are home to the only viable wild sturgeon populations left in the European Union, but unless this sophisticated illegal fishing is stopped, these fish are doomed" .[39]

2.17.7 Uses

Woman selling sturgeon at a market in Türkmenbaşy, Turkmenistan

Globally, sturgeon fisheries are of great value, primarily as a source for caviar, but also for flesh.

Before 1800, swim bladders of sturgeon (primarily Beluga sturgeon from Russia) were used as a source of isinglass, a form of collagen used historically for the clarification of wine and beer, as a predecessor for gelatin, and to preserve parchments.[40]

The Jewish law of kashrut, which only permits the consumption of fish with scales, forbids sturgeon, as they have ganoid scales instead of the permitted ctenoid and cycloid scales. While all Orthodox groups forbid the consumption of sturgeon, some conservative groups do allow it.[41][42] The theological debate over its kosher status can be traced back to such 19th-century reformers as Aron Chorin, though its consumption was already common in European Jewish communities.[43] It remains a high-end staple of many Jewish appetizing stores and some speciality food shops.

In England and Wales, the sturgeon, along with whales and porpoises, is a royal fish, and every sturgeon caught in those countries is the property of the Crown.

2.17.8 Classification

In currently accepted taxonomy, the family Acipenseridae is subdivided into two subfamilies, **Acipenserinae**, including the genera *Acipenser* and *Huso*, and **Scaphirhynchinae**, including the genera *Scaphirhynchus* and *Pseudosaphirhynchus*.[24]

*Pallid sturgeon (*Scaphirhynchus albus*) showing siphoning feeding behaviour*

2.17.9 Species

*A young lake sturgeon (*Acipenser fulvescens*)*

*European sturgeon (*Huso huso*) feeding on another fish*

- **Family Acipenseridae** Bonaparte, 1831
  - Subfamily Acipenserinae
    - Genus *Acipenser* Linnaeus, 1758
      - *Acipenser baerii* J. F. Brandt, 1869

- *Acipenser baerii baerii* J. F. Brandt, 1869 (Siberian sturgeon)
- *Acipenser baerii baicalensis* Nikolskii, 1896 (Baikal sturgeon)
- *Acipenser brevirostrum* Lesueur, 1818 (Shortnose sturgeon)
- *Acipenser dabryanus* A. H. A. Duméril, 1869 (Yangtze sturgeon)
- *Acipenser fulvescens* Rafinesque (Lake sturgeon)
- *Acipenser gueldenstaedtii* J. F. Brandt & Ratzeburg, 1833 (Russian sturgeon)
- *Acipenser medirostris* Ayres, 1854 (Green sturgeon)
- *Acipenser mikadoi* Hilgendorf, 1892 (Sakhalin sturgeon)
- *Acipenser naccarii* Bonaparte, 1836 (Adriatic sturgeon)
- *Acipenser nudiventris* Lovetsky, 1828 (Fringebarbel sturgeon)
- *Acipenser oxyrinchus* Mitchill, 1815
  - *Acipenser oxyrinchus desotoi* Vladykov, 1955 (Gulf sturgeon)
  - *Acipenser oxyrinchus oxyrinchus* Mitchill, 1815 (Atlantic sturgeon)
- *Acipenser persicus* Borodin, 1897 (Persian sturgeon)
- *Acipenser ruthenus* Linnaeus, 1758 (Sterlet)
- *Acipenser schrenckii* J. F. Brandt, 1869 (Amur sturgeon)
- *Acipenser sinensis* J. E. Gray, 1835 (Chinese sturgeon)

- *Acipenser stellatus* Pallas, 1771 (Starry sturgeon)
- *Acipenser sturio* Linnaeus, 1758 (European sea sturgeon)
- *Acipenser transmontanus* J. Richardson, 1836 (White sturgeon)
- Genus *Huso* J. F. Brandt & Ratzeburg, 1833
  - *Huso dauricus* (Georgi, 1775) (Kaluga sturgeon)
  - *Huso huso* (Linnaeus, 1758) (Beluga sturgeon)
- Subfamily Scaphirhynchinae
  - Genus *Scaphirhynchus* Heckel, 1835
    - *Scaphirhynchus albus* (Forbes & R. E. Richardson, 1905) (Pallid sturgeon)
    - *Scaphirhynchus platorynchus* (Rafinesque, 1820) (Shovelnose sturgeon)
    - *Scaphirhynchus suttkusi* J. D. Williams & Clemmer, 1991 (Alabama sturgeon)
  - Genus *Pseudoscaphirhynchus* Nikolskii, 1900
    - *Pseudoscaphirhynchus fedtschenkoi* (Kessler, 1872) (Syr Darya sturgeon)
    - *Pseudoscaphirhynchus hermanni* (Kessler, 1877) (Dwarf sturgeon)
    - *Pseudoscaphirhynchus kaufmanni* (Kessler, 1877) (Amu Darya sturgeon)

2.17.10   Notes

[1] Froese, Rainer, and Daniel Pauly, eds. (2009). "Acipenseridae" in FishBase. January 2009 version.

[2] Birstein, V.J., R. Hanner, and R. DeSalle. 1997. Phylogeny of the Acipenseriformes: cytogenic and molecular approaches. Environmental Biology of Fishes 48: 127-155.

[3] Chadwick, Niki; Drzewinski, Pia; Hurt, Leigh Ann (March 18, 2010). "Sturgeon More Critically Endangered Than Any Other Group of Species". *International News Release*. International Union for Conservation of Nature. Retrieved September 19, 2015.

[4] Chesapeake Bay Field Office. "Atlantic Sturgeon". U.S. Fish & Wildlife Service. Retrieved June 10, 2014.

[5] "Lake sturgeon". Minnesota Dept. of Natural Resources. Retrieved June 10, 2014.

[6] "Biology of Fishes (chapter: Biodiversity II: Primitive Bony Fishes and The Rise of Modern Teleosts)" (PDF). University of Washington. Retrieved May 30, 2014.

[7] "Sturgeons". Convention on International Trade in Endangered Species of Wild Fauna and Flora. Retrieved September 21, 2015.

[8] "Sturgeon more critically endangered than any other group of species". IUCN, the International Union for Conservation of Nature. 18 March 2010. Retrieved December 6, 2010.

[9] B. G. Gardiner (1984) Sturgeons as living fossils. Pp. 148–152 in N. Eldredge and S.M. Stanley, eds. Living fossils. Springer-Verlag, New York.

[10] J. Krieger and P.A. Fuerst. (2002) Evidence for a Slowed Rate of Molecular Evolution in the Order Acipenseriformes *Molecular Biology and Evolution* 19:891-897.

[11] Gene Helfman; Bruce B. Collette; Douglas E. Facey; Brian W. Bowen (3 April 2009). *The Diversity of Fishes: Biology, Evolution, and Ecology*. John Wiley & Sons. pp. 252–. ISBN 978-1-4443-1190-7.

[12] "Craniata, (2) Subclass Actinopterygii-the ray-finned fishes". San Francisco State University. Retrieved May 31, 2014.

[13] W. E. Bemis, E. K. Findeis, and L. Grande. (1997). An overview of Acipenseriformes. Environmental Biology of Fishes 48:25–71.

[14] F. Fontana, J. Tagliavini, L. Congiu (2001) Sturgeon genetics and cytogenetics: recent advancements and perspectives. *Genetica* 111: 359–373

[15] Caleb E. Finch (16 May 1994). *Longevity, Senescence, and the Genome*. University of Chicago Press. pp. 134–. ISBN 978-0-226-24889-9.

[16] J. D. McPhail (28 September 2007). *Freshwater Fishes of British Columbia (The)*. University of Alberta. pp. 23–. ISBN 978-0-88864-853-2.

[17] Frimodt, C., (1995). Multilingual illustrated guide to the world's commercial coldwater fish. Fishing News Books, Osney Mead, Oxford, England. 215 p.

[18] Krykhtin, M.L. and V.G. Svirskii (1997). Endemic sturgeons of the Amur River: kaluga, *Huso dauricus*, and Amur sturgeon, *Acipenser schrenckii*. Environ. Biol. Fish. 48(1/4):231-239.

[19] Berg, L.S. (1962). Freshwater fishes of the U.S.S.R. and adjacent countries. volume 1, 4th edition. Israel Program for Scientific Translations Ltd, Jerusalem. (Russian version published 1948).

[20] Anderson, Rachel (2004). "Shortnose Sturgeon". McGill University. Archived from the original on 2007-10-24. Retrieved 2007-08-23.

[21] "Fish & Habitats– White Sturgeon (Acipenser transmontanus) in British Columbia". British Columbia Ministry of Environment, Ecosystems Branch. Retrieved October 28, 2015.

[22] "Life Cycle of the White Sturgeon" (PDF). *HSBC Fraser River Sturgeon Education Program*. Fraser River Conservation Society. Retrieved October 28, 2015.

[23] LIFE 04NAT/IT/000126 "Conservation and Breeding of Italian Cobice Endemic Sturgeon"

[24] Froese, Rainer, and Daniel Pauly, eds. (2007). "Acipenseriformes" in FishBase. 12 2007 version.

[25] LA. Burtzev (1999) The History of Global Sturgeon Aquaculture. *Journal of Applied Ichthyology* 15 (4-5), 325–325. doi:10.1111/j.1439-0426.1999.tb00336.x

[26] S. Duke, P. Anders, G. Ennis, R. Hallock, J. Hammond, S. Ireland, J. Laufle, R. Lauzier, L. Lockhard, B. Marotz, V.L. Paragamian, R. Westerhof (1999) Recovery plan for Kootenai River white sturgeon (Acipenser transmontanus), *Journal of Applied Ichthyology* 15 (4-5), 157–163.

[27] G.I. Ruban, 1999. The Siberian Sturgeon *Acipenser baerii Brandt*: Structure and Ecology of the Species, Moscow, GEOS. 235 pp (in Russian).

[28] Sergei F. Zolotukhin and Nina F. Kaplanova. (2007) Injuries of Salmon in the Amur River and its Estuary as an Index of the Adult Fish Mortality in the Period of Sea Migrations. NPAFC Technical Report No. 4.

[29] Zhang, X., Song, J., Fan, C., Guo, H., Wang, X. and Bleckmann, H. (2012). "Use of electrosense in the feeding behavior of sturgeons". *Integrative Zoology* 7 (1): 74–82.

[30] Herzog, H. (2011). "Response properties of the electrosensory neurons in hindbrain of the white sturgeon, Acipenser transmontanus". *Neuroscience Bulletin* 27 (6): 422–429.

[31] Waldman, J. (2001). "Outdoors: The lofty mystery of why sturgeon leap". The New York Times.

[32] Video of leaping sturgeon can be see at approximately 6:50

[33] Sulak, K. J.; Edwards, R. E.; Hill, G. W.; Randall, M. T. (2002). "Why do sturgeons jump? Insights from acoustic investigations of the Gulf sturgeon in the Suwannee River, Florida, USA". *Journal of Applied Ichthyology* 18 (4-6): 617–620. doi:10.1046/j.1439-0426.2002.00401.x.

[34] Wilson, J.P., Burgess, G., Winfield, R.D. and Lottenberg, L. (2009). "Sturgeons versus surgeons: leaping fish injuries at a level I trauma center". *The American Surgeon* 75 (3): 220–222.

[35] "Leaping sturgeon kills girl in boat on Florida river". The Huffington Post. 2015.

[36] Clover, Charles. 2004. *The End of the Line: How overfishing is changing the world and what we eat*. Ebury Press, London. ISBN 0-09-189780-7

[37] Pallid Sturgeon - Montana Fish, Wildlife and Parks

[38] Species, status and population trend of Sturgeon on the IUCN Red List of Threatened Species (pdf)

[39] http://www.traffic.org/home/2013/6/18/europes-last-wild-sturgeons-threatened-by-ongoing-illegal-fi.html Sturgeon illegal fishing

[40] Davidson, Alan (1999). ""Isinglass"". *Oxford Companion to Food*. p. 407. ISBN 0-19-211579-0.

[41] http://cor.ca/en/15#12

[42] "Sturgeon: A controversial fish.". *bluethread.com*.

[43] Lupovich, Howard (2010). "7". *Jews and Judaism in World History*. p. 258. ISBN 0-203-86197-3.

[44] Froese, Rainer and Pauly, Daniel, eds. (2013). "Acipenser baerii" in FishBase. November 2013 version.

[45] *Acipenser baerii* (Brandt, 1869) FAO, Species Fact Sheet. Retrieved 11 November 2013.

[46] Ruban, G. & Bin Zhu (2010). "Acipenser baerii". *IUCN Red List of Threatened Species. Version 2013.1*. International Union for Conservation of Nature. Retrieved 11 November 2013.

[47] Froese, Rainer and Pauly, Daniel, eds. (2012). "Acipenser brevirostrum" in FishBase. November 2012 version.

[48] *Acipenser brevirostrum* (Lesueur, 1818) FAO, Species Fact Sheet. Retrieved 11 November 2013.

[49] Friedland, K.D. & Kynard, B. (2004). "Acipenser brevirostrum". *IUCN Red List of Threatened Species. Version 2011.2*. International Union for Conservation of Nature. Retrieved 11 November 2013.

[50] Froese, Rainer and Pauly, Daniel, eds. (2012). "Acipenser dabryanus" in FishBase. November 2012 version.

[51] *Acipenser dabryanus* (A. H. A. Duméril, 1869) FAO, Species Fact Sheet. Retrieved 11 November 2013.

[52] Qiwei, W. (2010). "Acipenser dabryanus". *IUCN Red List of Threatened Species. Version 2011.2*. International Union for Conservation of Nature. Retrieved 11 November 2013.

[53] Froese, Rainer and Pauly, Daniel, eds. (2012). "Acipenser fulvescens" in FishBase. November 2012 version.

[54] *Acipenser fulvescens* (Rafinesque) FAO, Species Fact Sheet. Retrieved 11 November 2013.

[55] St. Pierre, R. & Runstrom, A. (2004). "Acipenser fulvescens". *IUCN Red List of Threatened Species. Version 2011.2*. International Union for Conservation of Nature. Retrieved 11 November 2013.

[56] Froese, Rainer and Pauly, Daniel, eds. (2012). "Acipenser gueldenstaedtii" in FishBase. November 2012 version.

[57] *Acipenser gueldenstaedtii* (J. F. Brandt & Ratzeburg, 1833) FAO, Species Fact Sheet. Retrieved 11 November 2013.

[58] Gesner, J., Freyhof, J. & Kottelat, M. (2010). *"Acipenser gueldenstaedtii". IUCN Red List of Threatened Species. Version 2011.2.* International Union for Conservation of Nature. Retrieved 11 November 2013.

[59] Froese, Rainer and Pauly, Daniel, eds. (2012). *"Acipenser medirostris"* in FishBase. November 2012 version.

[60] *Acipenser medirostris* (Ayres, 1854) FAO, Species Fact Sheet. Retrieved 11 November 2013.

[61] St. Pierre, R. & Campbell, R.R. (2006). *"Acipenser medirostris". IUCN Red List of Threatened Species. Version 2011.2.* International Union for Conservation of Nature. Retrieved 11 November 2013.

[62] Froese, Rainer and Pauly, Daniel, eds. (2012). *"Acipenser mikadoi"* in FishBase. November 2012 version.

[63] *Acipenser mikadoi* (Hilgendorf, 1892) FAO, Species Fact Sheet. Retrieved 11 November 2013.

[64] Mugue, N. (2010). *"Acipenser mikadoi". IUCN Red List of Threatened Species. Version 2011.2.* International Union for Conservation of Nature. Retrieved 11 November 2013.

[65] Froese, Rainer and Pauly, Daniel, eds. (2012). *"Acipenser naccarii"* in FishBase. November 2012 version.

[66] *Acipenser naccarii* (Bonaparte, 1836) FAO, Species Fact Sheet. Retrieved 11 November 2013.

[67] Bronzi, P., Congiu, L., Rossi, R., Zerunian, S. & Arlati , G. (2011). *"Acipenser naccarii". IUCN Red List of Threatened Species. Version 2011.2.* International Union for Conservation of Nature. Retrieved 11 November 2013.

[68] Froese, Rainer and Pauly, Daniel, eds. (2012). *"Acipenser nudiventris"* in FishBase. November 2012 version.

[69] *Acipenser nudiventris* (Lovetsky, 1828) FAO, Species Fact Sheet. Retrieved 11 November 2013.

[70] Gesner, J., Freyhof, J. & Kottelat, M. (2010). *"Acipenser nudiventris". IUCN Red List of Threatened Species. Version 2011.2.* International Union for Conservation of Nature. Retrieved 11 November 2013.

[71] Froese, Rainer and Pauly, Daniel, eds. (2012). *"Acipenser oxyrinchus"* in FishBase. November 2012 version.

[72] *Acipenser oxyrinchus* (Vladykov, 1955) FAO, Species Fact Sheet. Retrieved 11 November 2013.

[73] St. Pierre, R. & Parauka, F.M. (2006). *"Acipenser oxyrinchus". IUCN Red List of Threatened Species. Version 2011.2.* International Union for Conservation of Nature. Retrieved 11 November 2013.

[74] Froese, Rainer and Pauly, Daniel, eds. (2012). *"Acipenser persicus"* in FishBase. November 2012 version.

[75] Gesner, J., Freyhof, J. & Kottelat, M. (2010). *"Acipenser persicus". IUCN Red List of Threatened Species. Version 2011.2.* International Union for Conservation of Nature. Retrieved 11 November 2013.

[76] Froese, Rainer and Pauly, Daniel, eds. (2012). *"Acipenser ruthenus"* in FishBase. November 2012 version.

[77] *Acipenser ruthenus* (Linnaeus, 1758) FAO, Species Fact Sheet. Retrieved 11 November 2013.

[78] Gesner, J., Freyhof, J. & Kottelat, M. (2010). *"Acipenser ruthenus". IUCN Red List of Threatened Species. Version 2011.2.* International Union for Conservation of Nature. Retrieved 11 November 2013.

[79] Froese, Rainer and Pauly, Daniel, eds. (2012). *"Acipenser schrenckii"* in FishBase. November 2012 version.

[80] *Acipenser schrenckii* (J. F. Brandt, 1869) FAO, Species Fact Sheet. Retrieved 11 November 2013.

[81] Ruban, G. & Qiwei, W. (2010). *"Acipenser schrenckii". IUCN Red List of Threatened Species. Version 2011.2.* International Union for Conservation of Nature. Retrieved 11 November 2013.

[82] Froese, Rainer and Pauly, Daniel, eds. (2012). *"Acipenser sinensis"* in FishBase. November 2012 version.

[83] *Acipenser sinensis* (J. E. Gray, 1835) FAO, Species Fact Sheet. Retrieved 11 November 2013.

[84] Qiwei, W. (2011). *"Acipenser sinensis". IUCN Red List of Threatened Species. Version 2011.2.* International Union for Conservation of Nature. Retrieved 11 November 2013.

[85] Froese, Rainer and Pauly, Daniel, eds. (2012). *"Acipenser stellatus"* in FishBase. November 2012 version.

[86] *Acipenser stellatus* (Pallas, 1771) FAO, Species Fact Sheet. Retrieved 11 November 2013.

[87] Qiwei, W. (2010). *"Acipenser stellatus". IUCN Red List of Threatened Species. Version 2011.2.* International Union for Conservation of Nature. Retrieved 11 November 2013.

[88] Froese, Rainer and Pauly, Daniel, eds. (2012). *"Acipenser sturio"* in FishBase. November 2012 version.

[89] *Acipenser sturio* (Linnaeus, 1758) FAO, Species Fact Sheet. Retrieved 11 November 2013.

[90] Gesner, J., Williot, P., Rochard, E., Freyhof, J. & Kottelat, M. (2010). *"Acipenser sturio". IUCN Red List of Threatened Species. Version 2011.2.* International Union for Conservation of Nature. Retrieved 11 November 2013.

[91] Froese, Rainer and Pauly, Daniel, eds. (2012). *"Acipenser transmontanus"* in FishBase. November 2012 version.

[92] *Acipenser transmontanus* (J. Richardson, 1836) FAO, Species Fact Sheet. Retrieved 11 November 2013.

[93] Duke, S., Down, T., Ptolemy, J., Hammond, J. & Spence, C. (2004). *"Acipenser transmontanus"*. *IUCN Red List of Threatened Species*. *Version 2011.2*. International Union for Conservation of Nature. Retrieved 11 November 2013.

[94] Froese, Rainer and Pauly, Daniel, eds. (2012). *"Huso dauricus"* in FishBase. November 2012 version.

[95] *Huso dauricus* (Georgi, 1775) FAO, Species Fact Sheet. Retrieved 11 November 2013.

[96] Ruban, G. & Qiwei, W. (2010). *"Huso dauricus"*. *IUCN Red List of Threatened Species*. *Version 2011.2*. International Union for Conservation of Nature. Retrieved 11 November 2013.

[97] Froese, Rainer and Pauly, Daniel, eds. (2012). *"Huso huso"* in FishBase. November 2012 version.

[98] *Huso huso* (Rafinesque, 1820) FAO, Species Fact Sheet. Retrieved 11 November 2013.

[99] Gesner, J., Chebanov, M. & Freyhof, J. (2010). *"Huso huso"*. *IUCN Red List of Threatened Species*. *Version 2011.2*. International Union for Conservation of Nature. Retrieved 11 November 2013.

[100] Froese, Rainer and Pauly, Daniel, eds. (2012). *"Scaphirhynchus albus"* in FishBase. November 2012 version.

[101] *Scaphirhynchus albus* (Forbes & R. E. Richardson, 1905) FAO, Species Fact Sheet. Retrieved 11 November 2013.

[102] Krentz, S. (2004). *"Scaphirhynchus albus"*. *IUCN Red List of Threatened Species*. *Version 2011.2*. International Union for Conservation of Nature. Retrieved 11 November 2013.

[103] Froese, Rainer and Pauly, Daniel, eds. (2012). *"Scaphirhynchus platorynchus"* in FishBase. November 2012 version.

[104] *Scaphirhynchus platorynchus* (Rafinesque, 1820) FAO, Species Fact Sheet. Retrieved 11 November 2013.

[105] Surprenant, C. (2004). *"Scaphirhynchus platorynchus"*. *IUCN Red List of Threatened Species*. *Version 2011.2*. International Union for Conservation of Nature. Retrieved 11 November 2013.

[106] Froese, Rainer and Pauly, Daniel, eds. (2012). *"Scaphirhynchus suttkusi"* in FishBase. November 2012 version.

[107] Collette B and 4 others (2011). *"Scaphirhynchus suttkusi"*. *IUCN Red List of Threatened Species*. *Version 2011.2*. International Union for Conservation of Nature. Retrieved 11 November 2013.

[108] Froese, Rainer and Pauly, Daniel, eds. (2012). *"Pseudoscaphirhynchus fedtschenkoi"* in FishBase. November 2012 version.

[109] Mugue, N. 2010. (2013). *"Pseudoscaphirhynchus fedtschenkoi"*. *IUCN Red List of Threatened Species*. *Version 2011.2*. International Union for Conservation of Nature. Retrieved 11 November 2013.

[110] Froese, Rainer and Pauly, Daniel, eds. (2012). *"Pseudoscaphirhynchus hermanni"* in FishBase. November 2012 version.

[111] *Pseudoscaphirhynchus hermanni* (Kessler, 1877) FAO, Species Fact Sheet. Retrieved 11 November 2013.

[112] Mugue, N. (2010). *"Pseudoscaphirhynchus hermanni"*. *IUCN Red List of Threatened Species*. *Version 2011.2*. International Union for Conservation of Nature. Retrieved 11 November 2013.

[113] Froese, Rainer and Pauly, Daniel, eds. (2012). *"Pseudoscaphirhynchus kaufmanni"* in FishBase. November 2012 version.

[114] *Pseudoscaphirhynchus kaufmanni* (Kessler, 1877) FAO, Species Fact Sheet. Retrieved 11 November 2013.

[115] Mugue, N. (2010). *"Pseudoscaphirhynchus kaufmanni"*. *IUCN Red List of Threatened Species*. *Version 2011.2*. International Union for Conservation of Nature. Retrieved 11 November 2013.

2.17.11 References

- This article incorporates text from a publication now in the public domain: Chisholm, Hugh, ed. (1911). "Sturgeon". *Encyclopædia Britannica* (11th ed.). Cambridge University Press.

2.17.12 External links

- FishBase info on Acipenser

- Official website of the World Sturgeon Conservation Society

- Sturgeon feeding on the remains of a fish at Eccleston Delph, Lancashire England – Set of images on Flickr

- Information on North American sturgeons with photographs

- Gallery of movie clips showing different species of sturgeon

2.18 Vitamin B12

Vitamin B$_{12}$, **vitamin B12** or **vitamin B-12**, also called **cobalamin**, is a water-soluble vitamin with a key role in the

Methylcobalamin (shown) is a form of vitamin B_{12}. Physically it resembles the other forms of vitamin B_{12}, occurring as dark red crystals that freely form cherry-colored transparent solutions in water.

normal functioning of the brain and nervous system, and for the formation of blood. It is one of the eight B vitamins. It is normally involved in the metabolism of every cell of the human body, especially affecting DNA synthesis and regulation, but also fatty acid metabolism and amino acid metabolism.*[1] Neither fungi, plants, nor animals (including humans) are capable of producing vitamin B_{12}. Only bacteria and archaea have the enzymes required for its synthesis, although many foods are a natural source of B_{12} because of bacterial symbiosis. The vitamin is the largest and most structurally complicated vitamin and can be produced industrially only through bacterial fermentation-synthesis.

Vitamin B_{12} consists of a class of chemically related compounds (vitamers), all of which have vitamin activity. It contains the biochemically rare element cobalt sitting in the center of a planar tetra-pyrrole ring called a corrin ring. Biosynthesis of the basic structure of the vitamin is accomplished only by bacteria and archaea (which usually produce hydroxocobalamin), but conversion between different forms of the vitamin can be accomplished in the human body. A common semi-synthetic form of the vitamin is cyanocobalamin, which does not occur in nature but is produced from bacterial hydroxocobalamin. Be-

cause of its stability and lower production cost, this form is then used in many pharmaceuticals and supplements as well as a food additive. In the body it is converted to the human physiological forms methylcobalamin and 5'-deoxyadenosylcobalamin, leaving behind the cyanide ion, albeit in a minimal concentration. More recently, hydroxocobalamin, methylcobalamin, and adenosylcobalamin can be found in more expensive pharmacological products and food supplements. Their extra utility is currently debated.

Vitamin B_{12} was discovered from its relationship to disease pernicious anemia, which is an autoimmune disease in which parietal cells of the stomach responsible for secreting intrinsic factor are destroyed (these cells are also responsible for secreting acid in the stomach). Because intrinsic factor is crucial for the normal absorption of B_{12}, its lack in pernicious anemia causes a vitamin B_{12} deficiency. Many other subtler kinds of vitamin B_{12} deficiency and their biochemical effects have since been elucidated.*[2]

2.18.1 Terminology

The names vitamin B_{12}, vitamin B12, or vitamin B-12, and the alternative name cobalamin, generally refer to all forms of the vitamin. Some medical practitioners have suggested that its use be split into two categories.

- In a broad sense, B_{12} refers to a group of cobalt-containing vitamer compounds known as cobalamins: these include cyanocobalamin (an artifact formed from using activated charcoal, which always contains trace cyanide, to purify hydroxycobalamin), hydroxocobalamin (another medicinal form, produced by bacteria), and finally, the two naturally occurring cofactor forms of B_{12} in the human body: 5'-deoxyadenosylcobalamin (adenosylcobalamin — AdoB12), the cofactor of Methylmalonyl Coenzyme A mutase (MUT), and methylcobalamin (MeB$_{12}$), the cofactor of enzyme Methionine synthase, which is responsible for conversion of homocysteine to methionine and of 5-methyltetrahydrofolate to tetrahydrofolate.

- The term B_{12} may be properly used to refer to cyanocobalamin, the principal B_{12} form used for foods and in nutritional supplements. This ordinarily creates no problem, except perhaps in rare cases of eye nerve damage, where the body is only marginally able to use this form due to high cyanide levels in the blood due to cigarette smoking; it thus requires cessation of smoking or B_{12} given in another form, for the optic symptoms to abate. However, tobacco amblyopia is a rare condition, and it is yet unclear whether it represents a peculiar B_{12} deficiency that is resistant to treatment with cyanocobalamin.

Finally, so-called pseudovitamin-B_{12} refers to B_{12}-like analogues that are biologically inactive in humans and yet found to be present alongside B_{12} in humans,[3][4] many food sources (including animals[5]), and possibly supplements and fortified foods.[6][7] In most cyanobacteria, including *Spirulina*, and some algae, such as dried Asakusa-nori (*Porphyra tenera*), pseudovitamin-B_{12} is found to predominate.[8][9]

2.18.2 Medical uses

Vitamin B_{12} is used to treat vitamin B_{12} deficiency, cyanide poisoning, and hereditary deficiency of transcobalamin II.[10] It is given as part of the Schilling test for detecting pernicious anemia.[10]

For cyanide poisoning, a large amount of hydroxocobalamin may be given intravenously and sometimes in combination with sodium thiosulfate.[11] The mechanism of action is straightforward: the hydroxycobalamin hydroxide ligand is displaced by the toxic cyanide ion, and the resulting harmless B_{12} complex is excreted in urine. In the United States, the Food and Drug Administration approved (in 2006) the use of hydroxocobalamin for acute treatment of cyanide poisoning.[12]

High vitamin B_{12} level in elderly individuals may protect against brain atrophy or shrinkage associated with Alzheimer's disease and impaired cognitive function.[13]

Recommended intake

The dietary reference intake for an adult ranges from 2 to 3 µg per day (US),[14] and 1.5 µg per day (UK).[15] But according to a new study,[16] the DRI should be 4 to 7 µg per day. The Center for Food Safety and Applied Nutrition recommends 6 µg per day, based on a caloric intake of 2,000 calories, for adults and children four or more years of age.[17]

Vitamin B_{12} is believed to be safe when used orally in amounts that do not exceed the recommended dietary allowance (RDA). There have been studies that showed no adverse consequences of doses above the RDA.[18]

The RDA for vitamin B_{12} in pregnant women is 2.6 µg per day and 2.8 µg during lactation periods.[19] There is insufficient reliable information available about the safety of consuming greater amounts of vitamin B_{12} during pregnancy.

The Institute of Medicine states that because 10 to 30% of older people may be unable to absorb naturally occurring vitamin B_{12} in foods, it is advisable for those 51 years old and older to consume B_{12}-fortified foods or B_{12} supplements to meet the recommended intake.[20]

Controversial sources in algae

The UK Vegan Society, the Vegetarian Resource Group, and the Physicians Committee for Responsible Medicine, among others, recommend that vegans either consistently eat B_{12}-fortified foods or take a daily or weekly B_{12} supplement to meet the recommended intake.[21][22][23]

It is important for vegans, whose food provides few sources of B_{12}, and anyone else wishing to obtain B_{12} from food sources other than animals, to consume foods that contain little or no pseudovitamin-B_{12} and are high in biologically active B_{12}. However, there have been no significant human trials of sufficient size to demonstrate enzymatic activity of B_{12} from nonbacterial sources, such as *Chlorella* and edible sea algae (seaweeds, such as lavers), although chemically some of these sources have been reported to contain B_{12} that seems chemically similar to active vitamin.[24][25] However, among these sources, only fresh sea algae such as Susabi-nori (*Porphyra yezoensis*)[26][27] have been reported to demonstrate vitamin B_{12} activity in B_{12} deficient rats. This has yet to be demonstrated for *Chlorella*, and no study in rats of any algal B_{12} source has yet to be confirmed by a second independent study. The possibility of algae-derived active forms of B_{12} presently remains an active topic of research, with no results that have yet reached consensus in the nutritional community.

Deficiency

Main article: Vitamin B12 deficiency

Vitamin B_{12} deficiency can potentially cause severe and irreversible damage, especially to the brain and nervous system. At levels only slightly lower than normal, a range of symptoms such as fatigue, depression, and poor memory may be experienced.[2] Vitamin B_{12} deficiency can also cause symptoms of mania and psychosis.[28][29]

Vitamin B_{12} deficiency is most commonly caused by low intakes, but can also result from malabsorption, certain intestinal disorders, low presence of binding proteins, and using of certain medications. Vitamin B_{12} is rare from plant sources, so vegetarians are most likely to suffer from vitamin B_{12} deficiency. Infants are at a higher risk of vitamin B_{12} deficiency if they were born to vegetarian mothers. The elderly who have diets with limited meat or animal products are vulnerable populations as well.[30] Vitamin B_{12} deficiency can manifest itself as anemia and in some cases cause permanent neurological damage. Recent studies showed depression is associated with vitamin B_{12} deficiency; sufficient vitamin B_{12} level was independently associated with a decreased risk of depression and better cognitive performance adjusted for confounders. Vitamin B_{12} is a cosubstrate of various cell reactions involved in methylation synthesis of nucleic acid and neurotransmitters. Synthesis of the trimonoamine neurotransmitters can enhance the effects of a traditional antidepressant.[31] The intracellular concentrations of vitamin B_{12} can be inferred through the total plasma concentration of homocysteine, which can be converted to methionine through an enzymatic reaction that uses 5-methyletetrahydrofolate as the methyl donor group. Consequently, the plasma concentration of homocysteine falls as the intracellular concentration of vitamin B_{12} rises. The active metabolite of vitamin B_{12} is required for the methylation of homocysteine in the production of methionine, which is involved in a number of biochemical processes including the monoamine neurotransmitters. Thus, a deficiency in vitamin B_{12} may impact the production and function of those neurotransmitters.[32]

Imerslund-Gräsbeck syndrome is a rare disease where there is selective malabsorption of cobalamine with proteinuria caused due to defect in ileal receptor.

2.18.3 Sources

Foods

Ultimately, animals must obtain vitamin B_{12} directly or indirectly from bacteria, and these bacteria may inhabit a section of the gut that is distal to the section where B_{12} is absorbed. Thus, herbivorous animals must either obtain B_{12} from bacteria in their rumens or (if fermenting plant material in the hindgut) by reingestion of cecotrope feces.

Vitamin B_{12} is found in most animal derived foods, including fish and shellfish, meat (especially liver), poultry, eggs, milk, and milk products.[2] However, the binding capacity of egg yolks and egg whites is markedly diminished after heat treatment.[33] An NIH fact sheet lists a variety of animal food sources of B_{12}.[2]

Besides certain fermented foods,[34][35] there are currently only a few non-animal food sources of biologically active B_{12} suggested, and none of these have been subjected to human trials.

A Japanese fermented black tea known as Batabata-cha has been found to contain biologically active B_{12}.[36] Unlike kombucha, which is made by fermenting already prepared tea, Batabata-cha is fermented while still in the tea leaf state.

Chlorella,[24][25][37] a fresh-water single cell green algae, has been suggested as a vitamin B_{12} source but not proven by any live animal assay. Algae are thought to acquire B_{12} through a symbiotic relationship with heterotrophic bacteria, in which the bacteria supply B_{12} in exchange for fixed carbon.[38][39] *Spirulina* and dried Asakusa-nori (*Porphyra tenera*) have been found to contain mostly pseudovitamin-B_{12} (see Terminology) instead of biologically active B_{12}.[8][9] While Asakusa-nori (*Porphyra tenera*) contains mostly pseudovitamin-B_{12} in the dry state, it has been reported to contain mostly biologically active B_{12} in the fresh state,[9] but even its fresh state vitamin activity has not been verified by animal enzyme assay.

One group of researchers has reported that the purple laver seaweed known as Susabi-nori (*Pyropia yezoensis*)[26][27] in its fresh state contains B_{12} activity in the rat model, which implies that source would be active in humans. These results have not been confirmed.

A single commensal bacteria present in the gut of many mammals has demonstrated an ability to perform all steps necessary to synthesize B_{12} from common metabolically available products.[40]

Foods fortified with B_{12} are also sources of the vitamin, although they cannot be regarded as true food sources of B_{12} since the vitamin is added in supplement form, from commercial bacterial production sources, such as cyanocobalamin. Foods for which B_{12}-fortified versions are widely available include breakfast cereals, soy products, energy bars, and nutritional yeast. The UK Vegan Society, the Vegetarian Resource Group, and the Physicians Committee for Responsible Medicine, among others, recommend that every vegan who is not consuming B_{12} foods fortify with supplements.[41][22][23] Not all of these may contain labeled amounts of vitamin activity. Supplemental B_{12} added to beverages in one study was found to degrade to contain varying levels of pseudovitamin-B_{12}. One report has found B_{12} analogues present in varying amounts in some multivitamins.[6][7]

Unconventional natural sources of B_{12} also exist, but their utility as food sources of B_{12} is doubtful. For example, plants pulled from the ground and not washed may contain remnants of B_{12} from the bacteria present in the surrounding soil.[42] B_{12} is also found in lakes if the water has not been sanitized.[43] Certain insects such as termites contain B_{12} produced by their gut bacteria, in a way analogous to ruminant animals.[44] The human intestinal tract itself may contain B_{12}-producing bacteria in the small intestine,[45] but it is unclear whether sufficient amounts of the vitamin could be produced to meet nutritional needs.

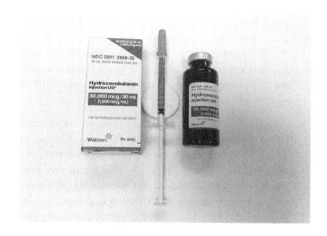

Hydroxocobalamin injection USP (1000 μg/mL) is a clear red liquid solution of hydroxocobalamin which is available in a 30 mL brown glass multidose vial packaged in a paper box. Shown is 500 μg B-12 (as 1/2 cc) drawn up in a 1/2 cc U-100 27 gauge x 1/2" insulin syringe, as prepared for subcutaneous injection.

Supplements

Vitamin B_{12} is provided as a supplement in many processed foods, and is also available in vitamin pill form, including multi-vitamins. Vitamin B_{12} can be supplemented in healthy subjects also by liquid, transdermal patch, nasal spray, or injection and is available singly or in combination with other supplements. It is a common ingredient in energy drinks and energy shots, usually at many times the minimum recommended daily allowance of B_{12}. Vitamin B_{12} supplements are effective for preventing deficiencies, especially in vegetarians, and are often marketed as weight loss supplements. However, no scientific studies have shown that B_{12} is effective for weight loss.

Cyanocobalamin is converted to its active forms, first hydroxocobalamin and then methylcobalamin and adenosylcobalamin in the liver.

The sublingual route, in which B_{12} is presumably or supposedly taken in more directly under the tongue, has not proven to be necessary or helpful, even though a number of lozenges, pills, and even a lollipop designed for sublingual absorption are being marketed. A 2003 study found no significant difference in absorption for serum levels from oral versus sublingual delivery of 0.5 mg of cobalamin.[46] Sublingual methods of replacement are effective only because of the typically high doses (0.5 mg), which are swallowed, not because of placement of the tablet. As noted below, such very high doses of oral B_{12} may be effective as treatments, even if gastro-intestinal tract absorption is impaired by gastric atrophy (pernicious anemia).

Injection and patches are sometimes used if digestive absorption is impaired, but there is evidence that this course

of action may not be necessary with modern high potency oral supplements (such as 0.5 to 1 mg or more). Even pernicious anemia can be treated entirely by the oral route.[47][48][49] These supplements carry such large doses of the vitamin that 1% to 5% of high oral doses of free crystalline B_{12} is absorbed along the entire intestine by passive diffusion.

However, if the patient has inborn errors in the methyl-transfer pathway (cobalamin C disease, combined methylmalonic aciduria and homocystinuria), treatment with intravenous, intramuscular hydroxocobalamin or transdermal B_{12} is needed.[50][51][52][53][54]

Non-cyano forms as supplements   Recently sublingual methylcobalamin has become available in 5 mg tablets. The metabolic fate and biological distribution of methylcobalamin are expected to be similar to that of other sources of vitamin B12 in the diet.[55] No cyanide is released with methylcobalamin, although the amount of cyanide (2% of the weight, or 20 *micrograms* cyanide in a 1 mg cyanocobalamin tab) is far less than ingested in many natural foods. Although the safety of cyanocobalamin has long been proven, the safety of the other types is also well established.[56]

2.18.4   Adverse effects

- Hematologic: Peripheral vascular thrombosis has been reported. Treatment of vitamin B_{12} deficiency can unmask polycythemia vera, which is characterized by an increase in blood volume and the number of red blood cells. The correction of megaloblastic anemia with vitamin B_{12} can result in fatal hypokalemia and gout in susceptible individuals, and it can obscure folate deficiency in megaloblastic anemia.

- Leber's disease: Vitamin B_{12} in the form of cyanocobalamin is contraindicated in early Leber's disease, which is hereditary optic nerve atrophy. Cyanocobalamin can cause severe and swift optic atrophy, but other forms of vitamin B_{12} are available. However, the sources of this statement are not clear, while an opposing view[57] concludes: "The clinical picture of optic neuropathy associated with vitamin B_{12} deficiency shows similarity to that of Leber's disease optic neuropathy. Both involve the nerve fibers of the papillomacular bundle. The present case reports suggest that optic neuropathy in patients carrying a primary LHON mtDNA mutation may be precipitated by vitamin B_{12} deficiency. Therefore, known carriers should take care to have an adequate dietary intake of vitamin B_{12} and malabsorption syndromes like those occurring in familial pernicious anaemia or after gastric surgery should be excluded."

Allergies

Vitamin B_{12} supplements in theory should be avoided in people sensitive or allergic to cobalamin, cobalt, or any other product ingredients. However, direct allergy to a vitamin or nutrient is extremely rare, and if reported, other causes should be sought.

Interactions

- Alcohol (ethanol): Excessive alcohol intake lasting longer than two weeks can decrease vitamin B_{12} absorption from the gastrointestinal tract.

- Aminosalicylic acid (para-aminosalicylic acid, PAS, Paser): Aminosalicylic acid can reduce oral vitamin B_{12} absorption, possibly by as much as 55%, as part of a general malabsorption syndrome. Megaloblastic changes, and occasional cases of symptomatic anemia have occurred, usually after doses of 8 to 12 g/day for several months. Vitamin B_{12} levels should be monitored in people taking aminosalicylic acid for more than one month.

- Antibiotics: An increased bacterial load can bind significant amounts of vitamin B_{12} in the gut, preventing its absorption. In people with bacterial overgrowth of the small bowel, antibiotics such as metronidazole (Flagyl) can actually improve vitamin B_{12} status. The effects of most antibiotics on gastrointestinal bacteria are unlikely to have clinically significant effects on vitamin B_{12} levels.

- Hormonal contraception: The data regarding the effects of oral contraceptives on vitamin B_{12} serum levels are conflicting. Some studies have found reduced serum levels in oral contraceptive users, but others have found no effect despite use of oral contraceptives for up to 6 months. When oral contraceptive use is stopped, normalization of vitamin B_{12} levels usually occurs. Lower vitamin B_{12} serum levels seen with oral contraceptives probably are not clinically significant.

- Chloramphenicol (Chloromycetin): Limited case reports suggest that chloramphenicol can delay or interrupt the reticulocyte response to supplemental vitamin B_{12} in some patients. Blood counts should be monitored closely if this combination cannot be avoided.

- Cobalt irradiation: Cobalt irradiation of the small bowel can decrease gastrointestinal (GI) absorption of vitamin B_{12}.

- Colchicine: Colchicine in doses of 1.9 to 3.9 mg/day can disrupt normal intestinal mucosal function, leading to malabsorption of several nutrients, including vitamin B_{12}. Lower doses do not seem to have a significant effect on vitamin B_{12} absorption after 3 years of colchicine therapy. The significance of this interaction is unclear. Vitamin B_{12} levels should be monitored in people taking large doses of colchicine for prolonged periods.

- Colestipol (Colestid), cholestyramine (Questran): These resins used for sequestering bile acids to decrease cholesterol, can decrease gastrointestinal (GI) absorption of vitamin B_{12}. It is unlikely this interaction will deplete body stores of vitamin B_{12} unless there are other factors contributing to deficiency. In a group of children treated with cholestyramine for up to 2.5 years, there was not any change in serum vitamin B_{12} levels. Routine supplements are not necessary.

- Folic acid: Folic acid, particularly in large doses, can mask vitamin B_{12} deficiency by completely correcting hematological abnormalities. In vitamin B_{12} deficiency, folic acid can produce complete resolution of the characteristic megaloblastic anemia, while allowing potentially irreversible neurological damage (from continued inactivity of methylmalonyl mutase) to progress. Thus, vitamin B_{12} status should be determined before folic acid is given as monotherapy.[58]

- H_2-receptor antagonists: include cimetidine (Tagamet), famotidine (Pepcid), nizatidine (Axid), and ranitidine (Zantac). Reduced secretion of gastric acid and pepsin produced by H_2 blockers can reduce absorption of protein-bound (dietary) vitamin B_{12}, but not of supplemental vitamin B_{12}. Gastric acid is needed to release vitamin B_{12} from protein for absorption. Clinically significant vitamin B_{12} deficiency and megaloblastic anemia are unlikely, unless H_2 blocker therapy is prolonged (2 years or more), or the person's diet is poor. It is also more likely if the person is rendered achlorhydric(with complete absence of gastric acid secretion), which occurs more frequently with proton pump inhibitors than H_2 blockers. Vitamin B_{12} levels should be monitored in people taking high doses of H_2 blockers for prolonged periods.

- Metformin (Glucophage): Metformin may reduce serum folic acid and vitamin B_{12} levels. Long-term use of metformin substantially increases the risk of B_{12} deficiency and (in those patients who become deficient) hyperhomocysteinemia, which is "an independent risk factor for cardiovascular disease, especially among individuals with type 2 diabetes."[59] There are also rare reports of megaloblastic anemia in people who have taken metformin for five years or more. Reduced serum levels of vitamin B_{12} occur in up to 30% of people taking metformin chronically.[60][61] However, clinically significant deficiency is not likely to develop if dietary intake of vitamin B_{12} is adequate. Deficiency can be corrected with vitamin B_{12} supplements even if metformin is continued. The metformin-induced malabsorption of vitamin B_{12} is reversible by oral calcium supplementation.*[62] The general clinical significance of metformin upon B_{12} levels is as yet unknown.*[63]

- Neomycin: Absorption of vitamin B_{12} can be reduced by neomycin, but prolonged use of large doses is needed to induce pernicious anemia. Supplements are not usually needed with normal doses.

- Nicotine: Nicotine can reduce serum vitamin B_{12} levels. The need for vitamin B_{12} supplementation in smokers has not been adequately studied.

- Nitrous oxide: Nitrous oxide inactivates the cobalamin form of vitamin B_{12} by oxidation. Symptoms of vitamin B_{12} deficiency, including sensory neuropathy, myelopathy, and encephalopathy, can occur within days or weeks of exposure to nitrous oxide anesthesia in people with subclinical vitamin B_{12} deficiency. Symptoms are treated with high doses of vitamin B_{12}, but recovery can be slow and incomplete. People with normal vitamin B_{12} levels have sufficient vitamin B_{12} stores to make the effects of nitrous oxide insignificant, unless exposure is repeated and prolonged (such as recreational use). Vitamin B_{12} levels should be checked in people with risk factors for vitamin B_{12} deficiency prior to using nitrous oxide anesthesia. Chronic nitrous oxide B_{12} poisoning (usually from use of nitrous oxide as a recreational drug), however, may result in B_{12} functional deficiency even with normal measured blood levels of B_{12}.*[64]

- Phenytoin (Dilantin), phenobarbital, primidone (Mysoline): These anticonvulsants have been associated with reduced vitamin B_{12} absorption, and reduced serum and cerebrospinal fluidlevels in some patients. This may contribute to the megaloblastic anemia, primarily caused by folate deficiency, associated with these drugs. It is also suggested that reduced vitamin B_{12} levels may contribute to the neuropsychiatric side effects of these drugs. Patients should be encouraged to maintain adequate dietary vitamin B_{12} intake. Folate and vitamin B_{12} status should be checked if symptoms of anemia develop.

- Potassium: Potassium supplements can reduce absorption of vitamin B_{12} in some people. This effect has been reported with potassium chloride and, to a lesser extent, with potassium citrate. Potassium might contribute to vitamin B_{12} deficiency in some people with other risk factors, but routine supplements are not necessary.*[65]

- Proton pump inhibitors (PPIs): The PPIs include omeprazole (Prilosec, Losec), lansoprazole (Prevacid), rabeprazole (Aciphex), pantoprazole (Protonix, Pantoloc), and esomeprazole (Nexium). The reduced secretion of gastric acid and pepsin produced by PPIs can reduce absorption of protein-bound (dietary) vitamin B_{12}, but not supplemental vitamin B_{12}. Gastric acid is needed to release vitamin B_{12} from protein for absorption. Reduced vitamin B_{12} levels may be more common with PPIs than with H2-blockers, because they are more likely to produce achlorhydria (complete absence of gastric acid secretion). However, clinically significant vitamin B_{12} deficiency is unlikely, unless PPI therapy is prolonged (2 years or more) or dietary vitamin intake is low. Vitamin B_{12} levels should be monitored in people taking high doses of PPIs for prolonged periods.

- Zidovudine (AZT, Combivir, Retrovir): Reduced serum vitamin B_{12} levels may occur when zidovudine therapy is started. This adds to other factors that cause low vitamin B_{12} levels in people with HIV, and might contribute to the hematological toxicity associated with zidovudine. However, the data suggest vitamin B_{12} supplements are not helpful for people taking zidovudine.

2.18.5 Structure

B_{12} is the most chemically complex of all the vitamins. The structure of B_{12} is based on a corrin ring, which is similar to the porphyrin ring found in heme, chlorophyll, and cytochrome. The central metal ion is cobalt. Four of the six coordination sites are provided by the corrin ring, and a fifth by a dimethylbenzimidazole group. The sixth coordination site, the center of reactivity, is variable, being a cyano group (-CN), a hydroxyl group (-OH), a methyl group (-CH_3) or a 5'-deoxyadenosyl group (here the C5' atom of the deoxyribose forms the covalent bond with Co), respectively, to yield the four B_{12} forms mentioned below. Historically, the covalent C-Co bond is one of first examples of carbon-metal bonds to be discovered in biology. The hydrogenases and, by necessity, enzymes associated with cobalt utilization, involve metal-carbon bonds.*[66]

Vitamin B_{12} is a generic descriptor name referring to a collection of cobalt and corrin ring molecules which are defined by their particular vitamin function in the body. All of the substrate cobalt-corrin molecules from which B_{12} is made, must be synthesized by bacteria. However, after this synthesis is complete, except in rare cases, the human body has the ability to convert any form of B_{12} to an active form, by means of enzymatically removing certain prosthetic chemical groups from the cobalt atom, and replacing them with others.

The four forms (vitamers) of B_{12} are all deeply red colored crystals and water solutions, due to the color of the cobalt-corrin complex.

Cyanocobalamin is one such form, i.e. "vitamer", of B_{12} because it can be metabolized in the body to an active co-enzyme form. However, the cyanocobalamin form of B_{12} does not occur in nature normally, but is a byproduct of the fact that other forms of B_{12} are avid binders of cyanide (-CN) which they pick up in the process of activated charcoal purification of the vitamin after it is made by bacteria in the commercial process. Since the cyanocobalamin form of B_{12} is easy to crystallize and is not sensitive to air-oxidation, it is typically used as a form of B_{12} for food additives and in many common multivitamins. Pure cyanocobalamin possesses the deep pink color associated with most octahedral cobalt(II) complexes and the crystals are well formed and easily grown up to millimeter size.

Hydroxocobalamin is another form of B_{12} commonly encountered in pharmacology, but which is not normally present in the human body. Hydroxocobalamin is sometimes denoted B_{12a}. This form of B_{12} is the form produced by bacteria, and is what is converted to cyanocobalmin in the commercial charcoal filtration step of production. Hydroxocobalamin has an avid affinity for cyanide ions and has been used as an antidote to cyanide poisoning. It is supplied typically in water solution for injection. Hydroxocobalamin is thought to be converted to the active enzymic forms of B_{12} more easily than cyanocobalamin, and since it is little more expensive than cyanocobalamin, and has longer retention times in the body, has been used for vitamin replacement in situations where added reassurance of activity is desired. Intramuscular administration of hydroxocobalamin is also the preferred treatment for pediatric patients with intrinsic cobalamin metabolic diseases, for vitamin B_{12} deficient patients with tobacco amblyopia (which is thought to perhaps have a component of cyanide poisoning from cyanide in cigarette smoke); and for treatment of patients with pernicious anemia who have optic neuropathy.

Adenosylcobalamin ($adoB_{12}$) and **methylcobalamin** (MeB_{12}) are the two enzymatically active cofactor forms of B_{12} that naturally occur in the body. Most of the body's reserves are stored as $adoB_{12}$ in the liver. These are converted to the other methylcobalamin form as needed.

2.18.6   Synthesis and industrial production

Neither plants nor animals are independently capable of constructing vitamin B_{12}.[67] Only bacteria and archaea[68] have the enzymes required for its biosynthesis. The total synthesis of B_{12} was reported by Robert Burns Woodward[69] and Albert Eschenmoser in 1972,[70][71] and remains one of the classic feats of organic synthesis. Species from the following genera are known to synthesize B_{12}: *Acetobacterium, Aerobacter, Agrobacterium, Alcaligenes, Azotobacter, Bacillus, Clostridium, Corynebacterium, Flavobacterium, Lactobacillus, Micromonospora, Mycobacterium, Nocardia, Propionibacterium, Protaminobacter, Proteus, Pseudomonas, Rhizobium, Salmonella, Serratia, Streptomyces, Streptococcus* and *Xanthomonas*.

Industrial production of B_{12} is achieved through fermentation of selected microorganisms.[72] *Streptomyces griseus*, a bacterium once thought to be a yeast, was the commercial source of vitamin B_{12} for many years.[73][74] The species *Pseudomonas denitrificans* and *Propionibacterium freudenreichii subsp. shermanii* are more commonly used today.[75] These are frequently grown under special conditions to enhance yield, and at least one company, Rhône-Poulenc of France, which has merged into Sanofi-Aventis, used genetically engineered versions of one or both of these species. Since a number of species of Propionibacterium produce no exotoxins or endotoxins and are **g**enerally **r**egarded **a**s **s**afe (have been granted GRAS status) by the Food and Drug Administration of the United States, they are presently the FDA-preferred bacterial fermentation organisms for vitamin B_{12} production.[76]

The total world production of vitamin B_{12}, by four companies (the French Sanofi-Aventis and three Chinese companies) is said to have been 35 tonnes in 2008.[77]

See cyanocobalamin for discussion of the chemical preparation of reduced-cobalt vitamin analogs and preparation of physiological forms of the vitamin such as adenosylcobalamin and methylcobalamin.

2.18.7   Mechanism of action

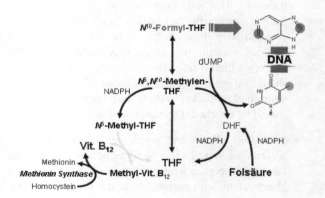

Metabolism of folic acid. The role of Vitamin B_{12} is seen at bottom-left.

Coenzyme B_{12}'s reactive C-Co bond participates in three main types of enzyme-catalyzed reactions.[78][79]

1. Isomerases

    Rearrangements in which a hydrogen atom is directly transferred between two adjacent atoms with concomitant exchange of the second substituent, X, which may be a carbon atom with substituents, an oxygen atom of an alcohol, or an amine. These use the $adoB_{12}$ (adenosylcobalamin) form of the vitamin.

2. Methyltransferases

    Methyl (-CH_3) group transfers between two molecules. These use MeB_{12} (methylcobalamin) form of the vitamin.

3. Dehalogenases

    Reactions in which a halogen atom is removed from an organic molecule. Enzymes in this class have not been identified in humans.

In humans, two major coenzyme B_{12}-dependent enzyme families corresponding to the first two reaction types, are known. These are typified by the following two enzymes:

1. MUT is an isomerase which uses the $AdoB_{12}$ form and reaction type 1 to catalyze a carbon skeleton rearrangement (the X group is -COSCoA). MUT's reaction converts MMl-CoA to Su-CoA, an important step in the extraction of energy from proteins and fats (for more see MUT's reaction mechanism). This functionality is lost in vitamin B_{12} deficiency, and can be measured clinically as an increased methylmalonic acid (MMA) level. Unfortunately, an elevated MMA, though sensitive to B_{12} deficiency, is probably overly sensitive, and not all who have it actually have B_{12} deficiency. For example, MMA is elevated in 90–98% of patients with B_{12} deficiency; however 20–25% of patients over the age of 70 have elevated levels of MMA, yet 25–33% of them do not have B_{12} deficiency. For this reason, assessment of MMA levels is not routinely recommended in the elderly. There is no "gold standard" test for B_{12} deficiency because as a B_{12} deficiency occurs, serum values may be maintained while tissue B_{12} stores become depleted. Therefore, serum B_{12} values above the cut-off point of deficiency do not necessarily indicate adequate B_{12} status[20] The MUT function is necessary for proper myelin synthesis (see mechanism below) and is not affected by folate supplementation.

2. MTR, also known as methionine synthase, is a methyltransferase enzyme, which uses the MeB_{12} and reaction type 2 to transfer a methyl group from 5-methyltetrahydrofolate to homocysteine, thereby generating tetrahydrofolate (THF) and methionine (for more see MTR's reaction mechanism).[80] This functionality is lost in vitamin B_{12} deficiency, resulting in an increased homocysteine level and the trapping of folate as 5-methyl-tetrahydrofolate, from which THF (the active form of folate) cannot be recovered. THF plays an important role in DNA synthesis so reduced availability of THF results in ineffective production of cells with rapid turnover, in particular red blood cells, and also intestinal wall cells which are responsible for absorption. THF may be regenerated via MTR or may be obtained from fresh folate in the diet. Thus all of the DNA synthetic effects of B12 deficiency, including the megaloblastic anemia of pernicious anemia, resolve if sufficient dietary folate is present.[58] Thus the best-known "function" of B_{12} (that which is involved with DNA synthesis, cell-division, and anemia) is actually a facultative function which is mediated by B_{12}-conservation of an active form of folate which is needed for efficient DNA production.[81] Other cobalamin-requiring methyltransferase enzymes are also known in bacteria, such as Me-H4-MPT, coenzyme M methyl transferase.

Enzyme function

If folate is present in quantity, then of the two absolutely vitamin B_{12}-dependent enzyme-family reactions in humans, the MUT-family reactions show the most direct and characteristic secondary effects, focusing on the nervous system (see below). This is because the MTR (methyltransferase-type) reactions are involved in regenerating folate, and thus are less evident when folate is in good supply.

Since the late 1990s, folic acid has begun to be added to fortify flour in many countries, so folate deficiency is now more rare. At the same time, since DNA synthetic-sensitive tests for anemia and erythrocyte size are routinely done in even simple medical test clinics (so that these folate-mediated biochemical effects are more often directly detected), the MTR-dependent effects of B_{12} deficiency are becoming apparent not as anemia due to DNA-synthetic problems (as they were classically), but now mainly as a simple and less obvious elevation of homocysteine in the blood and urine (homocysteinuria). This condition may result in long term damage to arteries and in clotting (stroke and heart attack), but this effect is difficult to separate from other common processes associated with atherosclerosis and aging.

The specific myelin damage resulting from B_{12} deficiency, even in the presence of adequate folate and methionine, is more specifically and clearly a vitamin deficiency problem. It has been connected to B_{12} most directly by reactions related to MUT, which is absolutely required to convert methylmalonyl coenzyme A into succinyl coenzyme A. Failure of this second reaction to occur results in elevated levels of MMA, a myelin destabilizer. Excessive MMA will prevent normal fatty acid synthesis, or it will be incorporated into fatty acid itself rather than normal malonic acid. If this abnormal fatty acid subsequently is incorporated into myelin, the resulting myelin will be too fragile, and demyelination will occur. Although the precise mechanism(s) are not known with certainty, the result is subacute combined degeneration of central nervous system and spinal cord.[82] Whatever the cause, it is known that B_{12} deficiency causes neuropathies, even if folic acid is present in good supply, and therefore anemia is not present.

Vitamin B_{12}-dependent MTR reactions may also have neurological effects, through an indirect mechanism. Adequate methionine (which, like folate, must otherwise be obtained in the diet, if it is not regenerated from homocysteine by a B_{12} dependent reaction) is needed to make S-adenosylmethionine (SAMe), which is in turn necessary for methylation of myelin sheath phospholipids. Although production of SAMe is not B_{12} dependent, help in recycling for provision of one adequate substrate for it (the essential amino acid methionine) is assisted by B_{12}. In addition, SAMe is involved in the manufacture of certain neurotransmitters, catecholamines and in brain metabolism. These neurotransmitters are important for maintaining mood, possibly explaining why depression is associated with B_{12} deficiency. Methylation of the myelin sheath phospholipids may also depend on adequate folate, which in turn is dependent on MTR recycling, unless ingested in relatively high amounts.

2.18.8   Absorption and distribution

Methyl-B_{12} is absorbed by an intestinal mechanism using intrinsic factor and by a diffusion process in which approximately 1% of the oral dose is absorbed.[83] The human physiology of vitamin B_{12} is complex, and therefore is prone to mishaps leading to vitamin B_{12} deficiency. Protein-bound vitamin B_{12} must be released from the proteins by the action of digestive proteases in both the stomach and small intestine.[84] Gastric acid releases the vitamin from food particles; therefore antacid and acid-blocking medications (especially proton-pump inhibitors) may inhibit absorption of B_{12}. In addition some elderly people produce less stomach acid as they age thereby increasing their probability of B_{12} deficiencies.[85]

B_{12} taken in a low-solubility, non-chewable supplement pill form may bypass the mouth and stomach and not mix with gastric acids, but these are not necessary for the absorption of free B_{12} not bound to protein.

R-protein (also known as haptocorrin and cobalophilin) is B_{12} binding protein that are produced in the salivary glands. It must wait until B_{12} has been freed from proteins in food by pepsin in the stomach. B_{12} then binds to the R-protein to avoid degradation of it in the acidic environment of the stomach.[86]

This pattern of secretion of a binding protein secreted in a previous digestive step is repeated once more before absorption. The next binding protein is intrinsic factor (IF), a protein synthesized by gastric parietal cells that is secreted in response to histamine, gastrin and pentagastrin, as well as the presence of food. In the duodenum, proteases digest R-proteins and release B_{12}, which then binds to IF, to form a complex (IF/B_{12}). B_{12} must be attached to IF for it to be absorbed, as receptors on the enterocytes in the terminal ileum of the small bowel only recognize the B_{12}-IF complex; in addition, intrinsic factor protects the vitamin from catabolism by intestinal bacteria.

Absorption of food vitamin B_{12} thus requires an intact and functioning stomach, exocrine pancreas, intrinsic factor, and small bowel. Problems with any one of these organs makes a vitamin B_{12} deficiency possible. Individuals who lack intrinsic factor have a decreased ability to absorb B_{12}. In pernicious anemia, there is a lack of IF due to autoimmune atrophic gastritis, in which antibodies form against parietal cells. Antibodies may alternately form against and bind to IF, inhibiting it from carrying out its B_{12} protective function. Due to the complexity of B_{12} absorption, geriatric patients, many of whom are hypoacidic due to reduced parietal cell function, have an increased risk of B_{12} deficiency.[87] This results in 80–100% excretion of oral doses in the feces versus 30–60% excretion in feces as seen in individuals with adequate IF.[87]

Once the IF/B_{12} complex is recognized by specialized ileal receptors, it is transported into the portal circulation. The vitamin is then transferred to transcobalamin II (TC-II/B_{12}), which serves as the plasma transporter. Hereditary defects in production of the transcobalamins and their receptors may produce functional deficiencies in B_{12} and infantile megaloblastic anemia, and abnormal B_{12} related biochemistry, even in some cases with normal blood B_{12} levels.[64] For the vitamin to serve inside cells, the TC-II/B_{12} complex must bind to a cell receptor, and be endocytosed. The transcobalamin-II is degraded within a lysosome, and free B_{12} is finally released into the cytoplasm, where it may be transformed into the proper coenzyme, by certain cellular enzymes (see above).

It's important to note that investigations into the intestinal absorption of B_{12} point out that the upper limit per single dose, under normal conditions, is about 1.5 µg: "Studies in normal persons indicated that about 1.5 μg is assimilated when a single dose varying from 5 to 50 μg is administered by mouth. In a similar study Swendseid *et al.* stated that the average maximum absorption was 1.6 μg [...]" [88]

The total amount of vitamin B_{12} stored in body is about 2–5 mg in adults. Around 50% of this is stored in the liver.[20] Approximately 0.1% of this is lost per day by secretions into the gut, as not all these secretions are reabsorbed. Bile is the main form of B_{12} excretion; however, most of the B_{12} secreted in the bile is recycled via enterohepatic circulation. Excess B_{12} beyond the blood's binding capacity is typically excreted in urine.[20] Owing to the extremely efficient enterohepatic circulation of B_{12}, the liver can store several years' worth of vitamin B_{12}; therefore, nutritional deficiency of this vitamin is rare. How fast B_{12} levels change depends on the balance between how much B_{12} is obtained from the diet, how much is secreted and how much is absorbed. B_{12} deficiency may arise in a year if initial stores are low and genetic factors unfavourable, or may not appear for decades. In infants, B_{12} deficiency can appear much more quickly.[89]

2.18.9 History

B_{12} deficiency is the cause of pernicious anemia, an anemic disease that was usually fatal and had unknown etiology when it was first described in medicine. The cure, and B_{12}, were discovered by accident. George Whipple had been doing experiments in which he induced anemia in dogs by bleeding them, and then fed them various foods to observe which diets allowed them fastest recovery from the anemia produced. In the process, he discovered that ingesting large amounts of liver seemed to most rapidly cure the anemia of blood loss. Thus, he hypothesized that liver ingestion might treat pernicious anemia. He tried this and reported some signs of success in 1920.

After a series of careful clinical studies, George Richards Minot and William Murphy set out to partly isolate the substance in liver which cured anemia in dogs, and found that it was iron. They also found that an entirely different liver substance cured pernicious anemia in humans, that had no effect on dogs under the conditions used. The specific factor treatment for pernicious anemia, found in liver juice, had been found by this coincidence. Minot and Murphy reported these experiments in 1926. This was the first real progress with this disease. Despite this discovery, for several years patients were still required to eat large amounts of raw liver or to drink considerable amounts of liver juice.

In 1928, the chemist Edwin Cohn prepared a liver extract that was 50 to 100 times more potent than the natural liver products. The extract was the first workable treatment for the disease. For their initial work in pointing the way to a working treatment, Whipple, Minot, and Murphy shared the 1934 Nobel Prize in Physiology or Medicine.

These events in turn eventually led to discovery of the soluble vitamin, called vitamin B_{12}, from bacterial broths. In 1947, while working for the Poultry Science Department at the University of Maryland, Mary Shaw Shorb (in a collaborative project with Karl Folkers from Merck.) was provided with a $400 grant to develop the so-called "LLD assay" for B_{12}. LLD stood for *Lactobacillus lactis* Dorner,[90] a strain of bacterium which required "LLD factor" for growth, which was eventually identified as B_{12}. Shorb and colleagues used the LLD assay to rapidly extract the antipernicious anemia factor from liver extracts, and pure B_{12} was isolated in this way by 1948, with the contributions of chemists Shorb,[91] Karl A. Folkers of the United States and Alexander R. Todd of Great Britain. For this discovery, in 1949 Mary Shorb and Karl Folkers received the Mead Johnson Award from the American Society of Nutritional Sciences.[91]

The chemical structure of the molecule was determined by Dorothy Crowfoot Hodgkin and her team in 1956, based on crystallographic data.[92] Eventually, methods of producing the vitamin in large quantities from bacteria cultures were developed in the 1950s, and these led to the modern form of treatment for the disease.

2.18.10 See also

- Cobamamide

- Cyanocobalamin includes discussion of chemistry of preparation of reduced-cobalt B_{12} analogs

- Hydroxocobalamin

- Methylcobalamin

2.18.11 References

[1] Yamada, Kazuhiro (2013). "Chapter 9. Cobalt: Its Role in Health and Disease". In Astrid Sigel, Helmut Sigel and Roland K. O. Sigel. *Interrelations between Essential Metal Ions and Human Diseases*. Metal Ions in Life Sciences **13**. Springer. pp. 295–320. doi:10.1007/978-94-007-7500-8_9.

[2] "Dietary Supplement Fact Sheet: Vitamin B12". Office of Dietary Supplements, National Institutes of Health. Retrieved 28 September 2011.

[3] Albert, M. J.; Mathan, V. I.; Baker, S. J. (1980). "Vitamin B12 synthesis by human small intestinal bacteria". *Nature* **283** (5749): 781–782. doi:10.1038/283781a0. PMID 7354869.

[4] Chanarin, I.; Muir, M. (1982). "Demonstration of vitamin B12 analogues in human sera not detected by microbiological assay". *British journal of haematology* **51** (1): 171–173. doi:10.1111/j.1365-2141.1982.tb07301.x. PMID 7041953.

[5] Kelly, R. J.; Gruner, T. M.; Furlong, J. M.; Sykes, A. R. (2006). "Analysis of corrinoids in ovine tissues". *Biomedical Chromatography* **20** (8): 806–814. doi:10.1002/bmc.604. PMID 16345011.

[6] Yamada, K.; Shimodaira, M.; Chida, S.; Yamada, N.; Matsushima, N.; Fukuda, M.; Yamada, S. (2008). "Degradation of Vitamin B12 in Dietary Supplements". *International Journal for Vitamin and Nutrition Research* **78** (45): 195–203. doi:10.1024/0300-9831.78.45.195. PMID 19326342.

[7] Herbert, V.; Drivas, G.; Foscaldi, R.; Manusselis, C.; Colman, N.; Kanazawa, S.; Das, K.; Gelernt, M.; Herzlich, B.; Jennings, J. (1982). "Multivitamin/Mineral Food Supplements Containing Vitamin B12May Also Contain Analogues of Vitamin B12". *New England Journal of Medicine* **307** (4): 255–256. doi:10.1056/NEJM198207223070424. PMID 7088084.

[8] Watanabe, F.; Katsura, H.; Takenaka, S.; Fujita, T.; Abe, K.; Tamura, Y.; Nakatsuka, T.; Nakano, Y. (1999). "Pseudovitamin B(12) is the predominant cobamide of an algal health food, spirulina tablets". *Journal of agricultural and food chemistry* **47** (11): 4736–4741. doi:10.1021/jf990541b. PMID 10552882.

[9] Yamada, K.; Yamada, Y.; Fukuda, M.; Yamada, S. (1999). "Bioavailability of dried asakusanori (porphyra tenera) as a source of Cobalamin (Vitamin B12)". *International journal for vitamin and nutrition research. Internationale Zeitschrift fur Vitamin- und Ernahrungsforschung. Journal international de vitaminologie et de nutrition* **69** (6): 412–418. doi:10.1024/0300-9831.69.6.412. PMID 10642899.

[10] "Vitamin B12". *The American Society of Health-System Pharmacists*. Retrieved 3 April 2011.

[11] Hall AH, Rumack BH (1987). "Hydroxycobalamin/sodium thiosulfate as a cyanide antidote". *The Journal of Emergency Medicine* **5** (2): 115–21. doi:10.1016/0736-4679(87)90074-6. PMID 3295013.

[12] Dart RC (2006). "Hydroxocobalamin for acute cyanide poisoning: new data from preclinical and clinical studies; new results from the prehospital emergency setting". *Clinical Toxicology* **44** (Suppl 1): 1–3. doi:10.1080/15563650600811607. PMID 16990188.

[13] Vogiatzoglou A, Refsum H, Johnston C, et al. (2008). "Vitamin B12 status and rate of brain volume loss in community-dwelling elderly". *Neurology* **71** (11): 826–32. doi:10.1212/01.wnl.0000325581.26991.f2. PMID 18779510.

[14] "Dietary Supplement Fact Sheet: Vitamin B12 —Health Professional Fact Sheet". *Office of Dietary Supplements.* National Institutes of Health. 2011-06-24. Retrieved 2012-11-02.

[15] "Vitamins and minerals – B vitamins and folic acid". *NHS*. National Health Service. 2012-11-26. Retrieved 2013-07-10.

[16] "Vitamin B12 recommendation change". *American Journal of Nutrition Facts*. NutritionFacts.org. 2010. Retrieved 2014-09-19.

[17] "Guidance for Industry: A Food Labeling Guide (14. Appendix F: Calculate the Percent Daily Value for the Appropriate Nutrients)". *U.S. Food and Drug Administration*. Retrieved 30 October 2014.

[18] Institute Of Medicine (Us) Standing Committee On The Scientific Evaluation Of Dietary Reference Intakes And Its Panel On Folate, Other B Vitamins (1998). "Dietary Reference Intakes: Thiamin, Riboflavin, Niacin, Vitamin B6, Folate, Vitamin B12, Pantothenic Acid, Biotin, and Choline". *Food and Nutrition Board, Institute of Medicine* (Washington, DC: National Academy Press). ISBN 0-309-06554-2.

[19] Institute of Medicine (1998). "Vitamin B12". *Dietary Reference Intakes for Thiamin, Riboflavin, Niacin, Vitamin B6, Folate, Vitamin B12, Pantothenic Acid, Biotin, and Choline*. Washington, DC: The National Academies Press. pp. 340–342. ISBN 0-309-06554-2. Retrieved 2012-02-07.

[20] Vitamin B12, usda.gov

[21] Walsh, Stephen. "What every vegan should know about vitamin B12". Vegan Society. Archived from the original on 2007-07-17. Retrieved 2007-12-03.

[22] Mangels, Reed. "Vitamin B12 in the Vegan Diet". Vegetarian Resource Group. Retrieved 2008-01-17.

[23] "Don't Vegetarians Have Trouble Getting Enough Vitamin B12?". Physicians Committee for Responsible Medicine. Retrieved 2008-01-17.

[24] Kittaka-Katsura, H.; Fujita, T.; Watanabe, F.; Nakano, Y. (2002). "Purification and characterization of a corrinoid compound from Chlorella tablets as an algal health food". *Journal of agricultural and food chemistry* **50** (17): 4994–4997. doi:10.1021/jf020345w. PMID 12166996.

[25] Watanabe, F.; Takenaka, S.; Kittaka-Katsura, H.; Ebara, S.; Miyamoto, E. (2002). "Characterization and bioavailability of vitamin B12-compounds from edible algae". *Journal of nutritional science and vitaminology* **48** (5): 325–331. doi:10.3177/jnsv.48.325. PMID 12656203.

[26] Watanabe, F.; Takenaka, S.; Katsura, H.; Miyamoto, E.; Abe, K.; Tamura, Y.; Nakatsuka, T.; Nakano, Y. (2000). "Characterization of a vitamin B12 compound in the edible purple laver, Porphyra yezoensis". *Bioscience, biotechnology, and biochemistry* **64** (12): 2712–2715. doi:10.1271/bbb.64.2712. PMID 11210144.

[27] Takenaka, S.; Sugiyama, S.; Ebara, S.; Miyamoto, E.; Abe, K.; Tamura, Y.; Watanabe, F.; Tsuyama, S.; Nakano, Y. (2001). "Feeding dried purple laver (nori) to vitamin B12-deficient rats significantly improves vitamin B12 status". *The British journal of nutrition* **85** (6): 699–703. doi:10.1079/BJN2001352. PMID 11430774.

[28] Sethi NK, Robilotti E, Sadan Y (2005). "Neurological Manifestations Of Vitamin B-12 Deficiency". *The Internet Journal of Nutrition and Wellness* **2** (1). doi:10.5580/5a9.

[29] Masalha R, Chudakov B, Muhamad M, Rudoy I, Volkov I, Wirguin I (2001). "Cobalamin-responsive psychosis as the sole manifestation of vitamin B$_{12}$ deficiency". *Israeli Medical Association Journal* **3**: 701–703. PMID 11574992.

[30] Killen, J. P.; Brenninger, V. L. (2013). "Vitamin B12 deficiency". *N. Engl. J. Med* **368**: 2040–1. doi:10.1056/nejmc1304350.

[31] Biemans, E.; Hart, H.E.; Rutten, G.E.; Renteria, V.G.C.; Kooijman-Buiting, A.M.; Beulens, J.W. (2014). "Cobalamin status has a relationship with depression, cognition and neuropathy in patients with Type 2 diabetes mellitus using metformin". *Acta diabetologica*: 1–11.

[32] Bottiglieri, T.; Laundy, M.; Crellin, R.; Toone, B.K.; Carney, M.W.; Reynolds, E.H. (2000). "Homocysteine, folate, methylation, and monoamine metabolism in depression". *Journal of Neurology, Neurosurgery & Psychiatry* **69** (2): 228–232. doi:10.1136/jnnp.69.2.228.

[33] Doscherholmen, A.; McMahon, J.; Ripley, D. (1975). "Vitamin B12 absorption from eggs". *Proceedings of the Society for Experimental Biology and Medicine. Society for Experimental Biology and Medicine* **149** (4): 987–990. doi:10.3181/00379727-149-38940. PMID 1172618.

[34] Kwak, C. S.; Lee, M. S.; Lee, H. J.; Whang, J. Y.; Park, S. C. (2010). "Dietary source of vitamin B12 intake and vitamin B12 status in female elderly Koreans aged 85 and older living in rural area". *Nutrition Research and Practice* **4** (3): 229–234. doi:10.4162/nrp.2010.4.3.229. PMC 2895704. PMID 20607069.

[35] Kwak, C. S.; Lee, M. S.; Oh, S. I.; Park, S. C. (2010). "Discovery of Novel Sources of Vitamin B12 in Traditional Korean Foods from Nutritional Surveys of Centenarians". *Current Gerontology and Geriatrics Research* **2010**: 1. doi:10.1155/2010/374897. PMC 3062981. PMID 21436999.

[36] Kittaka-Katsura, H.; Ebara, S.; Watanabe, F.; Nakano, Y. (2004). "Characterization of Corrinoid Compounds from a Japanese Black Tea (Batabata-cha) Fermented by Bacteria". *Journal of Agricultural and Food Chemistry* **52** (4): 909–911. doi:10.1021/jf030585r. PMID 14969549.

[37] Nakano, S.; Takekoshi, H.; Nakano, M. (2009). "Chlorella pyrenoidosa Supplementation Reduces the Risk of Anemia, Proteinuria and Edema in Pregnant Women". *Plant Foods for Human Nutrition* **65** (1): 25–30. doi:10.1007/s11130-009-0145-9. PMID 20013055.

[38] Croft, M. T.; Lawrence, A. D.; Raux-Deery, E.; Warren, M. J.; Smith, A. G. (2005). "Algae acquire vitamin B12 through a symbiotic relationship with bacteria". *Nature* **438** (7064): 90–93. doi:10.1038/nature04056. PMID 16267554.

[39] Kazamia, E.; Czesnick, H. R.; Nguyen, T. T. V.; Croft, M. T.; Sherwood, E.; Sasso, S.; Hodson, S. J.; Warren, M. J.; Smith, A. G. (2012). "Mutualistic interactions between vitamin B12-dependent algae and heterotrophic bacteria exhibit regulation". *Environmental Microbiology* **14** (6): 1466–1476. doi:10.1111/j.1462-2920.2012.02733.x. PMID 22463064.

[40] Moore, S. J.; Lawrence, A. D.; Biedendieck, R; Deery, E; Frank, S; Howard, M. J.; Rigby, S. E.; Warren, M. J. (2013). "Elucidation of the anaerobic pathway for the corrin component of cobalamin (vitamin B12)". *Proceedings of the National Academy of Sciences* **110** (37): 14906–11. doi:10.1073/pnas.1308098110. PMC 3773766. PMID 23922391.

[41] Walsh, Stephen, RD. "Vegan Society B$_{12}$ factsheet". Vegan Society. Retrieved 2008-01-17.

[42] Herbert, Victor (1988). "Vitamin B-12: Plant sources, requirements, and assay" (PDF). *The American journal of clinical nutrition* **48** (3 Suppl): 852–8. PMID 3046314.

[43] Daisley, K. W. (1969). "Monthly survey of vitamin B$_{12}$ concentration in some waters of the English Lake District" (PDF). *Limnol. Oceanogr.* **14** (2): 224–228. doi:10.4319/lo.1969.14.2.0224.

[44] Wakayama EJ, Dillwith JW, Howard RW, Blomquist GJ; Dillwith; Howard; Blomquist (1984). "Vitamin B$_{12}$ levels in selected insects". *Insect Biochemistry* **14** (2): 175–179. doi:10.1016/0020-1790(84)90027-1.

[45] Albert MJ, Mathan VI, Baker SJ; Mathan; Baker (1980). "Vitamin B$_{12}$ synthesis by human small intestinal bacteria". *INature* **283** (5749): 781–782. doi:10.1038/283781a0. PMID 7354869.

[46] Sharabi, A; Cohen, E; Sulkes, J; Garty, M (2003). "Replacement therapy for vitamin B12 deficiency: comparison between the sublingual and oral route". *British Journal of Clinical Pharmacology* **56** (6): 635–8. doi:10.1046/j.1365-2125.2003.01907.x. PMC 1884303. PMID 14616423.

[47] Bolaman Z, Kadikoylu G, Yukselen V, Yavasoglu I, Barutca S, Senturk T; Kadikoylu; Yukselen; Yavasoglu; Barutca; Senturk (2003). "Oral versus intramuscular cobalamin treatment in megaloblastic anemia: a single-center, prospective, randomized, open-label study". *Clin Ther* **25** (12): 3124–34. doi:10.1016/S0149-2918(03)90096-8. PMID 14749150.

[48] Lane LA, Rojas-Fernandez C; Rojas-Fernandez (2002). "Treatment of vitamin b(12)-deficiency anemia: oral versus parenteral therapy". *Ann Pharmacother* **36** (7–8): 1268–72. doi:10.1345/aph.1A122. PMID 12086562.

[49] Butler, C. C. (2006). "Oral vitamin B12 versus intramuscular vitamin B12 for vitamin B12 deficiency: A systematic review of randomized controlled trials". *Family Practice* **23** (3): 279. doi:10.1093/fampra/cml008.

[50] Andersson HC, Shapira E; Shapira (1998). "Biochemical and clinical response to hydroxocobalamin versus cyanocobalamin treatment in patients with methylmalonic acidemia and homocystinuria (cblC)". *J. Pediatr.* **132** (1): 121–4. doi:10.1016/S0022-3476(98)70496-2. PMID 9470012.

[51] Roze E, Gervais D, Demeret S; et al. (2003). "Neuropsychiatric disturbances in presumed late-onset cobalamin C disease". *Arch. Neurol.* **60** (10): 1457–62. doi:10.1001/archneur.60.10.1457. PMID 14568819.

[52] Thauvin-Robinet C, Roze E, Couvreur G; et al. (2008). "The adolescent and adult form of cobalamin C disease: clinical and molecular spectrum". *J. Neurol. Neurosurg. Psychiatr.* **79** (6): 725–8. doi:10.1136/jnnp.2007.133025. PMID 18245139.

[53] Heil SG, Hogeveen M, Kluijtmans LA; et al. (2007). "Marfanoid features in a child with combined methylmalonic aciduria and homocystinuria (CblC type)". *J. Inherit. Metab. Dis.* **30** (5): 811. doi:10.1007/s10545-007-0546-6. PMID 17768669.

[54] Tsai, A. C. H.; Morel, C. F.; Scharer, G.; Yang, M.; Lerner-Ellis, J. P.; Rosenblatt, D. S.; Thomas, J. A. (2007). "Late-onset combined homocystinuria and methylmalonic aciduria (cblC) and neuropsychiatric disturbance". *American Journal of Medical Genetics Part A* **143A** (20): 2430. doi:10.1002/ajmg.a.31932.

[55] "5′-deoxyadenosylcobalamin and methylcobalamin as sources for Vitamin B12 added as a nutritional substance in food supplements[1] - Scientific opinion of the Scientific Panel on Food Additives and Nutrient Sources added to food". *EFSA Journal* **815**: 1–21. 2008. doi:10.2903/j.efsa.2008.815. "the metabolic fate and biological distribution of methylcobalamin and 5′-deoxyadenosylcobalamin are expected to be similar to that of other sources of vitamin B12 in the diet."

[56] "5′-deoxyadenosylcobalamin and methylcobalamin as sources for Vitamin B12 added as a nutritional substance in food supplements[1] - Scientific opinion of the Scientific Panel on Food Additives and Nutrient Sources added to food". *EFSA Journal* **815**: 1–21. 2008. doi:10.2903/j.efsa.2008.815.

[57] Pott JW, Wong KH (2006). "Leber's hereditary optic neuropathy and vitamin B12 deficiency". *Graefe's Archive for Clinical and Experimental Ophthalmology* **244** (10): 1357–9. doi:10.1007/s00417-006-0269-7. PMID 16523300.

[58] "Argument for providing B12 with food fortification of folate, since otherwise folate will correct hematological symptoms while leaving neurological symptoms to progress". Victorherbert.com. Retrieved 2013-04-20.

[59] De Jager, J.; Kooy, A.; Lehert, P.; Wulffelé, M. G.; Van Der Kolk, J.; Bets, D.; Verburg, J.; Donker, A. J. M.; Stehouwer, C. D. A. (2010). "Long term treatment with metformin in patients with type 2 diabetes and risk of vitamin B-12 deficiency: Randomised placebo controlled trial". *BMJ* **340**: c2181. doi:10.1136/bmj.c2181. PMC 2874129. PMID 20488910.

[60] Andrès E, Noel E, Goichot B (2002). "Metformin-associated vitamin B12 deficiency". *Arch Intern Med* **162** (19): 2251–2. doi:10.1001/archinte.162.19.2251-a. PMID 12390080.

[61] Gilligan M (2002). "Metformin and vitamin B12 deficiency". *Arch Intern Med* **162** (4): 484–5. doi:10.1001/archinte.162.4.484. PMID 11863489.

[62] Bauman, WA; Shaw, S; Jayatilleke, E; Spungen, AM; Herbert, V (2000). "Increased intake of calcium reverses vitamin B12 malabsorption induced by metformin". *Diabetes Care* **23** (9): 1227–31. doi:10.2337/diacare.23.9.1227. PMID 10977010.

[63] Copp, Samantha (2007-12-01). "What effect does metformin have on vitamin B12 levels?". UK Medicines Information, NHS.

[64] *Pernicious Anemia* at eMedicine

[65] Palva, IP; Salokannel, SJ; Timonen, T; Palva, HL (1972). "Drug-induced malabsorption of vitamin B12: IV. Malabsorption and deficiency of B12 during treatment with slow-release potassium chloride". *Acta Medica Scandinavica* **191** (4): 355–7. PMID 5032681.

[66] Jaouen, G., ed. (2006). *Bioorganometallics: Biomolecules, Labeling, Medicine*. Weinheim: Wiley-VCH. ISBN 3-527-30990-X.

[67] Loeffler, G. (2005). *Basiswissen Biochemie*. Heidelberg: Springer. p. 606. ISBN 3-540-23885-9.

[68] Bertrand EM; Saito MA; Young JJ; Neilan BA (2011). "Vitamin B12 biosynthesis gene diversity in the Ross Sea: the identification of a new group of putative polar B12 biosynthes". *Environmental Microbiology* **13** (5): 1285–98. doi:10.1111/j.1462-2920.2011.02428.x. PMID 21410623.

[69] Khan, Adil Ghani; Eswaran, S. V. (2003). "Woodward's synthesis of vitamin B12". *Resonance* **8** (6): 8. doi:10.1007/BF02837864.

[70] Eschenmoser A, Wintner CE (June 1977). "Natural product synthesis and vitamin B12". *Science* **196** (4297): 1410–20. doi:10.1126/science.867037. PMID 867037.

[71] Riether, Doris; Mulzer, Johann (2003). "Total Synthesis of Cobyric Acid: Historical Development and Recent Synthetic Innovations". *European Journal of Organic Chemistry* **2003**: 30. doi:10.1002/1099-0690(200301)2003:1<30::AID-EJOC30>3.0.CO;2-I.

[72] Martens JH, Barg H, Warren MJ, Jahn D (2002). "Microbial production of vitamin B12". *Applied Microbiology and Biotechnology* **58** (3): 275–85. doi:10.1007/s00253-001-0902-7. PMID 11935176.

[73] Linnell JC, Matthews DM (1984). "Cobalamin metabolism and its clinical aspects". *Clinical Science* **66** (2): 113–21. PMID 6420106.

[74] Vitamin B12. Code of Federal Regulations. U.S. Government Printing Office. Title 21, Volume 3. Revised. April 1, 2001. CITE: 21CFR184.1945 p. 552

[75] De Baets S, Vandedrinck S, Vandamme EJ (2000). "Vitamins and Related Biofactors, Microbial Production". In Lederberg J. *Encyclopedia of Microbiology* **4** (2nd ed.). New York: Academic Press. pp. 837–853. ISBN 0-12-226800-8.

[76] Riaz, Muhammad; Iqbal, Fouzia; Akram, Muhammad (2007). "Microbial production of vitamin B12 by methanol utilizing strain of *Pseudomonas* specie". *Pak J. Biochem. Mol. Biol.* 1 **40**: 5–10.

[77] Yemei, Zhang (January 26, 2009) New round of price slashing in vitamin B12 sector. (Fine and Specialty). China Chemical Reporter.

[78] Voet, Judith G.; Voet, Donald (1995). *Biochemistry.* New York: J. Wiley & Sons. p. 675. ISBN 0-471-58651-X. OCLC 31819701.

[79] Banerjee, R; Ragsdale, SW (2003). "The many faces of vitamin B12: catalysis by cobalamin-dependent enzymes". *Annual review of biochemistry* **72**: 209–47. doi:10.1146/annurev.biochem.72.121801.161828. PMID 14527323.

[80] Banerjee RV, Matthews RG (1990). "Cobalamin-dependent methionine synthase". *The FASEB Journal* **4** (5): 1450–9. PMID 2407589.

[81] Wickramasinghe SN (1995). "Morphology, biology and biochemistry of cobalamin- and folate-deficient bone marrow cells". *Baillière's Clinical Haematology* **8** (3): 441–59. doi:10.1016/S0950-3536(05)80215-X. PMID 8534956.

[82] Naidich MJ, Ho SU (2005). "Case 87: Subacute combined degeneration". *Radiology* **237** (1): 101–5. doi:10.1148/radiol.2371031757. PMID 16183926.

[83] CerefolinNAC® Caplets. intetlab.com

[84] Marks, Allan D. (2009) *Basic Medical Biochemistry: A Clinical Approach,* 3rd ed., Lippincott Williams & Wilkins, p. 757, ISBN 078177022X.

[85] Beck, Melinda (January 18, 2011). "Sluggish? Confused? Vitamin B12 May Be Low". *The Wall Street Journal.*

[86] Allen, RH; Seetharam, B; Podell, E; Alpers, DH (1978). "Effect of Proteolytic Enzymes on the Binding of Cobalamin to R Protein and Intrinsic Factor". *The Journal of Clinical Investigation* **61** (1): 47–54. doi:10.1172/JCI108924. PMC 372512. PMID 22556.

[87] Combs, Gerald F. (2008). *The vitamins: fundamental aspects in nutrition and health* (3rd ed.). Amsterdam: Elsevier Academic Press. ISBN 0-12-183492-1. OCLC 150255807.

[88] Abels, J.; Vegter, J. J. M.; Woldring, M. G.; Jans, J. H.; Nieweg, H. O. (2009). "The Physiologic Mechanism of Vitamin B12 Absorption". *Acta Medica Scandinavica* **165** (2): 105. doi:10.1111/j.0954-6820.1959.tb14477.x.

[89] "B12: An essential part of a healthy plant-based diet". *International Vegetarian Union.*

[90] Mary Shorb Lecture in Nutrition

[91] "Dr. Mary Shaw Shorb – Annual Lecture". Department of Animal & Avian Sciences, University of Maryland. May 10, 2012.

[92] Kirkland, Kyle (2010). *Biological Sciences: Notable Research and Discoveries.* Facts on File, Inc. p. 87. ISBN 0816074399.

2.18.12 External links

- Vitamin B12 Fact Sheet from the U.S. National Institutes of Health

- Jane Higdon, "Vitamin B12", Micronutrient Information Center, *Linus Pauling Institute, Oregon State University*

- Oh, Robert C; Brown, David L (2003). "Vitamin B12 deficiency". *American Family Physician* **67** (5): 979–86. PMID 12643357.

- Vitamin B12 and Folate at Lab Tests Online

- Cyanocobalamin at the US National Library of Medicine Medical Subject Headings (MeSH)

Chapter 3

Text and image sources, contributors, and licenses

3.1 Text

- **Caviar** *Source:* https://en.wikipedia.org/wiki/Caviar?oldid=690600347 *Contributors:* Sfdan, Roybadami, Liftarn, Stan Shebs, Ronz, Tkinias, Wnissen, PaulinSaudi, Bemoeial, Tpbradbury, Bevo, Moriori, Sbisolo, Donreed, Psychonaut, Greudin, Academic Challenger, Nach0king, Rursus, Obli, Wyss, Revth, T0m, Bodnotbod, TreyHarris, Austin Hair, Marcus2, Burschik, Zondor, Squash, Dr.frog, Discospinster, Ivan Bajlo, Mani1, Bender235, Kwamikagami, Keno, Jpgordon, Bobo192, Iamunknown, Albinomonkey, Haham hanuka, HasharBot~enwiki, Jumbuck, Grutness, Alansohn, Anthony Appleyard, Ben James Ben, GrantNeufeld, DreamGuy, Garzo, Sciurinæ, T1980, Cmprince, Gene Nygaard, TheCoffee, ChrisJMoor, Nuno Tavares, Angr, Alvis, Garys67, Triddle, GregorB, SDC, Jwilder, J M Rice, Mandarax, RichardWeiss, Graham87, BD2412, Mendaliv, Canderson7, Rjwilmsi, Nightscream, Kazrak, Mlprater, Vuong Ngan Ha, Lebha, Margosbot~enwiki, Luckyj, Turidoth, Hitokirishinji, Gdrbot, Roboto de Ajvol, YurikBot, Jadon, Hairy Dude, RussBot, Pburka, Hellbus, Matt Fitzpatrick, Stephenb, Manop, Calicore, Bovineone, Varnav, NawlinWiki, The Ogre, Bobak, Epipelagic, Lockesdonkey, Nlu, Wd40, BorgQueen, Kingstonjr, Nimbex, Tom Morris, SmackBot, Dhockley, Sjhalasz~enwiki, Slashme, Dav2008, Vald, KocjoBot~enwiki, Alex earlier account, Yamaguchi 先 生, Peter Isotalo, Gilliam, Hmains, Bluebot, Deli nk, Wikipediatrix, Nbarth, Seifip, Eliezg, HeteroZellous, Atomskninja, BostonMA, Hannu-Makinen, T-borg, MartinRe, Derek R Bullamore, BlackTerror, Will Beback, Attys, Iliev, RomanSpa, Sohale, Voceditenore, JHunterJ, BillFlis, Red Alien, Dbertman, Succubus MacAstaroth, The2003s~enwiki, Marcipangris, Chezhiyan, Finneous, Dl2000, The-Pope, Iridescent, Lathrop1885, Tony Fox, Z220info, DavidOaks, Gilabrand, Tawkerbot2, Ghaly, TheHorseCollector, Afghana~enwiki, Greverod, Ksaraf, Van helsing, Stuart Drewer, Eric Le Bigot, Cydebot, RatatoskLemur, Thijs!bot, Epbr123, Fshando, Wompa99, Headbomb, Marek69, JohnPaulPagano, Visik, Mentifisto, Gossamers, AntiVandalBot, Dartrider, Fayenatic london, Petey21, Ran4, Leevclarke, Adeptitus, JAnDbot, Ericoides, Hut 8.5, Pedro, Bongwarrior, VoABot II, JNW, JamesBWatson, KConWiki, Catgut, Ngchikit, Mikenucklesii, Philg88, Nopira, Chapultepec, MartinBot, Dennisthe2, Cfrydj, Arjun01, R'n'B, CommonsDelinker, Aguynamededdy, Mooglemoogle, J.delanoy, Trusilver, Khathi, Icechyi, DJ1AM, Val92~enwiki, Sonabona, Donmike10, HighKing, CardinalDan, Idioma-bot, WWGB, Neuromath, Lights, Almw113, Hammersoft, Khochman, Iwavns, Ticklemygrits, Botol~enwiki, TXiKiBoT, Porkrind, Anna Lincoln, Tank2, Jackfork, SEY01, Plutonium27, SieBot, StAnselm, Coffee, Tresiden, Ham Pastrami, Ender qa, Flyer22 Reborn, Hxhbot, EditorInTheRye, Boromir123, Nn123645, Pinkadelica, Miyokan, ClueBot, ParlerVousWiki, Prinkipo71, Davidnqd, LizardJr8, BernardTom, Jusdafax, ParisianBlade, Oreenx519x, Promethean, Zharmad, Bleubeatle, Sharishirin, Trulystand700, DumZiBoT, Hibernia1700, XLinkBot, Mikebemka, Anturiaethwr, Skarebo, Netrat, Pianist ru, Badgernet, Alexius08, MatthewVanitas, Hoplophile, RN1970, Fluffernutter, Jim10701, MrOllie, LaaknorBot, CarsracBot, Favonian, Doniago, Ehrenkater, Lightbot, Jacob.l345, Luckas-bot, Yobot, WikiDan61, Richigi, AnomieBOT, Faethon Ghost, Hairhorn, Rubinbot, Jim1138, Jambobambo, Accuruss, Piano non troppo, Scythian77, Ufim, Crecy99, Bluee Mountain, Materialscientist, Bob Burkhardt, يدماغ.مد.محأ24, ArthurBot, Xqbot, JimVC3, Termininja, ITSENJOYABLE, Pb8330, Anna Frodesiak, GrouchoBot, ProtectionTaggingBot, Mathonius, Spongefrog, FrescoBot, Christos bacchus, AlexanderKaras, Weetoddid, Thriftytable, Armigo~enwiki, Buycaviar, Ver-bot, Trijnstel, ChristianD35, SpaceFlight89, Tofured, Christopher1968, Hessamnia, TobeBot, Mjnazari, Lotje, RPinney331, JenniferSimmons, DARTH SIDIOUS 2, Mean as custard, RjwilmsiBot, Foodiebuff, Emjohn71, Kamran the Great, DASHBot, Boghzo, EmausBot, John of Reading, Sergeiar, Deepsapphyr, GoingBatty, Ebe123, ZxxZxxZ, Scrabblensa, ZéroBot, Jenks24, Foodie2010, Erianna, Coasterlover1994, Noodleki, Donner60, Snusnusnu, ILikeCookies55, GermanJoe, ClueBot NG, Ykvach, Faizanalivarya, Newzynet, Joefromrandb, Hon-3s-T, ةذيغة التساوى, Wikigiovannini, Fabriziolalontra, Bukrafil, Itnat, Widr, El bandolero del sur, Helpful Pixie Bot, BG19bot, Toffanin, Northamerica1000, Eman2129, FakirNL, Ruosong, Iamchococake, Anyamuslimah, Minsbot, Azieglerjoens, Gylatshalit, Cyberbot II, Webclient101, Cookingchef, Will roarshock, Pratikswami, Sport and politics, John F. Lewis, Frosty, Marcionist, Black River Caviar, Provacitu74, Availingskink2, NorthernDivine, Eric Arrouzé, Giovanni-da-Ferrara, NorthernDivine1999, Param Mudgal, Skitman, Jameswelch5, Anonymous123456789101121314, KH-1, Wickedfrostguppy, Poopipupipupi, Anotherhelpfuldude, Deunanknute, 666armadillo666, Darenml88 and Anonymous: 390

- **Aquaculture** *Source:* https://en.wikipedia.org/wiki/Aquaculture?oldid=690600321 *Contributors:* Mav, Bryan Derksen, Rmhermen, Anthere, Heron, Jinian, Stevertigo, Michael Hardy, Ahoerstemeier, Mac, Suisui, Angela, Glenn, Nikai, Charles Matthews, Mjklin, DJ Clayworth, Marshman, Phoebe, Thue, J D, Jusjih, Johnleemk, Seglea, Modulatum, Hemanshu, Gidonb, Hadal, Lupo, Xanzzibar, GreatWhiteNortherner, Alan Liefting, Abigail-II, Chinasaur, Rpyle731, H-2-O, Bobblewik, Ebear422, Quadell, Antandrus, PDH, Plasma east, Brooker, TreyHarris, Paradoxian, DanielCD, Brianhe, Rich Farmbrough, Vsmith, Gronky, Bender235, ESkog, Nabla, Danieljackson, Germen, El C, EurekaLott, Orlady,

Aaronbrick, Femto, Vervin, Ypacaraí, Smalljim, Cmdrjameson, R. S. Shaw, ZayZayEM, Jumbuck, Arthena, Velella, Versageek, Gene Nygaard, MIT Trekkie, Drbreznjev, GringoInChile, Diamler, Ultramarine, Sfrantzman, Stemonitis, Kelly Martin, Pekinensis, Woohookitty, WadeSim-Miser, Paradon, Pufferfish101, Nktae, Tbyron, Wayward, Paxsimius, Porphyra, Graham87, Qwertyus, Rjwilmsi, Omnieiunium, StephanieM, Wareq, Ian Pitchford, SchuminWeb, Malhonen, Chobot, DaGizza, DVdm, Bgwhite, Dj Capricorn, YurikBot, Wavelength, Jamesmorrison, Pip2andahalf, RussBot, SpuriousQ, Stephenb, Gaius Cornelius, Ksyrie, Wimt, Saoshyant, Aaron Brenneman, Emersoni, Epipelagic, CLW, WAS 4.250, Closedmouth, Donald Albury, LeonardoRob0t, Fram, Owain.davies, Johnpseudo, Thomas Blomberg, Dleuck, Veinor, Smack-Bot, Fireworks, Davepape, Reedy, Lawrencekhoo, Delldot, Eskimbot, Jab843, Edgar181, SmartGuy Old, Perdita, Gilliam, Betacommand, Anwar saadat, Kurykh, Keegan, MK8, AussieLegend, Rrburke, Addshore, Jared, RJBurkhart, FelisLeo, Will Beback, Valfontis, Euchiasmus, Gobonobo, Butko, NathanLee, Shangrilaista, Beetstra, Avs5221, Mr Stephen, MainBody, Samwingkit, TastyPoutine, Qyd, Sifaka, Politepunk, Iridescent, Lakers, Joseph Solis in Australia, Shoeofdeath, Courcelles, Gilabrand, ChemicalBit, Tawkerbot2, Fishwww, A Born Cynic, Joostvan-deputte~enwiki, Van helsing, Como006, CBM, Kris Schnee, Rowellcf, BarraCuda, Basar, Cydebot, B, DumbBOT, ChrisIk02, UberScienceNerd, Thijs!bot, Epbr123, Lfrench, Davidj2054, Headbomb, Neil916, AntiVandalBot, Gioto, Luna Santin, Lfstevens, Aquaponics, JAnDbot, Dun-canHill, MER-C, The Transhumanist, Struthious Bandersnatch, Magioladitis, Pedro, VoABot II, Dentren, Websterwebfoot, Wikidudeman, Liverpool Scouse, Eilicea, Kajasudhakarababu, Think outside the box, Recurring dreams, Nposs, Dirac66, Patstuart, Fortunehunter, Mart-inBot, ExplicitImplicity, Asy oz, Penikett, David.j.james, R'n'B, CommonsDelinker, VirtualDelight, Paranomia, J.delanoy, M9jorodb, Un-cle Dick, Dlandeck, Albemarle24, Katalaveno, Melanochromis, Hellaenergy, Cobi, Vanished user 47736712, Akgb, Jevansen, Vanished user 39948282, Deweaver, Ja 62, Useight, James g2, Malik Shabazz, VolkovBot, Johnfos, AlnoktaBOT, Tenacious D Fan, Chafed, Philip Trueman, Mike Cline, Jomasecu, Java7837, Mussel~enwiki, Louieais, Wikiisawesome, Earthdirt, Telecineguy, Doug, Insanity Incarnate, Caltas, Lead-SongDog, Eikenhein, JerrySteal, Elfino, Flyer22 Reborn, Bob98133, Seacucumber06, Oxymoron83, AngelOfSadness, Lightmouse, Urvan25, Cngoulimis, ClueBot, Skyblue27, Mahograin, ImperfectlyInformed, Unbuttered Parsnip, R000t, Hysocc, Frmorrison, Blanchardb, Emorsso, Excirial, Gnome de plume, Jusdafax, Eeekster, Iner22, Iohannes Animosus, Snacks, Lorenzojuarez, Aitias, 7, Certes, Versus22, DumZiBoT, XLinkBot, Ec2rmngf, Dthomsen8, Little Mountain 5, Avoided, Doc9871, Drembody, Thatguyflint, Kembangraps, ERK, Mr0t1633, Wikeper-mie, Macarte1, Robadue, Hattar393, Ad23Lyall, Fluffernutter, CactusWriter, LinkFA-Bot, Tide rolls, Gail, Zorrobot, Innapoy, Snaily, Legobot, Luckas-bot, Yobot, Sanyi4, Spindoctor69, Gr8bushman, Sfucss, Eric-Wester, Tempodivalse, Onthewater, AnomieBOT, Tryptofish, JackieBot, LlywelynII, Kingpin13, Flewis, Bluerasberry, Materialscientist, Citation bot, ArthurBot, LilHelpa, Xqbot, Sionus, Jtravinternational, Capri-corn42, Nasnema, Mononomic, Hysilvinia, Anna Frodesiak, BulldogBeing, RibotBOT, 78.26, Con-struct, Asfarer, Pkrshark123, FrescoBot, Citation bot 1, Pinethicket, Peltirasia, Adlerbot, Onthegogo, MastiBot, Homo habilis, RazielZero, Kgrad, Jonwood2009, Changewords, To-beBot, DixonDBot, Yunshui, Kalaiarasy, Lotje, Venator, Louis thibault, Ellen243, Merlinsorca, Cmarz, The Utahraptor, RjwilmsiBot, Po-larpanda, DASHBot, Nwvsh, Look2See1, Usermandid, Starcheerspeaksnewslostwars, GoingBatty, Enviromet, JustinTeague, Aodhage, Werieth, AvicBot, ZéroBot, Codi727, مردود طارق إيهاب, RGwroc, Bamyers99, H3llBot, MollyAW, Wingman4l7, Δ, Wikiproject1400, Dotanbarnoy, Rangoon11, Scgillanders, ClueBot NG, Cwmhiraeth, CocuBot, Satellizer, Jba462, Movses-bot, Williamsr14, Sheaian, Valtermas, DrChrissy, Vibhijain, Helpful Pixie Bot, BG19bot, Arnavchaudhary, MKar, Mgraham22, Machage Chacha, AndyyParadise, Egertspirulina, R.moyle, Fishk-ingg, Perky15, Shellfishbiologist, BoathouseBob, Olojames25, ZephyrGem, Factsearch, Zoaelite, ChrisGualtieri, Ngoquangduong, EuroCarGT, Dexbot, Sminthopsis84, Frosty, ComfyKem, Epicgenius, Notaram, Kingofaces43, Pengolodhlerner, Stamptrader, Cooke aquaculture, CJCstu-dent, Bunoso, FourViolas, Xxxxx1239, JDEvergreen, Linkfixed, Mikeysdoyles, Andreagaion, Seasaler, Ayanaeliza, Conservation 436, Boat85, Soda Cqual and Anonymous: 404

- **Beluga caviar** *Source:* https://en.wikipedia.org/wiki/Beluga_caviar?oldid=676323287 *Contributors:* Stan Shebs, Andrewa, Xj14y, Donreed, OldakQuill, Mike R, Dr.frog, Iamunknown, Irrawaddy, Jeltz, Mendaliv, Rjwilmsi, Nightscream, YurikBot, Kafziel, The Ogre, Farmanesh, Bayerischermann, Closedmouth, Shawnc, Katieh5584, SmackBot, Dav2008, Jakz34, OrphanBot, Ser Amantio di Nicolao, The2003s~enwiki, Tawkerbot2, TheHorseCollector, Calmargulis, Anubis3, Porsche997SBS, Eeesh, Visik, HuntClubJoe, CommonsDelinker, Verdatum, Per Hede-tun, Donmike10, Pastordavid, 1812ahill, Gothbag, Philip Trueman, AronR, Humperdink13, Mojoworker, Traveler100, Blue954, AnomieBOT, Citation bot, Egracia, Speednat, Mjnazari, Hari7478, Innotata, DASHBot, Mjaumock, Avdonin, 2tuntony, ClueBot NG, Zed Orkin, KLBot2, Minderwinter, BattyBot, Chirag85, LH90569 and Anonymous: 54

- **Black Sea** *Source:* https://en.wikipedia.org/wiki/Black_Sea?oldid=685715018 *Contributors:* Paul Drye, The Epopt, WojPob, Mav, Bryan Derk-sen, Andre Engels, PierreAbbat, William Avery, SimonP, Peterlin~enwiki, Heron, N8chz, Olivier, Edward, Ixfd64, Iluvcapra, Looxix~enwiki, Ahoerstemeier, Dgaubin, Den fjättrade ankan~enwiki, Mihai~enwiki, Amcaja, Bogdangiusca, Djnjwd, Andres, Alex756, Davidzuccaro, Michaeln, Gutza, Rednblu, Wik, Haukurth, Peregrine981, Tpbradbury, Nv8200pa, Shizhao, Joy, Wetman, Shafei, Pollinator, Jeffq, Carlos-suarez46, Robbot, Altenmann, Romanm, Naddy, Mirv, GarnetRChaney, Alan Liefting, David Gerard, Arnout Steenhoek~enwiki, DocWatson42, Pmaguire, Lproven, Lethe, Monedula, Yak, Wwoods, Gilgamesh~enwiki, Dmmaus, Mboverload, Macrakis, Avala, Bobblewik, Mmm~enwiki, Ato, Utcursch, Pgan002, Knutux, Quadell, Antandrus, Bgbot, Eregli bob, Mzajac, Kesac, Dmaftei, Icairns, Irpen, Mschlindwein, Klemen Koc-jancic, Zeman, Lacrimosus, Thorwald, D6, Freakofnurture, Heryu~enwiki, Wfaulk, Jiy, Rich Farmbrough, Guanabot, Oska, Florian Blaschke, Leukonoe, Kostja, Dbachmann, Pavel Vozenilek, SpookyMulder, Bender235, El C, Kwamikagami, Chairboy, Jantangring, Aude, Art LaPella, Mentatus, Bobo192, Hurricane111, Elipongo, Cohesion, Man vyi, Nk, Obradovic Goran, Jumbuck, LibraryLion, Alansohn, Eric Kvaalen, Arthena, Alyeska, Geo Swan, JohnAlbertRigali, AzaToth, Alex '05, Cdc, Wdfarmer, Hu, Malo, Alinor, DreamGuy, Kober, Computerjoe, Ghirlandajo, Oleg Alexandrov, Postrach, Stemonitis, Woohookitty, Sinanozel, Georgia guy, Sburke, StradivariusTV, NormanEinstein, Steinbach, Arzachel, Sengkang, Arifhidayat, Dysepsion, BD2412, Qwertyus, Rjwilmsi, Ceinturion, Hiberniantears, MZMcBride, Tawker, Vegaswikian, Nneonneo, ElKevbo, Peripatetic, SeanMack, MapsMan, Titoxd, FlaBot, SchuminWeb, Latka, Itinerant1, Rune.welsh, RexNL, Gurch, Jere-mygbyrne, Goudzovski, Chobot, Moocha, Bgwhite, Roboto de Ajvol, YurikBot, RobotE, TodorBozhinov, Ilia~enwiki, RussBot, PetrosGreek, Fabartus, Red Slash, Amaltsev, Acefox, Cdbavg400, Gaius Cornelius, Macukali, Absolutadam802, Marcus Cyron, Shanel, Wiki alf, Aeusoes1, Grafen, Howcheng, Dppowell, Aldux, AdiJapan, Zwobot, Syrthiss, Gadget850, Smaines, TransUtopian, Culmination, Whitejay251, Orioane, Arthur Rubin, Josh3580, Barbatus, Argo Navis, Jonathan.s.kt, GrinBot~enwiki, KNHaw, Draicone, Vanka5, Attilios, RupertMillard, Smack-Bot, Unschool, David Kernow, Argyll Lassie, Unyoyega, Pgk, Holon67, Bomac, KocjoBot~enwiki, Big Adamsky, Clpo13, Nickst, Dandin1, Eskimbot, Onebravemonkey, Alsandro, Bertilvidet, Yamaguchi 先生, Gilliam, Hmains, Desiphral, IanDavies, Bluebot, D.Papuashvili, MK8, Enkyklios, Thumperward, Preslav, MalafayaBot, Roscelese, Timneu22, Hibernian, Cretanforever, Akanemoto, Bazonka, PureRED, DHN-bot~enwiki, Colonies Chris, Darth Panda, George Ho, Can't sleep, clown will eat me, KevM, Rrburke, Bardsandwarriors, SundarBot, Oli b, Seduisant, Khoikhoi, Jmlk17, Sirgregmac, Funky Monkey, EVula, Ryan Roos, Politis, Henning Makholm, Buidinhthiem, DDima, Sealevelns, Bejnar, SashatoBot, Lambiam, Mukadderat, Zahid Abdassabur, Vgy7ujm, J 1982, Mgiganteus1, Green Giant, Ckatz, The Man in Question,

Hvn0413, Tasc, Xiaphias, Don Alessandro, EdC~enwiki, Ginkgo100, Levineps, BranStark, Simon12, Iridescent, Dekaels~enwiki, Joseph Solis in Australia, Shoeofdeath, Mclowes, UncleDouggie, Twas Now, CapitalR, Courcelles, Chicho Ficho, KHasek, JForget, Stifynsemons, CmdrObot, Andrew Luimes, Van helsing, BeenAroundAWhile, Ldingley, Jgmccue, WATP, Marcelo Pinto, Jenniearcheo, CWY2190, Dgw, N2e, ProfessorPaul, Cydebot, TurcoGrande, Eerdem, A Softer Answer, Eu.stefan, Doug Weller, Jalen~enwiki, Throquzum, Omicronpersei8, Zalgo, Oleksii0, Mattisse, HJJHolm, JamesAM, Thijs!bot, Epbr123, Biruitorul, Olahus, Tsogo3, S Marshall, Headbomb, Marek69, Lethargy, Missvain, John254, Pmrobert49, Bethpage89, Dawnseeker2000, Escarbot, Mentifisto, Fedayee, Seaphoto, Erwin85Bot, Jj137, Madbehemoth, Cheater512, Kapustin, Yellowdesk, Krellkraver, Mikenorton, JAnDbot, Deflective, Husond, DuncanHill, MER-C, Gioleba, Tyrc, Calak~enwiki, .anacondabot, Pakord, Repku, KEKPΩΨ, Magioladitis, Bongwarrior, VoABot II, Meredyth, Shawiki, Think outside the box, Korenyuk, Gezegen1988, The Anomebot2, Zandweb~enwiki, Birelc, Catgut, Cmontero, DerHexer, GregU, Lenticel, Pax:Vobiscum, ScoreTanley, HolePen, Rickard Vogelberg, NatureA16, Zdf, MartinBot, Kaickul, Poeloq, R'n'B, MerryXIV, CommonsDelinker, AlexiusHoratius, Artcrp, Tgeairn, Gligan, J.delanoy, LordAnubisBOT, TheTrojanHought, Betswiki, Rosenknospe, Robertgreer, Erdeniss, Cometstyles, Squids and Chips, Idioma-bot, Wikieditor06, VolkovBot, Doktor Gonzo, Off-shell, ABF, Jmrowland, Shinju, Dom Kaos, TXiKiBoT, By ram~enwiki, Seboden, Rei-bot, Black Foil, Corvus cornix, Szlam, Leafyplant, Abdullais4u, Crònica~enwiki, Bearian, Maxim, Ratagosk, Doug, Levani110, Sensei333, Enviroboy, Cnilep, Kulikovsky, Insanity Incarnate, AlleborgoBot, Symane, Legoktm, Finnrind, NHRHS2010, EmxBot, SieBot, Matt.s.wise, Mycomp, Simplifier, Gerakibot, Phe-bot, Caltas, Blacktayf, Andrewjlockley, Til Eulenspiegel, Flyer22 Reborn, LibStar, Yerpo, KoshVorlon, Lightmouse, WacoJacko, BenoniBot~enwiki, Mátyás, Medievil ag, Jacob.jose, Aiaagna, Paulinho28, Addd wiki, ImageRemovalBot, Athenean, Martarius, Sfan00 IMG, ClueBot, Thewandererreturns, Binksternet, Badger Drink, Rodhullandemu, Cancelor, Drmies, Joao Xavier, CounterVandalismBot, Niceguyedc, The Wild West guy, Ashdod, Piledhigheranddeeper, Pras, DragonBot, Icotoi, Jotterbot, SchreiberBike, Thehelpfulone, Thingg, Avidius, Burner0718, DumZiBoT, Razvanus~enwiki, Janos Kurko, Helixweb, Xzibit911, Robveget, FellGleaming, Little Mountain 5, Olaffpomona, WikHead, NellieBly, Mifter, Rividian, Catgirl, Good Olfactory, Jadtnr1, Harjk, Mr0t1633, Rddddavid, Justloop, Shephia, Sergey mt guide, Blethering Scot, USchick, CarsracBot, Afxdgsdfg, AndersBot, Exor674, LinkFA-Bot, Numbo3-bot, Ehrenkater, Ondewelle, Yastanovog, HerculeBot, Geographyfanatic, Moni8909, Luckas-bot, BaldPark, Yobot, Amirobot, Yngvadottir, Mmxx, THEN WHO WAS PHONE?, Ayrton Prost, Mirgheca, Realjackal~enwiki, MacTire02, AnomieBOT, Piano non troppo, Ulric1313, Materialscientist, Citation bot, Koshmany, ArthurBot, საბაწმოა, Xqbot, Timir2, Gwaz, The Banner, Hanberke, Jeune17, Tyrol5, Levan666, Logos, Ruy Pugliesi, Fattonyni, J04n, GrouchoBot, Vincent pearse, Xuz, Shakarian141, Liuboznatelen, Omnipaedista, Haljordangl13, RibotBOT, Mttll, Nedim Ardoğa, Sophus Bie, GhalyBot, Shadowjams, Eugene-elgato, Soxfan522, Charity6ks, FrescoBot, Originalwana, Lothar von Richthofen, Truthishly, Tegel, Pinethicket, Rayshade, Metricmike, HRoestBot, Anonymous the Editor, Alonso de Mendoza, Trijnstel, Moryak, MJ94, Melba1, Rushbugled13, Seryo93, BRUTE, Midnight Comet, Turkishhistorian, Tralalix, Tim1357, TobeBot, Cazaresulina, Bogdan Muraru, Ollios, Mishae, Serdarozdil, Tbhotch, Reach Out to the Truth, Lolstarkey, TjBot, Fiftytwo thirty, Avatarion, EmausBot, WikitanvirBot, Immunize, Racerx11, SteveM123, Heljqfy, Winner 42, HarDNox, Wikipelli, Umumu, Ykraps, ZéroBot, BAICAN XXX, Naviguessor, \suicidalmidgit, Pokeyclap7, NataliyaVl, QEDK, Lothar Klaic, Brandmeister, Sahimrobot, KazekageTR, Ant12108, Ivannopulo, Puffin, ChuispastonBot, Forever Dusk, DASHBotAV, ClueBot NG, Ykvach, Again Backagain, Lemkey, Ryanbush2011, Observerq, This lousy T-shirt, Defooman, Me25.26, Frietjes, ComtesseDeMingrelie, Lucia lll, Sc135, Widr, WikiPuppies, Ρουθραμώτης, Helpful Pixie Bot, Alexandru M., Tholme, HMSSolent, Newyork1501, Curb Chain, Strike Eagle, Gob Lofa, Bibcode Bot, Hengist Pod, BG19bot, TheSockofAges, M0rphzone, Davidiad, Megakacktus, Rgbc2000, Utkhkm, Hillcrest98, Marcel.Melanson, Xxshannonrawrxx, Maurice Flesier, Glacialfox, Sergio zevs, Dourios, AndyKamy, Tntman34, Geohem, Eflatmajor7th, Cyberbot II, ChrisGualtieri, Khazar2, MadGuy7023, JYBot, E4024, Dexbot, SantoshBot, Saketsahu, Ukrained2012, Patlack, Pizzazzpizzazz123, AmaryllisGardener, Charles.millar, Hannah.abts, Mihai Pintilie, Loverbek, Cizlini, Kind Tennis Fan, Motique, Malinkimuk, Belasolve, Ahlert1500, Gts-tg, Centromax, Andrew J.Kurbiko, Ethically Yours, Aleksander Kaasik, Ddeggin1562, Monkbot, IsaColeman, Captcrissey, YoungLion88, Mikhael the Brave, Lies from the tablecloth, AwesomeSky, Sb2s3, Janissarywiki, Krastama, KasparBot, İslamic.Turk, Costinel 06 and Anonymous: 551

- **Caspian Sea** *Source:* https://en.wikipedia.org/wiki/Caspian_Sea?oldid=690594560 *Contributors:* Magnus Manske, Vicki Rosenzweig, Mav, Bryan Derksen, XJaM, Olivier, Fransvannes, Frecklefoot, Edward, Nealmcb, Patrick, Michael Hardy, Menchi, Mic, Ixfd64, Cyde, GTBacchus, Docu, Den fjättrade ankan~enwiki, K1, Lancevortex, Raven in Orbit, Jonadab~enwiki, WhisperToMe, Tpbradbury, Taxman, EikwaR, Joseaperez, Joy, Geraki, AnonMoos, Wetman, Bcorr, Proteus, Finlay McWalter, Shafei, Jeffq, Carlossuarez46, Robbot, Tomchiukc, Moncrief, Altenmann, Dann, Rholton, Ktotam, Mervyn, Guy Peters, Adam78, Alan Liefting, Decumanus, Connelly, Sina~enwiki, Ryanrs, Monedula, Tom Radulovich, Everyking, Wyss, Curps, Cantus, Beardo, Tokenizeman, Bobblewik, Edcolins, Golbez, Knutux, Zeimusu, Antandrus, Kichigai, Tothebarricades.tk, Zfr, Oknazevad, Mschlindwein, Demiurge, D6, Jayjg, DanielCD, Diagonalfish, Rich Farmbrough, Vsmith, Rupertslander, Parishan, Kostja, Dbachmann, Mani1, Byrial, SpookyMulder, Bender235, Kbh3rd, Doron, El C, Szquirrel, Kwamikagami, Bobo192, Teriyakipants, Foobaz, Darwinek, Firespeaker, QuantumEleven, Jumbuck, Red Winged Duck, Msh210, Gary, Anthony Appleyard, MrTree, Eleland, Duffman~enwiki, Buaidh, Arthena, Mr Adequate, Keenan Pepper, Pouya, Apoc2400, Theodore Kloba, Alinor, Wtmitchell, *Kat*, Zereshk, HenryLi, Deror avi, Thryduulf, Miaow Miaow, Jacobolus, Squibix, Benbest, SP-KP, Tabletop, Schzmo, NormanEinstein, Sengkang, Kralizec!, Xiong Chiamiov, TaivoLinguist, Chupon, Magister Mathematicae, BD2412, Rjwilmsi, Koavf, Kinu, Vary, Cxbrx, Rschen7754, Jehochman, FlaBot, Chiklit, Crazycomputers, Goudzovski, Malhonen, Russavia, Chobot, Metropolitan90, Bgwhite, PainMan, WriterHound, E Pluribus Anthony, Vmenkov, YurikBot, Wavelength, Radishes, RobotE, Brandmeister (old), RussBot, Anonymous editor, Hellbus, Hydrargyrum, Stephenb, Gaius Cornelius, Absolutadam802, Friday, NawlinWiki, ENeville, Boneheadmx, ChadThomson, Vika~enwiki, Rupert Clayton, Moe Epsilon, DeadEyeArrow, Bota47, Ali1986, Kmusser, Citynoise, Lt-wiki-bot, Mehrdadd, Arthur Rubin, Moogsi, SMcCandlish, Charlik, Mursel, Scoutersig, Ordinary Person, Nelson50, Otebig, Argo Navis, Eaefremov, Kungfuadam, Jonathan.s.kt, Roke, SmackBot, Ashenai, Unschool, Unyoyega, C.Fred, Grandmaster, Jacek Kendysz, Lsommerer, TimBits, Eskimbot, Brianski, Hmains, Betacommand, Carl.bunderson, Durova, Amatulic, Kurykh, MK8, Anchoress, MalafayaBot, Moshe Constantine Hassan Al-Silverburg, Akanemoto, Bazonka, Zinneke, DHN-bot~enwiki, Huji, Garydave, JustUser, OrphanBot, Nixeagle, MJCdetroit, JonHarder, Backspace, SundarBot, Khoikhoi, Nepaheshgar, DMacks, Ultraexactzz, Devoblue, Varg hashish, Deiz, Bejnar, Pilotguy, Snowgrouse, SashatoBot, Lambiam, Bcasterline, Ashinpt, Kuru, J 1982, Shadowlynk, JorisvS, Minna Sora no Shita, Mgiganteus1, Balladeer222, Mare Nostrum, Hvn0413, Geologyguy, Houshyar, Texas Dervish, Dabean, Jose77, Udibi, Levineps, Iridescent, Octane, Courcelles, Ziusudra, Tawkerbot2, Mrjahan, Shahbz, JForget, Lamiot, Woudloper, Georgiablue, Cydebot, Danrok, Parslad, Languagehat, Gogo Dodo, Foofiticus, Tec15, Scooteristi, Sloth monkey, Eu.stefan, Falcanary, Dyanega, CieloEstrellado, Bryan P. C. C., JamesAM, Thijs!bot, Barticus88, Tsogo3, HappyInGeneral, Tobz1000, Mojo Hand, Marek69, Lethargy, Ufwuct, CharlotteWebb, Zink53, Hajji Piruz, AntiVandalBot, Seaphoto, Paulatthehug, KP Botany, NSH001, College Watch, Noodlenut, Darklilac, Babakexorramdin, Sluzzelin, JAnDbot, MER-C, Skomorokh, MarkTwainOnIce, Andonic, Barefact, PhilKnight, Adamnyc77, .anacondabot, Steve Bob, Magioladitis, WolfmanSF, VoABot II, Wikidudeman, Hasek is the best, SSZ, Daarznieks, Taamu, AsgardBot, LorenzoB, Beagel, Halogenated, JaGa, Baristarim, NatureA16, Sicaspi, MartinBot, CommonsDelinker, AlexiusHoratius, Beit Or, J.delanoy, M samadi, DandyDan2007, Anoushirvan, Nimafade, Smeira, Scout1, Naniwako, Plasticup, LeighvsOptimvsMaximvs, Aliemadi, Boothferry, Saguamundi, Idioma-bot, Funandtrvl, VolkovBot, Gamer112, Halayman, Platinumsound, Firstorm, Gaianauta, Matterfoot, Zarcusian, TXiKiBoT, Mahaexp, Ryan shell, Argooya, JhsBot, Auzzyboy92, Mirimax Maiden, Fishhook, Alborz Fallah, Goirish4life, Ace Telephone, Spinningspark, Le Fou, Symane, Mohonu, EmxBot, GoonerDP, Arasha, SieBot, WereSpielChequers, Gerakibot, Juntiforces, Mazdakabedi, GlassCobra, Happysailor, Cojo55, Vmrgrsergr, Estropes, Jakejoh1, Rosiestep, Alefbe, Jacob.jose, Paulinho28, Vonones, Martarius, ClueBot, WurmWoode, Mild Bill Hiccup, DragonBot, Rhododendrites, MacedonianBoy, Mikalsvorsky, Jotterbot, Iohannes Animosus, Azerturku, Razorflame, JasonAQuest, BOTarate, Macabu~enwiki, Mlaffs, Ardeshire Babakan, Thingg, SoilMan2007, Versus22, Exuwon, Mrmpsy, Rosywounds, DumZiBoT, Kiensvay, Robveget, Pichpich, Koumz, Ihategv, Little Mountain 5, WikHead, Mifter, Fariborzh, Good Olfactory, Addbot, Mr0t1633, Roentgenium111, Willking1979, Micahmedia, Some jerk on the Internet, Lyr Sol, Timour Derevenko, CarsracBot, DFS454, CUSENZA Mario, LinkFA-Bot, Numbo3-bot, Lightbot, Zorrobot, Greyhood, Arbitrarily0, Tikar aurum, Everyme, Luckas-bot, Shannon1, Yobot, Fraggle81, Amirobot, Guy1890, Clíodhna-2, Azylber, KamikazeBot, MacTire02, AnomieBOT, Galoubet, Proger, Piano non troppo, Xufanc, Camfordwiki, Kingpin13, Hurtetusda, Materialscientist, Gamera1123, ArthurBot, DirlBot, Ayda D, Xqbot, Timir2, 康非字典, Asif Qasımov, DSisyphBot, Hanberke, Tyrol5, Almabot, GrouchoBot, Frosted14, Iranian agent006, ProtectionTaggingBot, RibotBOT, Nedim Ardoğa, Fattyfatsteve, Brutaldeluxe, Trafford09, GhalyBot, Chrisf122, Eugene-elgato, Bluekit, Thehelpfulbot, FrescoBot, Tobby72, Energyworm, Persia2, Kheo17, Pinethicket, I dream of horses, 10metreh, Jonesey95, Rameshngbot, Ghazne, MastiBot, Yutsi, MertyWiki, Vandidaad, Comancheros, 720-b.a.e.n., Imruz, TobeBot, NortyNort, Fama Clamosa, J-Scythian, AnastassiyaL, Fox Wilson, علی ویکی, Juybari, Phil A. Fry, Farhikht, Hari7478, Persia2099, DARTH SIDIOUS 2, Onel5969, RjwilmsiBot, Beyond My Ken, Slon02, CalicoCatLover, Kamran the Great, EmausBot, John of Reading, Orphan Wiki, Racerx11, GoingBatty, RA0808, Iranianson, مانفى, Wcwardrn, Rarevogel, Wikipelli, Sandielm, Maitreyo jatak, Evanh2008, HiW-Bot, ZéroBot, DragonTiger23, Shannon1, Sefer ibrahim, A930913, H3llBot, Condylarth, 2ravens, Alborzagros, ChuispastonBot, Teh klev, Saeedclever, Mjbmrbot, 2649pie, بزرگ شمال, ClueBot NG, Ykvach, GoetheFromm, Gareth Griffith-Jones, Osario~enwiki, Piast93, Joefromrandb, Movses-bot, Ebrahimi-amir, IfYouDoIfYouDon't, Rjbronn, Михаил Марчук, Kasirbot, AlwaysUnite, Helpful Pixie Bot, LuXou95, Calabe1992, Gob Lofa, Ymblanter, Vagobot, Petrarchan47, Jahani65, Oulipo2, Sasan Geranmehr, MusikAnimal, AvocatoBot, Carcajada, Abuubayda, Gazaneh, Xooon, Meatsgains, Farhang.amini, Pseudofusulina, Ray Garraty, Selcsia, Basp1, Saule83, Dexbot, राजेन्द्र मिश्र, ChemTerm, Jo-Jo Eumerus, Greenmenforpotus, HistoryofIran, Siktirgitir, Tentinator, Mitrakana, Alfinmiqradzcurrent, LouisAragon, Motique, Jellysandwich0, Filedelinkerbot, Tigercompanion25, M60801, Peter238, Poseidon Nep, Haßan, LOLrandompeople20, Mohammadgw, Njaredp, Last edited by:, Katenzz, Frank nl, Turcoman turk, KasparBot, Kavianrezaei, Promopersia, Laiza 123, Pterus, Jtesmer, Loïcdu92, Esmaeil mirzadeh, Lyarrr 2.0, Daniel0816 and Anonymous: 552

- **Caviar spoon** *Source:* https://en.wikipedia.org/wiki/Caviar_spoon?oldid=650553984 *Contributors:* Enric Naval, DoriSmith, Verne Equinox, Magioladitis, R'n'B, Maproom, Trilobitealive, Yobot, Richigi, AnomieBOT, RevelationDirect, GoingBatty, Richjordana, ClueBot NG, Tashif, BattyBot, Monkbot, Brenne and Anonymous: 8

- **Coregonus** *Source:* https://en.wikipedia.org/wiki/Coregonus?oldid=690453504 *Contributors:* Lee Daniel Crocker, Rmhermen, Nate Silva, Heron, Pcb21, Tkinias, Andres, Gdr, SwimmingLlama, Bobo192, Isfisk, Graham87, Eubot, Gdrbot, Dj Capricorn, Melly42, Alan Millar, Lt-wiki-bot, Pmaas, Kerripaul, Fralambert, Droll, DHN-bot~enwiki, Eliezg, Snowmanradio, SirIsaacBrock, Lokolskaia, GrahamBould, Bruinfan12, Ark-pl, Thijs!bot, Nipisiquit, OhanaUnited, Peter3, Balloonguy, R'n'B, CommonsDelinker, Idioma-bot, TXiKiBoT, A4bot, Mohonu, Lightmouse, OKBot, Niceguyedc, Addbot, Olaff, Lightbot, Luckas-bot, Yobot, ArthurBot, GrouchoBot, RibotBOT, Simuliid, MastiBot, Innotata, ZéroBot, Hwdenie, Ykvach, Divingpetrel, Caftaric and Anonymous: 10

- **Cristoforo di Messisbugo** *Source:* https://en.wikipedia.org/wiki/Cristoforo_di_Messisbugo?oldid=583077488 *Contributors:* Macrakis, Klemen Kocjancic, FeanorStar7, Bgwhite, Tony1, Ser Amantio di Nicolao, SchreiberBike, Addbot, RjwilmsiBot, Giovanni-da-Ferrara and Anonymous: 2

- **God Loves Caviar** *Source:* https://en.wikipedia.org/wiki/God_Loves_Caviar?oldid=690600540 *Contributors:* ISasha, Hairy Dude, Lugnuts, Addbot, Taketa, Eipnvn, RjwilmsiBot, ZéroBot, SporkBot, Odythal and Anonymous: 3

- **Ioannis Varvakis** *Source:* https://en.wikipedia.org/wiki/Ioannis_Varvakis?oldid=684765255 *Contributors:* Dimadick, Darwinek, Ghirlandajo, PANONIAN, Woohookitty, Rjwilmsi, ISasha, Damac, RussBot, Syrthiss, Segv11, SmackBot, FocalPoint, Commander Keane bot, Hmains, Colonies Chris, Egsan Bacon, Cplakidas, CmdrObot, Cydebot, JamesAM, BigrTex, MishaPan, Peeperman, Monegasque, Phso2, SchreiberBike, Dthomsen8, Addbot, Yobot, AnomieBOT, Erud, Omnipaedista, Full-date unlinking bot, Greco22, Lotje, RjwilmsiBot, John of Reading, ZéroBot, McZusatz, Psarrianos, Decathlete, HellenicLiverpudlianCR7, KasparBot and Anonymous: 7

- **Ossetra** *Source:* https://en.wikipedia.org/wiki/Ossetra?oldid=677920178 *Contributors:* Dominus, Dr.frog, GL, The Ogre, IceCreamAntisocial, BorgQueen, Patiwat, Verne Equinox, Jakz34, Bluebot, The2003s~enwiki, Mfield, Cydebot, Reywas92, Visik, Tahnan, CurranH, Legobot, Yobot, Champlax, Some standardized rigour, FrescoBot, Wymep, Mjnazari, Anfis Katechkin, Ebe123, Melic1313, Erianna, Helpful Pixie Bot, Northamerica1000, Vanishingcattle, Marcionist, Sahstar, Le Grand Bleu, Vieque, Falco525, Wickedfrostguppy and Anonymous: 9

- **Ovary** *Source:* https://en.wikipedia.org/wiki/Ovary?oldid=690198009 *Contributors:* AxelBoldt, Taw, Alex.tan, Andre Engels, Youssefsan, Vanderesch, PierreAbbat, Karen Johnson, Robert Foley, Someone else, Ixfd64, Karada, NuclearWinner, Ellywa, Habj, Emperorbma, Marshman, Saltine, Raul654, Pollinator, Robbot, RedWolf, Romanm, Nilmerg, Huckfinne, Isopropyl, Diberri, Marnanel, Barbara Shack, Mintleaf~enwiki, Leflyman, Jrquinlisk, Michael Devore, Slowking Man, Antandrus, Alteripse, Jossi, Tsemii, Szquirrel, Shanes, Bobo192, Arcadian, Kjkolb, Tritium6, Minghong, Ranveig, Alansohn, Anthony Appleyard, Keenan Pepper, Mysdaao, Osmodiar, Mauvila, Adrian.benko, Nuno Tavares, Macronyx~enwiki, MONGO, Isnow, Eras-mus, Wisq, Graham87, Paiste~enwiki, FreplySpang, BorgHunter, Rjwilmsi, RiseAbove, Tangotango, Uwe Gille, FlaBot, Naraht, CiaPan, Chobot, YurikBot, Chanlyn, Huw Powell, RussBot, Pigman, Hydrargyrum, Ajp, Rsrikanth05, Wimt, Bug42, Dysmorodrepanis~enwiki, Syrthiss, EEMIV, Mholland, Open2universe, Lt-wiki-bot, Kungfuadam, Lyrl, NeilN, Paul Erik, DVD R W, タチコマ robot, SmackBot, Andreas Erick~enwiki, Brya, Unyoyega, Rrius, KocjoBot~enwiki, Delldot, Eskimbot, Canthusus, Ohnoitsjamie, Agateller, Berton, Deli nk, Akanemoto, Colonies Chris, SundarBot, Ratel, Jóna Þorunn, Clicketyclack, Cyberevil, Rory096, CenozoicEra, Soumyasch, 041744, Waggers, Novangelis, Igoldste, Tawkerbot2, Filelakeshoe, The Letter J, Patho~enwiki, Di4gram, Dycedarg, Woudloper, Mcstrother, JohnCD, CWY2190, MarsRover, Cydebot, Treybien, Travelbird, Anthonyhcole, A Softer Answer, DumbBOT, Kozuch, Kobe91288, Didohotep~enwiki, Thijs!bot, Epbr123, Massimo Macconi, Escarbot, Mentifisto, AntiVandalBot, Ozgod, Joehall45, JAnDbot, Carolyns, Bongwarrior, VoABot II, QuizzicalBee, Jon f, Rivertorch, Gr1st, Janette.quennell, Edward321, Mmustafa~enwiki, Anaxial, Gidip, Keith D, R'n'B,

CommonsDelinker, AlexiusHoratius, Erkan Yilmaz, Watch37264, J.delanoy, Pharaoh of the Wizards, Trusilver, EscapingLife, Wilsbadkarma, Ginsengbomb, Mrob27, LEHarth, Mikael Häggström, Jasonasosa, Glacious, Vanished user 39948282, RJASE1, Idioma-bot, Spellcast, Petergreen12, PissonDemand, Jeff G., AlnoktaBOT, Philip Trueman, TXiKiBoT, GDonato, Loserbackpacker, Guldenat, Monkeynoze, Grafic, Gillyweed, Arm86, Neothe, Why Not A Duck, Alcmaeonid, AlleborgoBot, Sleep is good, SieBot, Flyer22 Reborn, Doctorfluffy, Oxymoron83, BenoniBot~enwiki, Patilsaurabhr, Into The Fray, Invertzoo, ClueBot, The Thing That Should Not Be, Jcpstud, DAStroh, Briankohl, Arunsingh16, Matticooper, Chrisbarnes20048, Walkingstick3, Thingg, Vanished User 1004, Rey101011, Avoided, WikHead, PL290, Addbot, Dryphi, DaughterofSun, Fieldday-sunday, Nilsonne, Download, CarsracBot, Bernstein0275, AndersBot, Christopher140691, 5 albert square, Numbo3-bot, Prim Ethics, Tide rolls, H3mcostlymilk, Maily812, David0811, Jarble, 2enable, Luckas-bot, Doctorruthshopeful, THEN WHO WAS PHONE?, IW.HG, XL2D, BLAKEWRAPP, Materialscientist, Driv3r89, Citation bot, Xqbot, Anders Torlind, Micemug, Datguydurr, Nuviapalomar, Pepemonbu, Amaury, Schekinov Alexey Victorovich, FrescoBot, VS6507, Recognizance, Pinethicket, I dream of horses, Adlerbot, BobJudy, Nicholascage69, Wikitanvir, SpaceFlight89, ScottMHoward, RandomStringOfCharacters, Ambenoxan, TobeBot, Fama Clamosa, MrX, Igotnolife, Rmcusc, A p3rson, Diannaa, Jhenderson777, DrBuzz2, Tbhotch, Fruitboot2009, DARTH SIDIOUS 2, RjwilmsiBot, Cornellalum, Agent Smith (The Matrix), Ibbn, YEloi, Tommy2010, Gailabby, K6ka, Kmoksy, Werieth, Imperial Monarch, Katherine.munn1, Zaher.Kadour, SporkBot, ChuispastonBot, ClueBot NG, Intoronto1125, Arne Saknussem, Skrawk, Brickmack, Jk2q3jrklse, Jorgenev, HMSSolent, BG19bot, JarritoFJ, John tickle, MusikAnimal, Goldster5, NotWith, Anatomist90, SaminTietokirja, Poongus, Jeanloujustine, Schafhirt, Turbo teabagger, MadGuy7023, MisterJS, Orangeflavoured99, Dexbot, Yogwi21, JakobSteenberg, Fox2k11, MyNipsGivMeTips, SANDQICH, Meena10, Zippedleader070, Ugog Nizdast, LT910001, Ginsuloft, Drstephen.kennedy, Tn9005, Quinnhelmig, Monkbot, TrollZayn, Karinpower, Royerlraph79, Tilifa Ocaufa, Mebutler443, Get333, KasparBot, Supdiop 2, Rd237, THEYROBBEDUS, Miladkarimii, S.pparkle and Anonymous: 283

- **Pasteurization** *Source:* https://en.wikipedia.org/wiki/Pasteurization?oldid=688576919 *Contributors:* Kpjas, WojPob, Tarquin, Koyaanis Qatsi, Alex.tan, LA2, William Avery, Ben-Zin~enwiki, Edward, Dwmyers, Ixfd64, TUF-KAT, Aarchiba, Julesd, Habj, Wnissen, Lommer, Timwi, Bemoeial, Ike9898, Pietrosperoni, Calieber, Robbot, RedWolf, Ancheta Wis, SmileyDude, BenFrantzDale, Tom harrison, Mboverload, Delta G, Wmahan, Chowbok, Utcursch, Antandrus, Beland, OverlordQ, Mukerjee, Jossi, Jokestress, JeffreyN, Jutta, Chrisbolt, Corti, Dr.frog, Jayjg, Wikiti, Mattman723, Rich Farmbrough, Alistair1978, ESkog, Andrejj, CanisRufus, Diomidis Spinellis, Bobo192, Spalding, Johnkarp, Smalljim, Ukeu, Jojit fb, Pschemp, Haham hanuka, Nsaa, Alansohn, Sligocki, Velella, Simbamangu, Harej, Gene Nygaard, Dan100, ChrisJMoor, Richard Arthur Norton (1958-), Plindberg, Woohookitty, Camw, JeremyA, BlaiseFEgan, Frungi, Eras-mus, Paullb, Jon Harald Søby, Palica, Mandarax, Graham87, Pmj, Ketiltrout, Rjwilmsi, Snowhare, Georgelazenby, TBHecht, Aerotheque, SchuminWeb, StephanCom, Nihiltres, RexNL, Redwolf24, Valermos, Quuxplusone, Stormwatch, Parutakupiu, King of Hearts, Emerymat, Chobot, UkPaolo, YurikBot, Wavelength, NTBot~enwiki, Jimp, Epolk, Mskfisher, RadioFan2 (usurped), Stephenb, Manop, CambridgeBayWeather, Wimt, NawlinWiki, Oberst, SigPig, Howcheng, Kkmurray, Vonfraginoff, Tom Sponheim, Closedmouth, Belgrano~enwiki, Johnsu01, 2fort5r, Chriswaterguy, Kungfuadam, Junglecat, Auroranorth, Dlainhart, NetRolller 3D, Rcronk, SmackBot, Vald, Sunkorg, Verne Equinox, Darklock, Likethesky, Gaff, Yamaguchi 先生, Gilliam, Tyciol, Jibbajabba, DavidJField, Postoak, Viewfinder, Gruzd, Can't sleep, clown will eat me, Vanis314, Sommers, Rmcgehee, Paolor, Thisisbossi, CanDo, Iridescence, Andrew c, Dan121377, SashatoBot, Sergiu.dumitriu, AThing, Stewie814, SilkTork, Bilby, Muadd, TJ Spyke, Shoeofdeath, Rhetth, Tdrng, Tawkerbot2, CmdrObot, Quaidbrown~enwiki, Valereee, Benightedbastard, Benwildeboer, Dgw, Redeem, Besieged, Khatru2, BlueAg09, Doug Weller, Cielovista, Bulmabriefs144, Krylonblue83, Click23, Epbr123, Kubanczyk, HappyInGeneral, PerfectStorm, Gamer007, Smile a While, Neil916, Bagofants, Uruiamme, Ctayfor, Mentifisto, JEBrown87544, AntiVandalBot, Luna Santin, MangoChicken, Tangerines, TimVickers, MER-C, Fetchcomms, 0s1r1s, Albany NY, Aryaghandikota, Tstrobaugh, Severo, Applescotty, Pablothegreat85, AuburnPilot, Brewhaha@edmc.net, MKFM, Boffob, Vssun, Seashorewiki, DerHexer, MartinBot, Neoprote, Bwtranch, Juansidious, Ccmolik, AlphaEta, J.delanoy, Trusilver, Aussie111, Southockendon, Ginsengbomb, Thegreenj, Tdadamemd, Katalaveno, Gkamel83, M-lemot-dit, Chiswick Chap, SmilesALot, Drdanny, Treisijs, HiEv, Pdcook, Evjammin, Epfleckl, Idioma-bot, X!, VolkovBot, Jeff G., OliviaGuest, Eedo Bee, Philip Trueman, DoorsAjar, TXiKiBoT, Xantar, Ask123, Biggy123456, Qxz, Oxfordwang, Tre1234, Broadbot, Jackfork, Cremepuff222, Joedamadman, DavesPlanet, Meters, Tamorlan, Rob Pommer, Why Not A Duck, Brianga, HiDrNick, Symane, LuigiManiac, Tumadoireacht, EmxBot, Metalmiser, Agvulpine, Tresiden, Andrarias, Sakkura, IanBushfield, Gerakibot, Timothy Cooper, Cwkmail, Calabraxthis, BDUAres, Keilana, Bentogoa, Flyer22 Reborn, Harry~enwiki, BenoniBot~enwiki, Dezwitser, Tony Webster, Denisarona, Ricklaman, MarsInSVG, ClueBot, Sirconnorstack, Fribbler, Traveler100, Binksternet, GorillaWarfare, The Thing That Should Not Be, Narutox82, Jan1nad, Unbuttered Parsnip, WDavis1911, Mizon, OccamzRazor, Bsimons, Mr Accountable, Rukee13, Alexbot, SpikeToronto, Vivio Testarossa, Shinkolobwe, The Founders Intent, Manohaupt~enwiki, Arjayay, Jotterbot, Kakofonous, La Pianista, Thingg, Catastrophicred, SoxBot III, MasterOfHisOwnDomain, Burubuz~enwiki, DumZiBoT, Piotron, Typographical Error, Rror, Ost316, Pediboi~enwiki, Zodon, Hoopingrl, Thatguyflint, Addbot, Proofreader77, Narayansg, Wildilocks, Elishabet, Fluffernutter, Ld100, Christopher140691, Tide rolls, Zorrobot, Billiondollartycoon, Angrysockhop, Legobot, Luckas-bot, Vedran12, Yobot, MattAldred, Fraggle81, Gambori, Donfbreed, Basil.williams, Daniel 1992, AnomieBOT, 1exec1, Six words, Jim1138, Kingpin13, Mostiquera, Materialscientist, RobertEves92, Xqbot, Janet Davis, Gigemag76, Nasnema, Hullo exclamation mark, SamSamSamSamSam, AbigailAbernathy, Loser987, RibotBOT, Jpbarbier, Peanutcactus, Bachcole, Prari, FreyGrimrod, MikeParniak, Arcendet, Pinethicket, LittleWink, Calmer Waters, Rushbugled13, RedBot, Robo Cop, Cubetronic, Celbia, Bogelund, Jashilo, ConcernedVancouverite, Thmc1, Polarbearjack, DARTH SIDIOUS 2, RjwilmsiBot, DASHBot, EmausBot, John of Reading, Axeavius, Tombx, Winner 42, TEHodson, K6ka, Ornithikos, ZéroBot, RaymondKertezc, Anir1uph, Kiwi128, Hazard-SJ, Inniverse, Erianna, Donner60, Melishe, Whoop whoop pull up, Petrb, ClueBot NG, Trainguy1, Gareth Griffith-Jones, CocuBot, MelbourneStar, Widr, Woofenstein, Helpful Pixie Bot, Curb Chain, BG19bot, Booch096, Spout5, Got'a go, Northamerica1000, Wiki13, AvocatoBot, Jenzum, Harizotoh9, Comfr, Testem, The Illusive Man, ChrisGualtieri, Codeh, Ngoquangduong, JYBot, Dexbot, Dkellab, Woombi, Webclient101, Mogism, Tony Mach, ComfyKem, Reatlas, Melonkelon, Tentinator, JustBerry, Jianhui67, I Đb, PortfolioMind, Monkbot, Plokmijnuhbygvtfcdxeszwaq, Grade X, El Chivo 2, Djtfoy, HMSLavender, Uniquemorley26, Rubbish computer, Eliasatahuichi, Jacquelineruizg, Denniscabrams, KasparBot, Kgerow16, MattRanieri and Anonymous: 655

- **Roe** *Source:* https://en.wikipedia.org/wiki/Roe?oldid=689537424 *Contributors:* Tarquin, Sfdan, Stevertigo, Dante Alighieri, Delirium, Timwi, Dysprosia, Selket, Robbot, Altenmann, Raeky, Macrakis, Solipsist, Andycjp, Sonjaaa, Demonslave, Evertype, Gscshoyru, Jcw69, Avihu, MementoVivere, Zondor, Dr.frog, Kyknos, Longhair, Tomgally, Hesperian, Caeruleancentaur, Pogo747, El Raki, Anthony Appleyard, Andrewpmk, Pippu d'Angelo, Bugg, Jefromi, GiovanniS, Japanese Searobin, Angr, Anish7, Woohookitty, Weevil, BD2412, Rjwilmsi, Vegaswikian, Lebha, Margosbot~enwiki, OpenToppedBus, Chobot, Marbot, Butsuri, Mongol, RussBot, Dysmorodrepanis~enwiki, Badagnani, Cquan, Epipelagic, Supten, JHCaufield, DeadEyeArrow, Sandstein, Sarefo, SmackBot, Espresso Addict, Nihonjoe, Lagalag, Ntk53s, Rojomoke, Xaosflux, Gilliam,

Chris the speller, RDBrown, Jon513, Moshe Constantine Hassan Al-Silverburg, 司徒天, Nbarth, VMS Mosaic, ColinKennedy, Rabidphage, Johan Jönsson, Hvn0413, Beetstra, SQGibbon, Bollinger, Beefyt, PaddyM, Mrjahan, Ghaly, The Haunted Angel, DanaMedic, Bonás, Gogo Dodo, Miyashita, Sagaciousuk, Nick Number, Amjaabc, Trabeculum001, Visik, WinBot, Dawsod, JAnDbot, Thylacinus cynocephalus, Richardw, Sukamusiru, ChrisBrunner, Retromatic, VoABot II, Monkeyvoodoo, Laubz83, Cocytus, Hemidemisemiquaver, Barrimundi, R'n'B, Creol, Petter Bøckman, Trusilver, AstroHurricane001, Khathi, Pilum, Idioma-bot, Alifshinobi, Caspian blue, Hamedgilan~enwiki, Davelapo555, Joakim589, Gpazpujalt, Lorangriel, EJF, Da Joe, Ouizardus, Peterbruce01, Nicklesh, Yerpo, Oxymoron83, Steven Crossin, Zac2333, Globe trotter4, Msjayhawk, Invertzoo, Mr. Granger, Faithlessthewonderboy, Annihilan, Helenabella, Darthveda, Viktorianec, Excirial, VictoiseC, Valchick07, Taranet, Dthomsen8, SilvonenBot, Fireinacrowdedtheatre, GDibyendu, Addbot, RN1970, DOI bot, ThisIsMyWikipediaName, MartinezMD, NjardarBot, BassplayerDAC, Koppas, Legobot, Ptbotgourou, Niclydon234, Tfcallahan1, NatFisherman, Melonbarmonster2, Dmarquard, Walrus heart, Xufanc, Xqbot, Anna Frodesiak, Coretheapple, RibotBOT, Sandcherry, FrescoBot, Citation bot 1, Skenar, Pinethicket, Angstorm, Ascap23, TobeBot, தமிழ்ச்செல்வன், Pjd2k9, Prasunkundu, EmausBot, WikitanvirBot, Milkunderwood, Newtdawg99, ClueBot NG, Frietjes, Pjimmej, Widr, MerlIwBot, Northamerica1000, Merovigla, LongLiveMusic, UmbreonPrince, Nitrobutane, Glavior, ChrisGualtieri, Gial Ackbar, Monkbot, Liance, Heymister6969669699, TheRottenEditor and Anonymous: 171

- **Royal fish** *Source:* https://en.wikipedia.org/wiki/Royal_fish?oldid=679119300 *Contributors:* Ihcoyc, Rich Farmbrough, Bdamokos, Dejvid, Tim!, Pburka, Eastlaw, Cydebot, Biruitorul, Ghmyrtle, VoABot II, Richard New Forest, StAnselm, Mangostar, Denisarona, Kbdankbot, Addbot, Salmon123, AnomieBOT, FrescoBot, Chrisdoyleorwell, BG19bot and Anonymous: 9

- **Sevruga** *Source:* https://en.wikipedia.org/wiki/Sevruga?oldid=649868159 *Contributors:* Altenmann, Utcursch, Dr.frog, Rsrikanth05, The Ogre, SmackBot, Jakz34, Panaqqa, Alaibot, Visik, Glane23, Erik9bot, DexDor, Anfis Katechkin, Ebe123, BG19bot, Albermaria and Anonymous: 8

- **Sterlet** *Source:* https://en.wikipedia.org/wiki/Sterlet?oldid=669686538 *Contributors:* Eugene van der Pijll, Fungus Guy, Art LaPella, RJFJR, Stemonitis, Firsfron, Woohookitty, Eubot, Karelj, Kummi, The Ogre, Clam0p, Apokryltaros, Shinmawa, SmackBot, Bluebot, Colonies Chris, LucVerhelst, SashatoBot, JonnyChance, JoeBot, Drinibot, Gustave G., Cydebot, Ark-pl, Jay934, Alphachimpbot, Bondolo, Jay942942, Soulbot, Konchevnik81, VolkovBot, TXiKiBoT, Jaguarlaser, Alcmaeonid, SieBot, DragonBot, Alexbot, Arthur chos, MystBot, Addbot, RN1970, LaaknorBot, Luckas-bot, Шнапс, AnomieBOT, Ipatrol, BritishWatcher, Erik9bot, TobeBot, Kamel.jones80, AgnesNutter, DexDor, Uanfala, Anfis Katechkin, EmausBot, ZéroBot, Citron, ClueBot NG, Ykvach, Štaki000, YFdyh-bot, Goulashthor, TidyUp and Anonymous: 20

- **Sturgeon** *Source:* https://en.wikipedia.org/wiki/Sturgeon?oldid=690468505 *Contributors:* Frecklefoot, Skysmith, Kingturtle, Aarchiba, Netsnipe, Tkinias, Alex756, Ptoniolo, Tpbradbury, Phoebe, Palefire, Jeffq, Robbot, Kristof vt, Naddy, Caknuck, UtherSRG, Rho~enwiki, Kent Wang, Cautious, Marc Venot, Ancheta Wis, Zigger, Robert Weemeyer, Mboverload, Bobblewik, Sca, Slavering.dog, Gdr, Zeimusu, LucasVB, Antandrus, PDH, Tothebarricades.tk, Burschik, Jh51681, Fanghong~enwiki, Trevor MacInnis, Koala man, Discospinster, Fungus Guy, YUL89YYZ, Khaldei, Bender235, Cyclopia, Fenevad, Gilgamesh he, Shanes, Cacophony, Bobo192, Smalljim, MPerel, Haham hanuka, Sean-Gustafson, Jumbuck, JYolkowski, Alfvaen, Bsadowski1, Pauli133, Gene Nygaard, TintoRetto, Japanese Searobin, TShilo12, Alkarex, Stemonitis, Nuno Tavares, Woohookitty, Richard Barlow, Daniel Case, StradivariusTV, WadeSimMiser, JeremyA, MONGO, John Hill, T34, BD2412, Rjwilmsi, Barklund, Seraphimblade, The wub, Dar-Ape, Vuong Ngan Ha, Eubot, HJV, Nihiltres, Crispyinstilly, Gdrbot, Bgwhite, Borgx, RussBot, Shell Kinney, Marcus Cyron, NawlinWiki, Dysmorodrepanis~enwiki, Commo1, Sylvain1972, Apokryltaros, Adamrush, Epipelagic, Moomoomoo, SmackBot, Vald, Kintetsubuffalo, Bluebot, Rorybowman, SailorfromNH, J. Spencer, Eliezg, Abyssal, Parent5446, NoIdeaNick, TheTallOne, Zzorse, Olsdude, JzG, F15x28, Kevmin, Minna Sora no Shita, Mgiganteus1, Chrisch, ErikTheRed13, HappyVR, Hu12, Dgmartin98, Courcelles, Jonathan W, Eastlaw, Makeemlighter, Rogersface, Neelix, Rifleman 82, GRBerry, יהודה, JamesAM, Thijs!bot, Epbr123, Janet Laurel, Neil916, Ajkr925, Dgies, Slaweks, DPdH, Vala M, Majorly, DKong, Dr. Blofeld, Moorematthews, Dryke, Sluzzelin, JAnDbot, Gcm, Bpmullins, WolfmanSF, VoABot II, Soulbot, Zatoichi26, Catgut, PenguinJockey, Animum, David Eppstein, Esanchez7587, Manasl, Atarr, Jmile69, Anaxial, Alro, CommonsDelinker, Wackyrussell, J.delanoy, Uncle Dick, Krisirk, Blotto adrift, James A. Stewart, MNRoss, Fk750, JavierMC, VolkovBot, Orphic, Jadea3, Philip Trueman, TXiKiBoT, Nxavar, Frog47, Brunton, Xarelete, Cremepuff222, BotKung, Maxim, FCStaehle, Falcon8765, Anarchist-t-t, Nathan B. Kitchen, Dominik92, Android Mouse Bot 3, Lightmouse, Astoni1950, Rabo3, Motyka, Zeitlinar, MBK004, ClueBot, Elephant Talk, Gunnar Mikalsen Kvifte~enwiki, Skäpperöd, Excirial, RCalabraro, Simon D M, Kaiba, Thingg, Smarkflea, RexxS, XLinkBot, Fastily, Jytdog, Freshbakedpie, SilvonenBot, Rishidigital1055, NellieBly, Scuttle14, Addbot, RN1970, Willking1979, Feelmeallnightlong, CanadianLinuxUser, Download, Tide rolls, ماني, Marcher 0018, Luckas-bot, Yobot, IW.HG, AnomieBOT, Badums, Jim1138, TheDigiPix, D barranco, Hammerdrill, Bob Burkhardt, Maxis ftw, GnawnBot, Xqbot, TinucherianBot II, Hspstudent, H123jump, RibotBOT, Jonesey95, Whyisjimbonotbuddha, DARTH SIDIOUS 2, Androstachys, J36miles, EmausBot, WikitanvirBot, Immunize, Gored82, RA0808, Winner 42, ZéroBot, PBS-AWB, Byronpat, H3llBot, Sakhalinio, Citron, Tot12, Awhitten, ClueBot NG, Ykvach, Chrisdoyleorwell, Atsme, Cntras, DrChrissy, DBigXray, Divingpetrel, Ternarius, BG19bot, Weeksnagzit, AvocatoBot, Vsleonardo, Joydeep, أحمد عصام الدين, Freelibyan96, Robin of the Hood, Minsbot, BattyBot, Justincheng12345-bot, Wes8383, Mrt3366, Ayhan981, The Illusive Man, Still1human, Karin Anker, Alexepic, Martin.psenda, Lemnaminor, Howicus, Michipedian, Jensen, George, Stamptrader, Alanyumaster, JaconaFrere, CourtCelts1988, Ca2james, Qwertyxp2000, Ecintron, Writerarticle, ImNotALier, KasparBot, Caftaric, Angrybirds707, SSTflyer, Commsvolunteer, GoldenTyper577 and Anonymous: 301

- **Vitamin B12** *Source:* https://en.wikipedia.org/wiki/Vitamin_B12?oldid=689179118 *Contributors:* AxelBoldt, Tarquin, Taw, Alex.tan, DavidLevinson, Rsabbatini, Quercusrobur, Olivier, Dwmyers, Chris~enwiki, Gabbe, Evanherk, Mkweise, Ahoerstemeier, William M. Connolley, Jpatokal, Julesd, Pratyeka, Aragorn2, Nikai, Andres, Tristanb, Jengod, Feedmecereal, Stone, Big Bob the Finder, Itai, Rei, Raul654, Pakaran, Pollinator, Carbuncle, Huangdi, Chuunen Baka, Donarreiskoffer, Gabb, RedWolf, Peak, Arkuat, Kn1kda, Rhombus, Bkell, Fuelbottle, Mandel, Anthony, Wayland, GreatWhiteNortherner, Matt Gies, Crculver, Nunh-huh, Bork, Zigger, Alterego, Ds13, Jfdwolff, FrYGuY, Ans, Jens Schriver, Foobar, DryGrain, Pne, Delta G, Gyrofrog, Adenosine, Chowbok, Pgan002, Andycjp, Knutux, Onco p53, Semenko, Urhixidur, Ensrifraff, Ukexpat, Pearla~enwiki, Freakofnurture, MattKingston, O'Dea, Meta~enwiki, Solitude, Rich Farmbrough, Guanabot, Qutezuce, GoD, Francis Davey, Bender235, Eric Forste, CanisRufus, Koenige, Thortful, BrokenSegue, Davidruben, Cmdrjameson, Arcadian, Kjkolb, Jumbuck, Alansohn, Andkaha, Nchase, Doopokko, Andrewpmk, Benjah-bmm27, SlimVirgin, Noosphere, Ltbarcly, ClockworkSoul, Lerdsuwa, Fantumphool, Kenyon, Woohookitty, Linas, Mindmatrix, WadeSimMiser, Tabletop, Firien, Pmm1221, Uvo, Deltabeignet, Taestell, V8rik, Galwhaa, LanguageMan, FreplySpang, BorisTM, Seventh Holy Scripture, Mendaliv, Rjwilmsi, Ian the younger, Arisa, Bubba73, Bleees, Tommy Kronkvist, Cyclometh, FlaBot, Ground Zero, Nihiltres, Theuedimaster, Ralphael, Fresheneesz, Stevenfruitsmaak, Sderose, Physchim62, Imnotminkus, Chobot, Bgwhite, WriterHound, YurikBot, Wavelength, Mikalra, Hairy Dude, Sillybilly, Anonymous editor, Chris Capoccia, Epolk, Eleassar, Pseudomonas, Complainer, Keithonearth, Trovatore, Długosz, Dogcow, Azazell0, Dbfirs, Samir, BOT-Superzerocool, Zephalis, Bota47,

Zzuuzz, Lt-wiki-bot, Nikkimaria, GraemeL, Ghetteaux, Limhes, Tsiaojian lee, Selkem, Lyrl, John Broughton, Andrew73, Veinor, A13ean, SmackBot, Mangoe, Slashme, KnowledgeOfSelf, Shoy, Bomac, Eskimbot, Edgar181, Slixi, Perdita, Xaosflux, Ohnoitsjamie, Hmains, Eug, Lovecz, MK8, SweetP112, DroEsperanto, Snori, Billmarrs, Tree Biting Conspiracy, EncMstr, Deli nk, Uthbrian, Sbharris, Darth Panda, Vdavisson, HoodedMan, Addshore, Ratznium, Kingdon, Xcomradex, Mrpark01, Smokefoot, DMacks, Fredgoat, Henning Makholm, Sammy1339, Acdx, Ligulembot, Vina-iwbot~enwiki, Clicketyclack, SashatoBot, Writtenonsand, Gobonobo, Minna Sora no Shita, Kylle22, Stwalkerster, The-HYPO, Libera~enwiki, Beetstra, Xiaphias, MTSbot~enwiki, Rickington, Hu12, Olivierd, Mig77, Iridescent, Dagoldman, Shoeofdeath, Ewulp, Chovain, Alegoo92, Scienthomas, ChrisCork, Winston Spencer, J Milburn, CmdrObot, Dycedarg, Vuzman, Baiji, Sack36, Johner, Cydebot, Kupirijo, Matrix61312, Reywas92, Cunningpal, Webaware, Rifleman 82, Gogo Dodo, MysticMetal, Carstensen, Clovis Sangrail, Now might i do it pat, Asteen~enwiki, Epbr123, Molix~enwiki, Electron9, James086, Kborer, Leon7, Escarbot, David D., Luna Santin, Opelio, SummerPhD, Belljaf, Jj137, Pro crast in a tor, TimVickers, Darklilac, Gdo01, Iandron, Blacksun1942, Astavats, Dougher, Jordan Rothstein, Amberroom, Ncity, JAnDbot, Kingadrock, BlindEagle, Plantsurfer, QuantumEngineer, PhilKnight, WolfmanSF, Wopb24, XZeddx, VoABot II, Soulbot, Becksguy, Caesarjbsquitti, BOne, SLWatson, JMyrleFuller, WLU, Erpbridge, Yobol, MartinBot, Nehwyn, ChemNerd, Wowaconia, R'n'B, Zylstra, J.delanoy, Tmallard, Ian.thomson, Ijustam, Rod57, Naniwako, Mikael Häggström, Belovedfreak, NewEnglandYankee, DadaNeem, Enix150, Mathdeveloper, WJBscribe, Ymwang42, Brvman, Million Moments, Blood Oath Bot, CardinalDan, Szalzala, Clafouti, Lights, Jeff G., Shalomi, Philip Trueman, Mkcmkc, Zimirk, January192007, WatchAndObserve, DocGratis, Tyge, Cbass94, Muleattack, Elyada, Shadowlapis, Max.coke, ACEOREVIVED, Dr.michael.benjamin, Madhero88, בל יבול, Eubulides, Q Science, Ar-wiki, Võitkutõde, Jpeeling, Sce1313, Cgosh, HiDrNick, Doc James, Shplongl, Petergans, My4lane, Nubiatech, Scarian, BotMultichill, Yintan, Keilana, BlueCerinthe, N96, Jangolawless, Drowner1979, Florentino floro, Hordaland, Juliakbird, Denisarona, Tsoul, Canglesea, Chem-awb, RobinHood70, Invertzoo, Faithlessthewonderboy, WikiBotas, ClueBot, Fyyer, Wikievil666, The Thing That Should Not Be, Dagron12345, Rb1248, Abe (or Abraham), Gastro guy, Sfiga, Drmies, AirdishStraus, Niceguyedc, CandleInTheDark, Gre9 s, Kurumban, Burleigh2, Excirial, GraybeardBiochemist, U0224006, Versus22, RedSox2008, Wnt, Ostinato2, Paco10000, DumZiBoT, Ean5533, XLinkBot, Drop the soap!, D1ma5ad, Winterkrieg, Mifter, Noctibus, RyanCross, Addbot, Bennnh, Jacopo Werther, Some jerk on the Internet, DOI bot, Lewashinton, Tcncv, Blethering Scot, Shawnar, Ez2rmbr, Krocheford12, Diptanshu.D, Download, Ld100, Favonian, ChenzwBot, Equine-man, Zorrobot, Dr.queso, Legobot, Yobot, UltraMagnus, CheMoBot, DisillusionedBitterAndKnackered, Lisafyfe, Jetbundle, KamikazeBot, BeBoldInEdits, Tempodivalse, AnomieBOT, DemocraticLuntz, Wikieditoroftoday, Casforty, Akhran, Piano non troppo, AdjustShift, Jtonejc, Materialscientist, Are you ready for IPv6?, The High Fin Sperm Whale, WordBounce, Citation bot, Larsanders, PCurve, ArthurBot, LilHelpa, Carturo222, Gymnophoria, Transity, Tomdo08, Horseprerace, Rasmudsaagaard, Micropion, Basket of Puppies, Rocosm, Loolololol, Quikfastgoninja, Globe Collector, Coffeerules9999, BobFijiwinkle, Chaseandjonathan, Wikiania, FrescoBot, Hobsonlane, Thefoodlady, Ianphil397, Citation bot 1, Wuthering123, Nirmos, Gfcvoice, Klubbit, Pinethicket, Serols, Dobror, Xsxixmx, Jdweller, Fartherred, BogBot, Kgrad, WPPilot, Raidon Kane, Noz777, Rhinoman99, HealthMind, DARTH SIDIOUS 2, Kgsheppard, RjwilmsiBot, Becritical, Lexorh, EmausBot, John of Reading, Cinosaur, Vaevictis Asmadi, RawrMage, Kriswarner, Cnscaevola, Misty MH, Traxs7, H3llBot, Nihods, AManWithNoPlan, Jesanj, Herlao, Donner60, Johnveinger, Cakoy08, Spicemix, 28bot, Louisajb, Teaktl17, Verticalstall, ClueBot NG, Smtchahal, Horoporo, Morgankevinj huggle, Edouard Albert, Pashihiko, SVCDuval, Frietjes, Thatguywhobreaths, O.Koslowski, Eyesighter, Helpful Pixie Bot, Faus, LargeVirus, Curb Chain, BG19bot, Andreacarol57, Wiki13, NevermindWiki, Bubbliciousgurl, TacticalMaster, Leshraq, Thechristin, Ctconnolly, Cglion, JPAO44, Ethanwarshow, W.D., Jimw338, Mrt3366, Erh2103, GoShow, Tyler-Durden8823, Lucialauteria, AK456, Stoneglasgow, Dexbot, Mysterious Whisper, Keystones, NotoriousPyro, Andrux, Jmvernay, Corn cheese, JustAMuggle, David Martin Zeegen Roth, Gooseman143, Sucremusts, Cobgenius, WoodyinNYC, Klkuo, RainCity471, Quenhitran, Arripay, Rusty94114, Pankajbatham, Stamptrader, NitaiPrasad, Lindseyragoczy, Monkbot, Fench, Soma.netic, Dr pauline, Dr.Jagadish.R, Wbmsclife, Mouthbodyconnection, HMSLavender, Alrich44, A8v, Pigi5, KH-1, Thorlewis, LL221W, Wimbartx, Umxu68, KasparBot, Nahtexo, SummerPhDv2.0, Jpniciforos, Brian heim composer and Anonymous: 622

3.2 Images

- **File:Abalone-farm1web.jpg** *Source:* https://upload.wikimedia.org/wikipedia/commons/f/fa/Abalone-farm1web.jpg *License:* Public domain *Contributors:* ? *Original artist:* ?

- **File:Acipenser_baerii.jpg** *Source:* https://upload.wikimedia.org/wikipedia/commons/5/5d/Acipenser_baerii.jpg *License:* CC BY-SA 3.0 *Contributors:* Own work *Original artist:*

- **File:Acipenser_brevirostrum_(NY).jpg** *Source:* https://upload.wikimedia.org/wikipedia/commons/a/a0/Acipenser_brevirostrum_%28NY%29.jpg *License:* Public domain *Contributors:* http://pond.dnr.cornell.edu/nyfish/fish.html *Original artist:* Ellen Edmonson and Hugh Chrisp

- **File:Acipenser_dabryanus.jpg** *Source:* https://upload.wikimedia.org/wikipedia/commons/0/07/Acipenser_dabryanus.jpg *License:* Public domain *Contributors:* *Nouvelles Archives du Muséum d'histoire Naturelle* url *Original artist:* Josephe Huët

- **File:Acipenser_fulvescens_1908.jpg** *Source:* https://upload.wikimedia.org/wikipedia/commons/0/00/Acipenser_fulvescens_1908.jpg *License:* Public domain *Contributors:* *The fishes of Illinois* Forbes, Stephen Alfred, 1844-1930; Richardson, Robert Earl, b. 1877 *Original artist:* unknown

- **File:Acipenser_gueldenstaedtii.jpg** *Source:* https://upload.wikimedia.org/wikipedia/commons/6/60/Acipenser_gueldenstaedtii.jpg *License:* Public domain *Contributors:* <a data-x-rel='nofollow' class='external text' href='http://openlibrary.org/books/OL17968292M/Die_S%C2%A9sswasserfische_der_%C2%A9streichischen_Monarchie_mit_r%C2%A9cksicht_auf_die_angr%C2%A9%C3%9Enzenden_l%C2%A9%C3%9Ender'>*Die Süsswasserfische der üstreichischen Monarchie mit rücksicht auf die angrüÞnzenden lüÞnder*</a> Jakob Heckel & Rudolf Kner. *Original artist:* Unknown

- **File:Acipenser_medirostris.jpg** *Source:* https://upload.wikimedia.org/wikipedia/commons/d/d8/Acipenser_medirostris.jpg *License:* Public domain *Contributors:* *Nouvelles Archives du Muséum d'histoire Naturelle* *Original artist:* Muséum d'histoire Naturelle

- **File:Acipenser_naccarii.jpg** *Source:* https://upload.wikimedia.org/wikipedia/commons/d/d7/Acipenser_naccarii.jpg *License:* Public domain *Contributors:* <a data-x-rel='nofollow' class='external text' href='http://openlibrary.org/books/OL17968292M/Die_S%C2%A9sswasserfische_der_%C2%A9streichischen_Monarchie_mit_r%C2%A9cksicht_auf_die_angr%C2%A9%C3%9Enzenden_l%C2%A9%C3%9Ender'>*Die*

Süsswasserfische der üstreichischen Monarchie mit rücksicht auf die angrüÞnzenden lüÞnder</a> Jakob Heckel & Rudolf Kner. *Original artist:* Unknown

- **File:Acipenser_nudiventris.jpg** *Source:* https://upload.wikimedia.org/wikipedia/commons/d/d2/Acipenser_nudiventris.jpg *License:* Public domain *Contributors:* <a data-x-rel='nofollow' class='external text' href='http://openlibrary.org/books/OL17968292M/Die_S%C2% A9sswasserfische_der_%C2%A9streichischen_Monarchie_mit_r%C2%A9cksicht_auf_die_angr%C2%A9%C3%9Enzenden_l%C2%A9% C3%9Ender'>*Die Süsswasserfische der üstreichischen Monarchie mit rücksicht auf die angrüÞnzenden lüÞnder</a>* Jakob Heckel & Rudolf Kner. *Original artist:* Unknown

- **File:Acipenser_oxyrhynchus.jpg** *Source:* https://upload.wikimedia.org/wikipedia/commons/b/b8/Acipenser_oxyrhynchus.jpg *License:* Public domain *Contributors:* fws.gov *Original artist:* Duane Raver/U.S. Fish and Wildlife Service

- **File:Acipenser_oxyrhynchus_(edit).png** *Source:* https://upload.wikimedia.org/wikipedia/commons/6/65/Acipenser_oxyrhynchus_ %28edit%29.png *License:* Public domain *Contributors:* Derived from: File:Acipenser oxyrhynchus.jpg *Original artist:* Duane Raver/U.S. Fish and Wildlife Service

- **File:Acipenser_persicus.jpg** *Source:* https://upload.wikimedia.org/wikipedia/commons/3/3b/Acipenser_persicus.jpg *License:* CC0 *Contributors:* http://www.ittiofauna.org/webmuseum/pesciossei/acipenseriformes/acipenseridae/acipenser/acipenser_persicus/index_big.htm *Original artist:* A. Abdoli

- **File:Acipenser_ruthenus1.jpg** *Source:* https://upload.wikimedia.org/wikipedia/commons/d/d4/Acipenser_ruthenus1.jpg *License:* Public domain *Contributors:* Illustrations de Ichtyologie ou histoire naturelle générale et particulière des Poissons Bloch, Marcus Elieser, J. F. Hennig, Plumier, Krüger, Pater, Schmidt, Ludwig, Bodenehr, Moritz 1795-1797 (<a data-x-rel='nofollow' class='external text' href='http://gallica.bnf.fr/ark: /12148/btv1b2300245v/'>Bibliothèque nationale de France</a>) *Original artist:* Krüger

- **File:Acipenser_ruthenus3.jpg** *Source:* https://upload.wikimedia.org/wikipedia/commons/f/ff/Acipenser_ruthenus3.jpg *License:* Public domain *Contributors:* <a data-x-rel='nofollow' class='external text' href='http://openlibrary.org/books/OL17968292M/Die_S%C2% A9sswasserfische_der_%C2%A9streichischen_Monarchie_mit_r%C2%A9cksicht_auf_die_angr%C2%A9%C3%9Enzenden_l%C2%A9% C3%9Ender'>*Die Süsswasserfische der üstreichischen Monarchie mit rücksicht auf die angrüÞnzenden lüÞnder</a>* Jakob Heckel & Rudolf Kner. *Original artist:* Unknown

- **File:Acipenser_ruthenus_Prague_Vltava_3.jpg** *Source:* https://upload.wikimedia.org/wikipedia/commons/b/b5/Acipenser_ruthenus_ Prague_Vltava_3.jpg *License:* Public domain *Contributors:* Own work *Original artist:* Karelj

- **File:Acipenser_sinensis.JPG** *Source:* https://upload.wikimedia.org/wikipedia/commons/a/aa/Acipenser_sinensis.JPG *License:* CC BY-SA 3.0 *Contributors:* Own work *Original artist:* Shizhao

- **File:Acipenser_stellatus.jpg** *Source:* https://upload.wikimedia.org/wikipedia/commons/a/af/Acipenser_stellatus.jpg *License:* Public domain *Contributors:* <a data-x-rel='nofollow' class='external text' href='http://openlibrary.org/books/OL17968292M/Die_S%C2%A9sswasserfische_ der_%C2%A9streichischen_Monarchie_mit_r%C2%A9cksicht_auf_die_angr%C2%A9%C3%9Enzenden_l%C2%A9%C3%9Ender'>*Die Süsswasserfische der üstreichischen Monarchie mit rücksicht auf die angrüÞnzenden lüÞnder</a>* Jakob Heckel & Rudolf Kner. *Original artist:* Unknown

- **File:Acipenser_sturio.jpg** *Source:* https://upload.wikimedia.org/wikipedia/commons/e/e2/Acipenser_sturio.jpg *License:* Public domain *Contributors:* Illustrations de Ichtyologie ou histoire naturelle générale et particulière des Poissons Bloch, Marcus Elieser, J. F. Hennig, Plumier, Krüger, Pater, Schmidt, Ludwig, Bodenehr, Moritz 1795-1797 (<a data-x-rel='nofollow' class='external text' href='http://gallica.bnf.fr/ark: /12148/btv1b2300245v/'>Bibliothèque nationale de France</a>) *Original artist:* Krüger

- **File:Acipenser_transmontanus1.jpg** *Source:* https://upload.wikimedia.org/wikipedia/commons/9/96/Acipenser_transmontanus1.jpg *License:* Public domain *Contributors:* Nouvelles Archives du Muséum d'histoire Naturelle url *Original artist:* Josephe Huët

- **File:Aivazovsky_-_Black_Sea_Fleet_in_the_Bay_of_Theodosia.jpg** *Source:* https://upload.wikimedia.org/wikipedia/commons/5/57/ Aivazovsky_-_Black_Sea_Fleet_in_the_Bay_of_Theodosia.jpg *License:* Public domain *Contributors:* http://lj.rossia.org/users/john_petrov/ 500773.html *Original artist:* Ivan Aivazovsky

- **File:Amasra,_Bartın,_Turkey.jpg** *Source:* https://upload.wikimedia.org/wikipedia/commons/d/d1/Amasra%2C_Bart%C4% B1n%2C_Turkey.jpg *License:* CC BY 2.0 *Contributors:* http://www.flickr.com/photos/lukas/2745765427/ *Original artist:* http://www.flickr.com/photos/lukas/

- **File:Antennarius_striatus.jpg** *Source:* https://upload.wikimedia.org/wikipedia/commons/3/3d/Antennarius_striatus.jpg *License:* Public domain *Contributors:* ? *Original artist:* ?

- **File:Aquaculturechile.jpg** *Source:* https://upload.wikimedia.org/wikipedia/commons/9/9a/Aquaculturechile.jpg *License:* CC BY-SA 3.0 *Contributors:* Transferred from en.wikipedia to Commons. *Original artist:* <a href='//en.wikipedia.org/wiki/User:Dentren' class='extiw' title='en: User:Dentren'>Dentren</a> | <a href='//en.wikipedia.org/wiki/User_talk:Dentren' class='extiw' title='en:User talk:Dentren'>*Talk</a>

- **File:Atlantic_cod.jpg** *Source:* https://upload.wikimedia.org/wikipedia/commons/a/a3/Atlantic_cod.jpg *License:* Public domain *Contributors:* ? *Original artist:* ?

- **File:B12_methylcobalamin.jpg** *Source:* https://upload.wikimedia.org/wikipedia/commons/8/83/B12_methylcobalamin.jpg *License:* CC BY-SA 3.0 *Contributors:* Own work *Original artist:* Sbharris (Steven B. Harris)

- **File:Baku_Bulvar.jpg** *Source:* https://upload.wikimedia.org/wikipedia/commons/7/7c/Baku_Bulvar.jpg *License:* Public domain *Contributors:* Own work *Original artist:* Samir Rəsulov

- **File:Barbakeios_Sxoli_1867_003.JPG** *Source:* https://upload.wikimedia.org/wikipedia/commons/8/84/Barbakeios_Sxoli_1867_003.JPG *License:* Public domain *Contributors:* Magazine Ethnikon Imerologion Bretou, Vol 7, No 1 (1867) *Original artist:* Marinos Bretos (1828 - 1871)

- **File:Beluga_sturgeon.png** *Source:* https://upload.wikimedia.org/wikipedia/commons/e/e7/Beluga_sturgeon.png *License:* Public domain *Contributors:* ? *Original artist:* ?

- **File:The_Danube_Spills_into_the_Black_Sea.jpg** *Source:* https://upload.wikimedia.org/wikipedia/commons/0/0d/The_Danube_Spills_into_the_Black_Sea.jpg *License:* Public domain *Contributors:* NASA Earth Observatory *Original artist:* The SeaWiFS Project

- **File:Trawer_Hauling_Nets.jpg** *Source:* https://upload.wikimedia.org/wikipedia/commons/1/1e/Trawer_Hauling_Nets.jpg *License:* Public domain *Contributors:* http://www.photolib.noaa.gov/htmls/fish0813.htm (was http://www.photolib.noaa.gov/fish/fish0813.htm). Transferred from en.wikipedia to Commons by Faisal Hasan using CommonsHelper. *Original artist:* ?

- **File:USS_Yorktown_collision.jpg** *Source:* https://upload.wikimedia.org/wikipedia/commons/3/36/USS_Yorktown_collision.jpg *License:* Public domain *Contributors:* http://www.defenseimagery.mil/imagery.html#guid=3fbec26218ee63044a583fa43631f40681be4e95 *Original artist:* Unknown

- **File:VU_IUCN_3_1.svg** *Source:* https://upload.wikimedia.org/wikipedia/commons/0/04/VU_IUCN_3_1.svg *License:* CC BY 2.5 *Contributors:*

- Status_iucn3.1.svg *Original artist:*

- derivative work: Mareklug <a href='//commons.wikimedia.org/wiki/User_talk:Mareklug' title='User talk:Mareklug'>*talk</a>

- **File:Veleka-sinemorets-mouth-dinev.jpg** *Source:* https://upload.wikimedia.org/wikipedia/commons/7/7e/Veleka-sinemorets-mouth-dinev.jpg *License:* CC BY 2.0 *Contributors:* ? *Original artist:* ?

- **File:View_of_night_Baku,_2010.jpg** *Source:* https://upload.wikimedia.org/wikipedia/commons/3/3f/View_of_night_Baku%2C_2010.jpg *License:* CC BY-SA 3.0 *Contributors:* Own work *Original artist:* Gulustan

- **File:Widok_na_Jałtę_ze_statku_06.JPG** *Source:* https://upload.wikimedia.org/wikipedia/commons/2/29/Widok_na_Ja%C5%82t%C4%99_ze_statku_06.JPG *License:* CC BY-SA 4.0 *Contributors:* Own work *Original artist:* Hons084

- **File:Wikibooks-logo.svg** *Source:* https://upload.wikimedia.org/wikipedia/commons/f/fa/Wikibooks-logo.svg *License:* CC BY-SA 3.0 *Contributors:* Own work *Original artist:* User:Bastique, User:Ramac et al.

- **File:Wikiquote-logo.svg** *Source:* https://upload.wikimedia.org/wikipedia/commons/f/fa/Wikiquote-logo.svg *License:* Public domain *Contributors:* ? *Original artist:* ?

- **File:Wikisource-logo.svg** *Source:* https://upload.wikimedia.org/wikipedia/commons/4/4c/Wikisource-logo.svg *License:* CC BY-SA 3.0 *Contributors:* Rei-artur *Original artist:* Nicholas Moreau

- **File:Wiktionary-logo-en.svg** *Source:* https://upload.wikimedia.org/wikipedia/commons/f/f8/Wiktionary-logo-en.svg *License:* Public domain *Contributors:* Vector version of Image:Wiktionary-logo-en.png. *Original artist:* Vectorized by Fvasconcellos (talk · contribs), based on original logo tossed together by Brion Vibber

- **File:Woodcut_Italian_Kitchen.png** *Source:* https://upload.wikimedia.org/wikipedia/commons/b/bb/Woodcut_Italian_Kitchen.png *License:* Public domain *Contributors:* Paul Lacroix, <a data-x-rel='nofollow' class='external text' href='http://www.gutenberg.org/ebooks/%7B%7B%7Bno%7D%7D%7D'>Manners, Custom and Dress During the Middle Ages and During the Renaissance Period</a>, available freely at Project Gutenberg *Original artist:* Unknown

- **File:X_mark.svg** *Source:* https://upload.wikimedia.org/wikipedia/commons/a/a2/X_mark.svg *License:* Public domain *Contributors:* Own work *Original artist:* User:Gmaxwell

- **File:Yangzhuanghe_-_CIMG3404.JPG** *Source:* https://upload.wikimedia.org/wikipedia/commons/4/43/Yangzhuanghe_-_CIMG3404.JPG *License:* CC BY-SA 3.0 *Contributors:* Own work *Original artist:* User:Vmenkov

- **File:Yellow.tang.arp.jpg** *Source:* https://upload.wikimedia.org/wikipedia/commons/a/a0/Yellow.tang.arp.jpg *License:* Public domain *Contributors:* Photographed by Adrian Pingstone in December 2005 *Original artist:* Adrian Pingstone

- **File:Yes_check.svg** *Source:* https://upload.wikimedia.org/wikipedia/en/f/fb/Yes_check.svg *License:* PD *Contributors:* ? *Original artist:* ?

- **File:Young_lake_sturgeon.jpg** *Source:* https://upload.wikimedia.org/wikipedia/commons/2/24/Young_lake_sturgeon.jpg *License:* Public domain *Contributors:* This image originates from the National Digital Library of the United States Fish and Wildlife Service *Original artist:* ?

- **File:Астрахань._набережная_1_мая._1.jpg** *Source:* https://upload.wikimedia.org/wikipedia/commons/9/97/%D0%90%D1%81%D1%82%D1%80%D0%B0%D1%85%D0%B0%D0%BD%D1%8C._%D0%BD%D0%B0%D0%B1%D0%B5%D1%80%D0%B5%D0%B6%D0%BD%D0%B0%D1%8F_1_%D0%BC%D0%B0%D1%8F._1.jpg *License:* CC BY-SA 3.0 *Contributors:* Own work *Original artist:* Ludushka

- **File:Здание_санатория_«Орджоникидзе»_(Сочи,_курортный_пр.)102.jpg** *Source:* https://upload.wikimedia.org/wikipedia/commons/0/0f/%D0%97%D0%B4%D0%B0%D0%BD%D0%B8%D0%B5_%D1%81%D0%B0%D0%BD%D0%B0%D1%82%D0%BE%D1%80%D0%B8%D1%8F_%C2%AB%D0%9E%D1%80%D0%B4%D0%B6%D0%BE%D0%BD%D0%B8%D0%BA%D0%B8%D0%B4%D0%B7%D0%B5%C2%BB_%28%D0%A1%D0%BE%D1%87%D0%B8%2C_%D0%BA%D1%83%D1%80%D0%BE%D1%80%D1%82%D0%BD%D1%8B%D0%B9_%D0%BF%D1%80.%29102.jpg *License:* CC BY-SA 3.0 *Contributors:* Own work *Original artist:* Ганощенко Роман (Ganoshenko Roman)

- **File:Морской_порт_г_Евпатория.jpg** *Source:* https://upload.wikimedia.org/wikipedia/commons/5/57/%D0%9C%D0%BE%D1%80%D1%81%D0%BA%D0%BE%D0%B9_%D0%BF%D0%BE%D1%80%D1%82_%D0%B3_%D0%95%D0%B2%D0%BF%D0%B0%D1%82%D0%BE%D1%80%D0%B8%D1%8F.jpg *License:* CC BY-SA 4.0 *Contributors:* Own work *Original artist:* Aleksander Kaasik

- **File:Палац_«Ластівчине_гніздо»_2.JPG** *Source:* https://upload.wikimedia.org/wikipedia/commons/e/e4/%D0%9F%D0%B0%D0%BB%D0%B0%D1%86_%C2%AB%D0%9B%D0%B0%D1%81%D1%82%D1%96%D0%B2%D1%87%D0%B8%D0%BD%D0%B5_%D0%B3%D0%BD%D1%96%D0%B7%D0%B4%D0%BE%C2%BB_2.JPG *License:* CC BY-SA 3.0 *Contributors:* Own work *Original artist:* Derevyagin Igor

- **File:Судак.jpg** *Source:* https://upload.wikimedia.org/wikipedia/commons/e/e5/%D0%A1%D1%83%D0%B4%D0%B0%D0%BA.jpg *License:* CC BY-SA 3.0 *Contributors:* http://500px.com/photo/61284774 *Original artist:* Alexander Vovchenko

3.3 Content license

Made in the USA
Las Vegas, NV
03 July 2024